THE-ANTI VIRGINITY PACT

KATIE WISMER

Ahimsa Press

THE ANTI-VIRGINITY PACT

Copyright © 2020 by Katie Wismer

All rights reserved. Printed in the United States of America. No part of this book may be used or reproduced in any manner whatsoever without written permission of the publisher, except in the case of brief quotations embodied in critical articles and certain other noncommercial uses permitted by copyright law.

This book is a work of fiction. All names, characters, businesses, organizations, places, events and incidents either are the product of the author's imagination or are used fictitiously. Any resemblance to actual persons, living or dead, events, or locales is entirely coincidental.

For information contact:

www.katiewismer.com

Cover design by MoorBooks Design

Editing by Nina Denison

ISBN: 978-1-7346115-0-2

First published June 2020

10 9 8 7 6 5 4 3 2 1

ALSO BY KATIE WISMER

The Anti-Relationship Year
Poems for the End of the World
The Sweetest Kind of Poison

This book contains material that may be triggering for some readers. Reader discretion is advised. For a complete list of trigger warnings, please visit katiewismer.com/trigger-warnings

INTRODUCTION

To be the first to know about new releases, giveaways, exclusive content, and more, make sure to sign up for my newsletter:
www.katiewismer.com

Playlist is available on Spotify:
shorturl.at/entO1

THE PACT

For the record, I don't normally have a predisposition for making bad decisions. I think it's important for you to know that. Maybe that makes me boring, but the one thing I've always had going for me—at least according to all of my parents' incredibly condescending friends—is how smart I am. How responsible. How I have always been a good girl.

And maybe that's why I did it.

The point is, please don't judge me until you know the whole story. Because you might think you know, but you don't. Unless you've spent the last eighteen years feeling like you're drowning inside of yourself, you don't know. And even then, I'm not so sure.

It happened on a Saturday night. Johanna's parents were out of town—Shanghai, I think it was this time—so we were sitting in her bedroom with a bottle of vodka she'd swiped from their liquor cabinet and a crazy plan scrawled on the page between us.

Johanna's room was more akin to the penthouse suite of a five-star hotel—vaulted ceilings, full-length windows, sleek, modern furniture. Besides the photo wall displaying her best photography and collection of hanging plants, everything was black and white. She said she preferred the simplicity of it, that it made her feel like she was living inside an old photograph.

Johanna swallowed the last of her drink and immediately grabbed the bottles from the floor so she could pour herself another—three-fourths cranberry juice, one-fourth vodka—only this time, it looked closer to half and half. She took another sip before offering the bottles to me.

I hadn't had that much to drink yet. Not enough to give me the spins. But enough to make Jo's words resonate with something in my chest. Enough to make me want to keep drinking until her empty promises came true, and that scared me more than anything else.

Jo downed the next drink in two gulps as she spun around and around in her hanging bubble chair. I was sprawled out on her massive four-poster bed, getting dizzy from watching her. Then she planted her feet, yanked out the pen securing her hair atop her head, allowing the thick red waves to collapse around her face, and pointed to the papers she'd gathered in her lap.

"Mare, we have to do this," she said.

I laughed, but not because it was funny.

She waved her arms impatiently. "No, I'm serious!

Here, I'll go first." After a quick scribble at the bottom of the first page, she flipped to the second and held it out to me. "Your turn."

I took another sip of my drink. I couldn't even taste the alcohol anymore, just the syrupy aftertaste of the juice and the nauseating bubble of panic growing in the pit of my stomach. "You can't be serious."

"Come on, Mare, just sign the contract." Johanna plopped herself beside me and pushed the papers into my lap. Her breath smelled like the overly-sweet perfume usually reserved for the halls of a middle school. "You know I'm right about this."

Johanna always thought she was right about everything. I rolled my eyes. "I'm not signing that thing."

Even as the words left my mouth, a heavy feeling of inevitability had started to cling to my skin. Because Johanna didn't have to convince me with reminders of our looming graduation—reminders of all the things I hadn't done, or the things people whispered in the halls.

I looked down at the papers in my lap. When laid out like this, sure, they held a kind of sparkle in their potential. She was absolutely right. All my life, I'd been the quiet one. The one people teased about why I never talked, and when I did, they feigned shock that I had the capability to speak. I was the girl with a yearbook full of flippant *have a good summer* messages because no one had anything better to say. My shyness had always been a self-imposed cage that left me crippled to all that was high school.

High school. It had a way of making you feel so small.

It wasn't even the judgmental looks or the snarky comments. It was the absence of them. Sometimes, not being seen at all was worse. The way kids you'd gone to school with since kindergarten couldn't remember your name. The way they walked into you in the hallway because they expected you to be the one to move. The way your whole body would deflate when teachers commented on how you never talked, even when you were so proud of yourself for working up the courage to raise your hand that day.

My finger ran over the last line of Johanna's contract. *By the end of senior year, I vow to no longer be a virgin.*

I was eighteen years old and I'd never been kissed. Never even been on a date. Honestly, none of the guys in our class had probably *thought* of me that way. All while I watched every other girl, freshmen and seniors alike, burn through relationship after relationship. I couldn't help but think if it was so easy for them, then maybe there was something wrong with me.

Johanna must have seen the indecision on my face because she jumped at my hesitation. "Come *on!*" she urged. "Take a risk for once. Do something that scares you. You've played it safe all through high school. We're *eighteen fucking years old*. And we're about to be out of here, anyway, and then it won't even matter what these losers think of us."

Johanna had always been dangerously impulsive, and if I were being honest, it was part of the reason we became friends. Even as a kid, she had this mysterious allure. There was something intoxicating about her presence, something that made you want to be brave, too. I didn't know if it was the alcohol or her words that made me do it, but either way, I held out my hand. "Give me the pen."

1

Sunday mornings at the Beaumont house are grand events. Papa spends the morning practicing his sermon by mumbling it into his coffee; Maman prances around the kitchen making breakfast, humming as she goes, because Sundays are the only days she has time to cook; and my younger sister, Harper, sits at the kitchen table, glued to her phone, glaring at everyone and everything because she's pissed Maman made her wear a dress. Meanwhile, I scramble to get my homework done before school tomorrow while simultaneously doing everything in my power to avoid catching my parents' attention.

Because the thing about Sundays is they're what my parents live for. They're the one day Maman doesn't have to work, Harper doesn't have dance class, and I'm not working at the shelter. To them, Sundays are holy days in more ways than one. To Harper and me, they are the ultimate test of patience.

The kitchen table is tucked in the far corner so it backs up to the bay window for extra seating. Harper sits in the chair closest to the stairs, her entire body slouched over her phone. Papa sits across from her on the bench, and the rest of the seats are occupied by Maman's various pairs of discarded high heels.

When I tug on one of Harper's dark braids to get her attention, she glances up, quickly locking the screen so I can't see what she was looking at, and scowls at me. "What?"

My gaze flickers to the phone, just for a second. Harper's pinched expression glares back at me in the reflection.

"Have you seen my book?" I ask.

"You can read?"

I glare at her smug little face—pursed glossy lips, haughtily elevated brows—an expression I've grown all too familiar with since she started high school this past fall. Someone ought to tell her that her eyebrow pencil is the wrong shade.

It's not going to be me.

"Very funny. Have you seen it? I left it there last night." I point at the table in front of her.

"I didn't take it, if that's what you're implying."

"I wasn't implying anything. I just need the book so I can do my homework."

She shrugs and turns back to her phone. "Looks like you're screwed then."

"Harper Beaumont," Maman gasps from across the kitchen. She's standing with an oven mitt on each hand, one pressed to her chest in horror. She clearly hasn't realized doing so smeared melted cheese on her white dress. "*Language.*"

I turn my back so Maman can't see me roll my eyes and decide to rope me in on this lecture.

Harper scrunches up her nose. "It isn't even a bad word."

"We don't say it in this house," Papa says without looking up. He's counting something off on his fingers, mouthing the numbers as he goes, but keeps getting stuck on the fourth finger for some reason, his face creasing in agitation each time. His reading glasses have slipped so far down his nose, I think he's forgotten he's wearing them.

Harper throws her arms up and slaps them against her thighs. "Why are you yelling at me? Mare says it—and worse—all the time!"

"I do not." I wave my hand as if she's being ridiculous and start searching for my book in the mess on the island. "Have you ever heard me say that word?"

Maman shakes her head. "I haven't."

I shoot a quick grin at Harper over my shoulder. I totally have.

"Come on!" Harper exclaims, pointing at me, but I've already resumed my innocent book-hunting.

Maman sighs, oozing disappointment, and rips the oven mitts off one by one. She throws them onto the island, exposing the extremely intimidating pattern of kittens playing with a ball of yellow yarn. Really, it's a mystery where Harper gets her dramatic flair.

"Harper," she says. "We don't point the blame at others for our mistakes. We accept responsibility." Maman uses her overly calm, lecturing voice that makes me want to scream whenever it's directed at me. I'd feel bad for Harper if she hadn't just tried to throw me under the bus.

"*Ugh.*" Harper gets up from the table and storms upstairs.

"Harper, sit back down! Breakfast is almost ready," Maman calls after her.

"I'm not hungry!"

Maman shoots an exasperated look to Papa, but he's not even paying attention. In fact, I think he might be laughing at something on his phone. "We're leaving in ten minutes!" she yells.

Harper replies with a slammed door.

A faint burnt scent reaches my nose, and I glance across the kitchen to see plumes of smoke escaping the oven.

"*Maman!*" I yell.

"*Oh, non! Non, non, non! Zoot!*" In her well-practiced routine, she flicks the oven off, turns on the hood vent, and has the situation under control in seconds, though the kitchen is now smoky enough to burn my eyes.

This, finally, gets Papa's attention. He leaps up from his seat, glasses falling from his face and clattering to the table in the process, and hurries over to the windows above the sink. He throws them open, and the decorative metal cross *clings* against the glass.

"*Je suis désolée.*" Maman sets the charcoaled breakfast foods on the counter, body deflated, and wipes the sweat from her brow. The quiches are scorched, but at least it's not as bad as last week. "Who wants cereal?"

The moment we reach the church, I split off from my family. Papa needs to get set up, anyway, and as long as I rejoin Maman and Harper before the service starts so we can all sit together in the front—Maman says it gives the appearance of a united front, as if this is some kind of political election—they don't mind.

If you didn't already know it was a church, you probably wouldn't be able to tell from the outside, what with its modern architecture and Papa's weird infatuation with trying to seem hip to attract younger people. I think the building used to be a concert hall before it was repurposed.

I pause at the cluster of tables a few yards from the entrance to wait for Johanna, who is headed towards me from the opposite direction in dark jeans and a white T-shirt, her fiery hair knotted messily atop her head. She spots me a moment later and lifts her hand as if to wave, and then proceeds to flip me off. I glance around to make sure no one else saw before allowing myself to laugh.

"You're looking...chaste," she says by way of greeting. We prop ourselves atop the tables, staking our claim in the sunny spots since it's still super chilly in the shade. It's midway through April, but Colorado never fails to surprise us with random snow storms every other week.

There's still a good half-hour before the service starts, and I don't think either of us wants to go inside until we absolutely have to. Jo's even less religious than I am but shows up on occasion for moral support. Also because my dad's best friend drags his ridiculously attractive son here every Sunday.

Yeah, it probably has more to do with that.

I don't even want to talk about the white dress my mother insisted I wear today. I've always thought wearing white in contrast to my ash blonde hair and pale skin makes me look like a ghost, but Maman swears it's her favorite color on me and is constantly bringing back white things from her boutique.

"You're looking...casual," I reply.

Johanna lets out a mighty yawn and stretches her arms over her head. "How much longer are you going to keep up the perfect daughter act and make me get up at the butt crack of dawn?"

"The service starts at ten."

She shrugs. "The question still remains."

I glance at the church over my shoulder, squinting my eyes against the sun. *The perfect daughter act.* "I'm moving out soon anyway. I don't see the point in stirring up trouble."

She slaps her arms back to her sides. "Whatever, it's your life. Just seems like Jesus might have a problem with a non-believer being his poster-child, but okay—oh my God, is Danielle Owens *crying?*"

Johanna points to the parking lot, where two girls are heading toward us. Danielle Owens and Ricki Paige—both are in the youth program here, but they're closer to Harper's age than mine, and I've never gotten to know them that well beyond reputation. Papa *loves* them, which kind of makes me assume I wouldn't. Ricki and Harper were friends at one point, but they don't seem to talk much anymore.

Both girls are in the standard church pastel and floral attire, but Ricki has her arm braced around Danielle's shaking shoulders. Danielle looks like some kind of grieving widow, with dark circles stamped beneath her eyes and a tissue pressed against her face. Honestly, I wouldn't be surprised if this is about her not getting the lead in the church's latest theater production or something.

"Are you okay?" I ask as they near the curb.

Ricki glances around when they reach us. She's gotten a lot prettier as she's gotten older. Dark golden hair, freckled cheeks. Looks like she finally grew into her nose, too. "Have you heard about Silvia?" she asks.

Now that she mentioned it, it was kind of odd to just see the two of them. Silvia was the usual third member of their trio.

"What about her?" Jo asks, popping her gum, oblivious to the tension lining their faces.

Ricki lowers her voice. "Her parents say she's spending a few months with her grandparents in Montana, but *we* think they found out she was smoking pot and hooking up with this guy, Patrick, so they hired one of those Jesus camps that kidnaps you in the middle of the night to *reform you*."

"Wait, *what?*" Johanna makes a small choking sound like she just swallowed her gum. "That's a real thing?"

I raise an eyebrow. Their jump from point A to point B seems like a bit of a stretch. Silvia's mom is also president of the church's knitting club, which pretty much makes her the picture of innocence. "Why would you think that?"

"She hasn't returned any of my texts or DMs," Danielle wails, as if this proves everything. She sniffles a few times before pulling a new tissue out of her purse.

"And she told us weeks ago that she found one of those camps on their computer's search history," adds Ricki. "So of course she totally freaked out. And then suddenly she just disappears? And in the middle of the semester? Tell me that's not sketchy."

"And now look at them!" Danielle glares over our heads at Silvia's parents standing in the church lobby, arm in arm, smiling and chatting with their friends. "They're smiling and lying to everyone like some kind of *psychopaths*." Danielle practically spits the word.

"Did you tell anyone about this?" I ask.

"Like who?" Ricki demands.

"Uh, like the *police?*"

"Oh, so we can be next?" Danielle dots the tissue under her eyes, but it does little to help the puddles of smeared mascara. "Plus, who would believe us? Everyone here loves them. And we don't have any proof."

"Danielle! Ricki!"

Silvia's mom has stepped away from the group and is now waving her arms dramatically overhead like she's signaling a plane, trying to get their attention.

Danielle's face twists, glaring at the woman like she just sprouted devil's horns. Though as Silvia's mom stands there with her pink polka dot cardigan and matching kitten heels, waving at us with wide eyes and an equally wide smile, I'm having a hard time seeing it. Ricki tugs on Danielle's arm.

"Come on," Ricki says. "Let's just go inside."

They both mutter their goodbyes, but it's Silvia's mom who I can't stop staring at as they walk away. Her expression shifts as Danielle and Ricki disappear into the atrium. It looks almost like longing. She just doesn't look capable of heartlessly shipping off her daughter. Not to mention, I'm pretty sure Silvia is only sixteen. What kind of a parent could actually do that? Especially after all of the horror stories? Just last year, there was a story on the news of a couple of girls in those camps getting abused and *dying* out in the woods. And for what? Because she liked a guy?

"Do you think that actually happened?" I mutter.

"I hope not," says Jo. "Can you imagine?"

Silvia's mom's gaze drifts over to us, and I grab Jo's arm to turn away before she catches us staring at her, my stomach suddenly uneasy.

Jo clears her throat. "Okay, so like, not to be insensitive or anything, but look who just pulled into the parking lot."

I look up to see a sleek black car park just a few spaces away. Jo grabs my arm, forcing me to stand. Her posture is suddenly impeccable, shoulders thrown back, chest pushed out. She adjusts the bun atop her head and tucks the loose strays behind her ears. "Do you think you could rub your non-believing off on *him*?"

"It's not contagious," I mutter as a gray-headed man in an expensive black suit emerges from the car and waits for his passenger. His son, Sam, steps out in gray fitted pants, a navy button-down shirt, and tinted sunglasses. Unlike his father, Sam's hair is dark and thick, tousled like he just rolled out of bed. It makes me wonder if Mr. Johnson was handsome when he was younger, or if Sam just favors his mom.

Not that I would know. I've never seen the woman.

What are the odds they'll just keep walking and I won't have to talk to them?

Sam's dad waves at me and Johanna as he approaches. "Howdy, Meredith. How's your daddy?"

Zero, apparently.

My teeth grind together, but I give him a tight smile and pretend not to notice the way he speaks to me like I'm a five-year-old. "Good, Mr. Johnson. He's inside."

Sam—or as Jo likes to call him, Sexy Sam—just shoves his hands in his pockets and raises his eyebrows in greeting. There is nothing threatening about him standing there, but my anxiety and logic have never been well acquainted. It's like the switch on my fight-or-flight response is faulty and flips whenever it damn well feels like it. Right now, for instance. My body coils itself tight, like its preparing to get thrown into a lion's den. Not that I should be surprised—my anxiety has always been an unwanted but expected houseguest. I can usually anticipate it long before it starts to manifest, but no matter how hard I try to prepare or reason with my body, it still reacts as if the millions of times before haven't taught it this is not a life or death situation. That it is, in fact, only making things even more difficult than necessary.

Right on time, my anxiety rears its head in the forms of clammy palms, a skittering heartbeat, and a flood of heat to my face. I can only hope the liquid foundation I put on this morning is thick enough that no one else can tell.

Mr. Johnson nods and starts to turn away, but then whips back around as if he just remembered something. "How do you say 'daddy' in French?"

He asks this like he's doing me a favor, giving me the opportunity to show off my knowledge even though he very well knows the answer. I can't see Sam's eyes through his sunglasses, but I can *feel* his gaze. This, of course, only makes my heartbeat panic more. I pointedly avoid looking at him.

"It's *papa*, sir," I say.

He nods, satisfied, and heads inside, Sam following close behind. Even after they're gone, my body doesn't relax, not at first. My hands shake a bit as if trying to burn off the lingering nervous energy. I hope to God they didn't notice.

Jo smacks my arm.

That snaps me out of it.

"Ouch! What was that for?"

"Sorry. But did you see that? Sexy Sam totally just gave you a look."

I rub my arm. "Yeah, an *I'd rather be anywhere but here* look."

"No." She rolls her eyes like I'm being unusually dense. "He gave you an eyebrow raise. Any eyebrow action, by definition, is flirty."

As if Sexy Sam Johnson *would ever be interested in me.*

"If you say so."

"You know..." Johanna's mouth curls into a slow smile.

She leans in and lowers her voice. "Sexy Sam would be an awfully good choice for our pact."

"Oh my God, Johanna." I cross my arms and glance over my shoulder to make sure no one is within hearing range. It had only been a week, but a part of me was hoping she'd forget about the pact. "Do *not* go after Sam. For one thing, he would never. And for another, Mr. Johnson and my dad are best friends. What if that got back to my dad?" I honestly think I might throw up just at the thought.

She snorts. "Yeah, I'm sure that's exactly what would happen. You know, most guys go running to tell their parents *all* about their sexual escapades."

"You are not having any *sexual escapades*," I whisper-scream, "with Sam Johnson!"

"You're right!" She grins and starts walking backwards toward the church. "You are."

"Jo!"

"See you later!" She winks and whips around before I can respond, disappearing into the crowd now beginning to trickle in. She hates sitting in the front, mostly because then she can't play on her phone the entire time, and tends to sit with some other friends from school in the back. I tried to talk Maman into letting me sit with them one time, but no such luck.

A chatty-looking older couple starts heading toward me, smiling, so I quickly duck away and follow Jo into the church to avoid having to talk to them. The lobby is full of people mingling and laughing, the line to the coffee cart stretching all the way into the back hall where the youth programs and daycare are held. Papa thinks the modern look attracts a wider demographic, so the atrium still looks more like a concert hall than a church. Chairs fan out in a semi-circle around the stage, where shiny music equipment is set up for the band and illuminated by various colored lights. Worship music trickles through the speakers, a countdown to the start of the service projected on the screen behind the stage.

After I slide into my place between Harper and Maman, my eyes do a quick scan of the room. Sam is sitting beside his dad in the front row on the other side of the atrium, sans sunglasses. He glances up and I freeze, feeling caught. He holds my gaze for a moment, his expression impossible to read. I quickly face forward again.

"What were you and Jo doing?" Harper asks.

I smooth down my dress with shaky hands and breathe deeply through my nose, willing the looming heat out of my face. "None of your business," I say without looking at her.

She jabs her elbow into my side until I glance her way. "What do you think Maman would say if she saw Jo give you the finger?"

I quickly glance over my shoulder to make sure Maman doesn't overhear, but she's absorbed in conversation with the lady on her right. "For once in your life, could you try not to be a little snitch?" I hiss.

Her dark eyes narrow at me. "It'd be what you deserved after this morning."

"*You're* the one who tried to get me in trouble to save your own skin! And besides, go ahead and tell her. She's not too happy with you right now, so who do you think she'd believe if I said you were lying?"

"She'd believe me because it's the truth," she snaps.

"She'd believe *me* because I'm the favorite."

She sniffs and turns away, her jaw clenched. I sigh. I hit a nerve, and should probably apologize, but then Papa walks onto the stage and applause fills the church, saving me.

2

When I pull into the school's parking lot on Monday morning, the clock on my dash reads 6:25 a.m. First bell doesn't ring until 7:00, but since I didn't end up finding my book until this morning, I need to get some homework done before class. Also, I like getting here early. I have to deal with fewer people that way.

Harper doesn't ride with me to school for three reasons: one, she doesn't want to come in early; two, she'd rather carpool with her friend Melanie; and three, she's embarrassed to be seen in my 1996 red Pathfinder when everyone else at school drives cars with the price tag of an entire college education. I don't see what her problem is. Stew looks great for his age, and only breaks down every once in a while. He cost me two whole summers' worth of triple-shift babysitting, but the freedom of having my own car was one-hundred percent worth letting three-year-old boys beat me up with action figures for a few months. Harper just doesn't understand our relationship.

It's fine by me. Harper is always in a dreadful mood in the mornings. Not that it's much different from her mood the rest of the time.

I park in the second row, despite the first being nearly empty. It's close enough that it's still convenient but prevents someone from keying my car for parking in the prime spots. Those spots are for the popular crowd—no one has to say it; we all just respect the rule. And poor Stew is already beat up enough as it is.

I pass through the halls, surrounded by dark green lockers and colorful posters advertising clubs, events, and the upcoming prom until I reach my locker and pull out the materials I need for my classes: AP French, AP Latin, AP Bio, and World History. I also pull down my anti-anxiety meds, pop one of the pills in my mouth, and wash it down with a gulp from my water bottle. They upset my stomach if I don't eat breakfast beforehand, which usually consists of a granola bar on the drive to school. I've gotten in the habit of keeping them in my locker so I don't forget to take them.

After closing my locker, I hesitate and stare at the prom poster a second too long.

But then a couple of kids appear at the end of the hall, spurring me into motion. I duck out of the building before they can notice me. As I head to the library, I mentally plan the French paper I need to write in my head. Thanks to Maman's French side of the family (ironic, since Papa's the one with the French last name), I'm practically fluent in the language, so I pretty much never do the work for that class until the last minute. It's not the best habit, but I get good enough grades.

I scout out my favorite table in the back, half-hidden by the shelves of books, and make sure to get a seat with my back against the wall. I hate the feeling of people sitting behind me. It's also right next to the wall of windows, so I can look out at the field across the street. Several runners and people walking their dogs crowd the paths as the sun rises behind them, painting the sky a soft pink.

Only two other students are in here, one crouched in the stacks with his head cocked to the side, looking for a book, the other hunched over one of the computers in the back, playing some kind of video game. They both look like freshmen, so at least I know they won't bother me. Another unspoken yet universally acknowledged rule: freshmen and seniors do not intermingle unless instigated by the older party.

I pull out a sheet of paper and my French book. The assignment is to write a paper about the pros and cons of nuclear energy based on the provided sources, which are stupid. The author clearly doesn't understand the science behind it at all. After skimming for a few minutes, I get to bullshitting the essay.

"Look at you, being all studious. How cute. Say 'soy cheese.'"

The camera flash goes off the moment I raise my eyes. Johanna grins, returning the cap to the lens.

"Are you even allowed to have that thing in here?" I ask, blinking away the spots from my vision.

Johanna rolls her eyes and slides into the seat opposite me. "It's a camera, not a Bluetooth speaker. I'm not disrupting anyone. I even have the shutter on silent." She gingerly returns the camera to its bag and sets it on the table. "You know I need to build up my portfolio some more before college. I need candids." Her red hair is in a long side-braid, which she tosses over her shoulder as she leans toward me, hitting me with a wave of her peach perfume.

"What are you even doing here?" I ask. It's still at least ten minutes until first period, and Jo is usually here no earlier than ten minutes *after*.

"I was up all night, thinking about our pact—"

I roll my eyes. "*Mon Dieu*, Jo."

"Hey." She holds up a hand. "We found your guy, but I still need one. And that's the thing. I think I found him—I was so excited about it, I couldn't even sleep in this morning." She grins like she's proud of herself.

"Pray tell. Who's the lucky guy?"

Her grin twists into something mischievous. "Mr. Graham."

I give her a *yeah, right* look and turn back to my essay.

She just keeps smiling.

I open and close my mouth a few times before finally leaning forward and whispering, "You can't be serious! You can't pick a *teacher*."

She looks genuinely confused. "Why not?"

I shake my head a few times. "Please tell me you're not seriously asking that question."

"What? I'm eighteen, so it's legal. And he's only, like, twenty-five or something. If I were twenty-one and he were twenty-eight, no one would give it a second thought. And, I mean, can you seriously look me in the eye and tell me you wouldn't do him if you had the chance?"

She's clearly given this way too much thought.

"No, I wouldn't!" I glance around to make sure no librarians have snuck up to eavesdrop, as they commonly like to do. "We're in high school, Jo. It's different. He would get into so much trouble—both of you would."

She rolls her eyes. "Only if people find out—which they won't."

"Oh, don't be stupid. Stuff like that always gets out eventually."

"Would you stop being a goody-two-shoes for five seconds," she whines. "Can't you just appreciate how awesome it would be to have those hands—God, he has nice hands—running all over—"

"*Ugh!*" I wave my hands in front of my face as if I can swat the mental images away. "No. Please keep your fantasies to yourself."

"Come *on*. We're about to be out of here anyway. If we don't take these risks now, we never will."

"Okay, *'taking a risk*—'" I actually air-quote the words because she clearly needs the distinction, "—by asking some guy out or whatever, and doing something that could put Mr. Graham in *jail* are two totally separate things."

She rolls her eyes and pulls some lip gloss out of her backpack. "That's a little dramatic, don't you think?"

"If you really want someone older, can't you just find a college guy or something?"

"Where would the fun be in that?" She reaches across the table and squeezes my wrist. "And just think about what a *great* first-time story this would make. So much better than some meat-head football player under the bleachers. He'd probably be a lot better at it, too."

Johanna always did love herself a good story.

I shake my head again, pulling my arm away. "I can't believe I'm even validating this idea by talking about it."

Suddenly, the low, droning tones of first bell fill the silence of the library, and when I look up, I realize a few other students trickled in while I wasn't paying attention.

I point a finger at Jo. "We are not done talking about this. So don't do anything stupid today."

She holds up her palms. "I'd never." In one fluid motion, she's standing, her bag tossed over one shoulder, her braid back in place across the other. "See you in fourth." She winks and takes off.

Fourth period is the only class we have together. It also happens to be taught by Mr. Graham.

MY FIRST TWO CLASSES PASS WITHOUT MUCH EVENT. Madam Fournier gives me an arched eyebrow at the sight of my hastily-scrawled essay, but I hurry to my seat before she can say anything. I'm a straight-A student and a second-semester senior. Compared to the rest of the people in this class, I'm Mother-freaking-Teresa.

Latin passes in a blur, then I head to the admin building for an appointment during my third-period open block. It's only a few months until graduation, and this is my first time in the guidance counselor's office. And if the meeting weren't required, I'd probably never step foot in here at all. Honestly, I'd kind of forgotten it was here. It's more of a department, with a spacious lobby and a dozen or so private cubicles Tetris-ed together behind the front desk. The receptionist glances up at me as I step inside. A pair of cheetah-print horn-rimmed glasses take up the majority of her face, complemented by bright red lipstick.

"Can I help you?" she asks. She doesn't smile.

"Um, yeah." I walk up to her desk, though she looks like she'd rather I didn't. "I have an appointment with Mrs. Russell?"

She looks away and starts typing, her acrylics aggressively tapping against the keyboard. "Name?"

"Meredith Beaumont." I adjust my backpack's straps on my shoulders, though there was nothing wrong with them in the first place.

"It's your senior exit interview?" she asks.

"Yeah."

She lets out a heavy sigh as if I've caused her a major inconvenience and pulls the glasses from her face. They hang around her neck on a purple-jeweled chain. No one wearing lipstick that affrontingly bright should be this grumpy. "Have a seat."

I hesitate for a second, and there's something hostile

about the way she raises her eyebrows at me. I scuttle away to the half-dozen chairs lined up against the wall. All but one are full, their occupants scrolling through their phones in various slumped-over positions. Unfortunately, the only remaining seat is between two guys. I avoid making eye contact and slip between them, setting my backpack in my lap and clutching it to my chest.

"What do you think her deal is?" The guy on my right nods his head toward the receptionist. "My guess is divorce."

At first, I'm not sure he's talking to me, but no one else has looked up from their phones, and now he's *definitely* looking at me, waiting for a response. He has short dark hair and those invisible braces on his upper teeth, and I'm pretty sure he's on the basketball team, though I'm certain we've never spoken before.

"Uh—" As usual, my brain fails me in coming up with a witty response. Or in this case, any response. Heat slowly creeps up my ears.

In some small act of grace, a woman appears around the corner and calls, "Meredith?"

I quickly hoist my backpack up and hurry after her, not looking back at the boy who now probably thinks I'm mentally deficient.

"I'm Mrs. Russell." The woman offers me a hand to shake, and I cringe a little because I know mine's sweaty. She pretends like she doesn't notice and leads me to her cubicle, which is the farthest one in the back. She's tall, her height further exaggerated by the six-inch heels she's wearing—bright yellow to match her blouse. Maybe wearing bright colors is some psychological job requirement.

Her cubicle is minimally decorated with a few plants and crayon drawings probably done by her kids. The one closest to me looks like a top-heavy giraffe with pink-painted nails, but I'm honestly not sure. She sinks into the seat behind her desk and motions for me to take one of the plush chairs across from her. The entire office reeks of lemon-scented cleaning supplies.

"Let me just pull up your file," she says, her typing much quieter than the receptionist's was. "Are you excited about graduation?"

"Very." I offer her a closed-lip smile.

"Well, your grades look great, and that's quite the impressive ACT score. I see here that you're interested in pursuing a pre-vet program? Are you still looking at the schools you have listed here?"

I wring my hands together in my lap. I'm focusing so hard on keeping eye contact with her that I almost don't process what she's saying. "Yeah, but now I'm just trying to find somewhere I can get a good scholarship." I break our eye contact and look at the picture of her golden retriever on the desk instead. "My parents don't really like the schools I'm looking at, so they're not going to help pay."

She leans back in her chair. "That's surprising. Most parents would be thrilled. UC-Davis, Cornell—these are all great schools."

"They're not all-girls, Christian, or close by." The words come out a lot harsher than I intend.

For a moment we just stare at each other.

Mrs. Russell nods slowly. "Beaumont. As in Pastor Beaumont?" Her voice sounds oddly sour when she says it.

"That would be the one." The closed-lip smile again.

"Well." She rolls her chair back and sifts through the brochures on her back wall. "You definitely have the grades to be a strong contender for a scholarship. You'll also need a good essay. A lot of schools offer merit scholarships, but you could also look for private ones. Have you already started applying? A lot of them have early deadlines. I think a lot have passed. Do you have any extracurriculars, volunteer work, work experience, anything like that? Good grades and test scores are great, but they won't be enough to make you to stand out." All of this comes out without her taking a single breath.

She hands me the stack of brochures, then rolls back over to her computer and starts typing again.

"I volunteer at the animal shelter," I say weakly.

"That's good." She nods, though it's less than enthusiastic. "Anything else?"

I shrug. "Not really."

"Hm." She purses her lips and scrolls on her computer. "You have a lot of AP classes, which is good. But colleges are really looking for more well-rounded and interesting candidates."

Did this woman seriously just call me boring?

"People with interesting hobbies, accomplishments, awards," she continues. "I'd work on padding your resume some more, and make sure you have a really impressive essay." She keeps nodding, though it seems to be more to herself than me, and leans forward to read something on her screen. Maybe she's reading from a script. "You should also apply pretty widely. For as many as you can. There's a big book in the library full of private scholarships you should check out. Did you apply to any smaller schools? You might want to aim lower—they might be more generous with their financial aid."

When she finally looks back at me, we stare at each other in silence for a couple of seconds before I realize I've been dismissed.

"Oh. Yeah. Thanks." I stand and slip my backpack over my shoulder.

"Don't forget your brochures!" She shoves the papers I'd left on her desk at me. "And good luck with everything!" She glances at her watch, stands, and follows me to the door. "Now, if you'll excuse me, I have another appointment."

The moment I take a step out of her cubicle, she passes me and heads back to the lobby. I shuffle through the papers in my hands, all of which are for local community colleges, and promptly shove them in the trashcan before following.

I'M HALFWAY TO MR. GRAHAM'S CLASSROOM FOR WORLD History when the bell rings, and the hallways instantly clog with people, as they always do during passing period. I flatten myself against the lockers as I attempt to slip through the jostling mass of bodies. The high-fives, loud conversations, and slamming lockers are just static in my ears. Usually, my anxiety would be going crazy in this crowd, but my mind keeps getting stuck on that look on Mrs. Russell's face, like I was completely delusional and out of my depths. Like I had *no chance* of going somewhere good. If my straight A's, near-perfect test scores, and volunteer experiences aren't enough for colleges, then what possibly is? If I weren't so angry by how dismissive and completely *unhelpful* she'd been, I'd probably be crying.

Jo was smart and scheduled her appointment earlier in the semester, but from what she told me, they hadn't been much help for her either. Once she dropped her aspiration bomb of art school and a photography degree, she pegged herself as an alumn unlikely to become a success story for their newsletter, and they sent her off with a pat on the back and a *good luck!* But Johanna's family has money, so at least they didn't tell her *don't bother*.

When I finally reach my destination, I nearly run into the door because the boy in front of me couldn't be bothered to hold it.

I slip inside, and Mr. Graham is standing at the front of the room in his fancy Mr. Graham attire—he always looks like he just stepped out of a Calvin Klein catalog—with his back to the class as he writes something on the whiteboard. You'd have to be blind not to notice how attractive he is, but I'd never really given it much thought. After that conversation with Jo this morning, however, I am hyperaware of him. My eyes fall on the way his hand grips the dry erase marker as I enter the room, and I quickly look away, heat prickling the back of my neck.

I head for my desk in the back, head down. Johanna's

seat is next to mine, but she's not here yet. The girls who sit in front of us, both members of what Johanna has labeled the Pretty Committee, are twisted toward each other in their chairs, chatting, blocking the entire aisle so I can't get through. I wait beside them, obviously trying to get past, but they don't move.

Finally, I say, "Excuse me."

They pull away from each other without looking at me, but they don't stop talking. The movement is so minor that I basically have to climb over the combination of bags, feet, and knees still blocking my path.

When Jo shows up, it's a completely different story. She doesn't bother waiting; she just pushes the girls aside and forces her way through.

"Excuse me!" Ashley, the blonde who sits in front of me, says.

"Yeah," Jo replies as she sinks into the seat beside me. "Excuse *you*. You're blocking the whole goddamn aisle."

Jo and I are not popular for two very different reasons. Me, because I'm invisible. Her, because she calls out bullshit when she sees it, hates everything about the Pretty Committee, and isn't shy about letting them know it. I, on the other hand, have nightmares at just the thought of confrontation.

Ashley levels Jo with a chilling look and then turns it on me, as if I'm guilty by association, before turning back to her friend. Johanna and I exchange a sideways glance.

While digging out my World History stuff from my backpack, I hear Jo make a drawn-out hum. She's watching Mr. Graham, shaking her head a little.

"*Damn*, he has a nice ass," she whispers to me. "Have you ever noticed how nice his ass is?"

I stare at her. "You're seriously starting to weird me out."

She sighs, rests her cheek in her hand, and continues to watch Mr. Graham as he strolls over to his desk and picks up a stack of papers. "I just appreciate nice things," she muses.

"Does someone want to help pass these out?" Mr. Graham asks the class.

"I'll do it!" Ashley pops up from her seat, smoothes down her plaid skirt, and hurries over to Mr. Graham. He hands her half the stack and she flips her hair over her shoulder.

"His first name is Oliver. Oliver Graham. God, even his name is attractive," Jo whispers.

I try to think of a nice way to tell Johanna she needs to stop wasting her time. It would be one thing if she just had a crush on him—and in all honesty, that would be justifiable—but she actually wants something to happen. And there's no way Mr. Graham would ever go there with her, or any student for that matter. Just look at the way he's ignored Ashley's obvious flirting the past few months.

"Jo—"

"Who is...*Meredith Beaumont?*" Ashley stands at the front, squinting at the paper on the top of her stack.

I lift my hand a little. "Over here."

It's not like I sit behind you. Or have had at least one class with you every year since fourth grade.

"Oh." She struts over to our seats and plops the old

worksheet on my desk. "Sorry." Funny. She doesn't look the least bit sorry. "You're just so *quiet.*" She pauses and smiles like she's waiting for me to laugh with her. Like she just said something clever. As if she's unique in pointing out the one thing every fucking person feels the need to point out, as if I of all people am not cripplingly aware of this fact.

Extroverted people like to point out shyness like it's the punchline to the ultimate joke. A joke that just never seems to get funny, despite hearing it thirty times a day. But every time someone points it out, I feel myself shrink just a little bit smaller. Because no matter how hard I try to break out of my comfort zone, to talk just a little bit more—hell, even if I did a complete 180 and turned into the bubbliest of extroverts—it wouldn't matter. Once people have decided you're a "quiet one," they never let it go.

They never let you forget it.

As she flips away and moves on to the next paper in her hands, one of her friends—another member of the Pretty Committee—leans toward her and whispers, "Has she been in our class the whole year?"

Ashley giggles. "Right?"

Suddenly my whole body feels hot, and I hear their laughter like it's crawled inside of my bones. But I do what I always do. I grit my teeth, pretend I didn't hear, and turn back to Jo.

Mr. Graham stops beside my desk to drop off my latest test. Ninety-four. Relieved, I snatch it off my desk and do a quick flip through of the pages. History has never been my strongest subject, but I studied for this one for *weeks*.

While he shuffles through the remaining papers in his hands, I glance over to catch Jo shamelessly staring at him. He pulls one from the pile and hands it to her, facedown.

"Johanna, could you see me after class?" he asks.

She sits up taller, smiling. "Of course."

As soon as he's gone, Jo leans across the aisle and whispers, "Did you hear that? He wants to *see me* after class." She wiggles her eyebrows.

I flip her test over. Fifty-two.

I grimace. "I think it might have more to do with that."

Her lips pucker.

"What do you have in this class right now?" I ask. "You know you need to pass to graduate."

The pucker intensifies. "History really isn't my forte."

"If you want, I could tutor you—"

She gasps and slams her hands down on her desk, her eyes lit with excitement. Blonde Number Two whips around to glare, but Jo just waves her off with a middle finger and turns back to me. "Thanks for the offer—really, Mare, I love you forever—but I just got a better idea. What if I ask Mr. Graham to tutor me? Then we'd have all this alone time, and...*you know*," she mouths. "This couldn't have worked out better if I'd planned it."

I'm shaking my head before she even finishes speaking. "Jo, please let this go."

But Mr. Graham has already returned to his place at the front of the class to begin teaching, and Jo turns away, fully engrossed.

"Today is the day I know you've all been looking

forward to." Mr. Graham holds up a stack of papers. "Group projects."

The class makes no effort to hide their groans as Mr. Graham starts working his way through the aisles again, assigning group members and passing out papers. I say a silent prayer that I don't end up with a group that makes me do all of the work. Usually, when that happens, it's not that big of a deal. But apparently, at least according to our esteemed guidance counselors, I have a lot of work to do if I want any hope of getting into college, so I don't have time to carry a bunch of dead weight for a project that's worth half our grade.

"Meredith." Mr. Graham appears at my side and hands me the assignment. "You'll be with Johanna and Ashley." He hands each of them a sheet of paper and moves on before my brain has the chance to fully process this information.

"I am so sorry," Ashley's friend mutters and lays her hand on Ashley's arm before turning away to her own group.

Ashley turns around in her seat to face us, her upper lip curled back.

"Don't worry," Johanna says flatly. "We're just as happy about this as you are."

"That's doubtful," Ashley snips.

"Look at it this way," Johanna replies. "You just lucked out. You've got a group who'll do everything for you so we don't turn in anything stupid."

Ashley's jaw sets. "Did you just call me dumb?"

"We just both need a good grade on this," I cut in

before Jo can say anything else. Judging by how high her eyebrows have risen, it wouldn't have been anything pleasant.

Ashley turns her glare on me, nostrils flared. "And you think I'm incapable of getting a good grade?"

I open my mouth, but nothing comes out.

"We can meet at my house," Johanna offers. "This isn't due for a while, so how about next week?"

"Fine," Ashley says through her teeth. "And since you two are so smart, why don't you start brainstorming topics? Now if you'll excuse me, I'm going to go be stupid in the bathroom." She storms out of the room, a tube of lip gloss in hand.

"I think we just made her hate us even more than she already did," I mutter.

"I didn't think that was possible." Johanna grins like this is an accomplishment.

"Everything okay back there?" Mr. Graham calls from his desk.

Johanna just grins wider and gives him a thumbs up. "Oh, everything is great."

3

I've been staring at my laptop screen for so long that even after I blink my eyes shut, I can still see the webpage burned into my eyelids. Immediately after getting home from school, I'd set myself up in my room and gotten to work. And after two hours of sitting here, all I've learned is there are about a million different ways I can write my college essay, but unless I've already won an Olympic medal, started a successful nonprofit, or starred in a Hollywood movie, none of them are going to do me much good.

I've drafted the essay approximately fifty-six times at this point, all about my life, my passions, my goals. Which should be good enough, given this is a *personal statement*, but I can't stop replaying that stupid guidance counselor's words in my mind. There's nothing about my life that'll make my essay stand out from however many thousands of applicants. There's nothing that interesting. Nothing they haven't already seen before. I'm a kid who likes animals and has good grades. But so does every other applicant now. Everyone has straight A's. Everyone takes AP classes. Everyone gets a thirty-five on the ACT. Maybe I *am* just boring.

With a frustrated groan, I minimize the now overly-revised Word doc and pull up my most frequented bookmark: the link to Closet Atheists.

My eyes immediately dart to the door. Even though I know it's closed, I still double check. Maman's still at work at the boutique, but I can hear Papa's gospel music downstairs and Harper working out next door. It's very unlikely either will come check on me.

I keep the link hidden three-folders-deep on my computer, so just in case someone borrows it, they don't stumble across the site accidentally. The red bubble at the top of the page informs me there are four new posts in a forum I'm following. The thread is about atheists and nonbelievers trapped in religious households. I've never posted anything out of paranoia that it would somehow, someway get traced back to me. Even though the site uses anonymous usernames, I'm terrified Papa will somehow find out, as if my internet search history is tattooed on my forehead.

One of the chat rooms shows recent activity, so I pull it up and start scrolling.

Fallen2Reason009: *If I'm forced to lead prayer at the dinner table one more time I swear I'm going to scream.*

JesusInTheHizhouse: *My grandma won't stop buying*

me bibles. This is the seventh she's given me this year. We've passed annoying and now it's just downright insulting. I AM AN ATHIEST. DEAL WITH IT.

Alice_in_atheist_land: *Came out of the atheist closet to my mom today. She looked at me like I spontaneously caught on fire.*

Nope_NoGod746: *The prison wardens—ie my parents—have given up on trying to convert me. Looks like they're sending me off to live with my uncle in the middle of nowhere Montana to "find my way back." No internet there. Probably won't be able to post for a while. They may even just off me while I'm out there. I guess you'll never know. It was nice knowing ya'll. Stay strong.*

A text notification *dings* onto the screen, making me jump. My gaze darts to the door for a second before I dig around in my backpack for my phone. Johanna.

Johanna: *Guess who has an afterschool meeting with Mr. Hot Stuff tomorrow?? ;)*

Meredith: *I still vote abort mission*

Johanna: *If it were up to you I'd die a virgin!*

Meredith: *If it were up to you we'd all end up in prison!*

Johanna: *Mare Bear, this is happening. Get on board.*

The use of correct punctuation makes me pause. She never uses periods.

Meredith: *Okay, honestly Jo, idk why you're doing this. What do you have to prove?*

Johanna: *I don't have to prove anything! I'm doing this because I want to. And if you're just gonna bitch about it every time it comes up, then I guess we have nothing left to talk about*

Meredith: *Come on, Jo*

Johanna: *I've already made up my mind.*
Meredith: *This is just so needlessly risky! It's not smart, Jo.*
Johanna: *Just call me stupid then.*
Meredith: *You know that's not what I'm saying*

Three dots appear as she starts typing something else, but they disappear just as quickly. They appear and disappear three more times, but she never responds. I sigh and toss my phone across my bed, not wanting to deal with it right now. If she's asking me to support her hooking up with our teacher, it's just not going to happen. And the fact that she's mad at me like *I'm* the one being unreasonable is ridiculous.

Propping myself against my headboard, I pull my laptop into my lap and resume scrolling through the chatroom, though my heart's not really in it anymore.

____o_o____replied: *Yo, Fallen2Reason009, start off real serious, praising Jesus or some shit, then make a complete 180 and start talking about Satan or something before they realize what's happening. They'll never ask you to do the prayer again. Bonus points if it's some big family gathering. Worked for me ;)*

SufferInSilence303 replied: *Don't do that. There's no need to be insensitive and insulting.*

____o_o____replied: *Yeah, cuz obviously they're being real sensitive to* his *beliefs.*

Oblivion replied: *Have you tried telling them how it makes you uncomfortable? Say you don't mind if they partake in their religious practices at the table, and you'll respect that, but you won't participate. If you stay calm and level-headed, they'll take you more seriously and be more susceptible to reason.*

___o_o____replied: *Still think you should start pledging your allegiance to the Dark One.*

It was freshman year when I first found the site. Back then, there were only seventy or so people who frequented the forums. In the past four years, that number has jumped to over a thousand, and now it's kind of become my after-school tradition to do a quick read-through of the updates. Even though I never post anything, I've weirdly started to think of the posters as my friends.

And even though I admire the people brave enough to tell their parents—though more often than not the situation ends poorly—I just don't think I could ever do it. There's a lot of things my parents could forgive me for, but this isn't one of them.

"Hey!"

The door to my room swings open and Harper's head pops in. I jump and slam my laptop shut, my heart lurching in my chest.

Harper's eyes dart from the computer to my face, a single eyebrow raised. Her hair is tied back in a sweaty ponytail, and she's still in her running shorts and lime green sneakers.

"What's up?" I ask, brushing my laptop off my legs casually as if I hadn't just acted incredibly suspicious.

She narrows her eyes. "Papa wants help with dinner."

"Great!" My voice comes out too loud and too high. "I'll be right down!"

Harper stares at me a moment longer before walking away, leaving the door open.

The moment she's gone, I let out a long, slow breath,

and open my laptop to clear the history before heading downstairs. Harper immediately plops down at the kitchen table, which is currently buried beneath a mountain of her belongings. Her backpack lays discarded on its side, bright highlighters and loose-leaf paper spilling out dangerously close to the edge of the table. An empty plastic water bottle lays on its side on the floor, a casualty of Harper's workout. I've been nagging her for years to switch to something reusable because of the waste and what single-use plastic is doing to the planet, but she seems to conveniently *forget* nearly every day.

Papa is standing at the kitchen island in his tall white chef's hat, a handprint of flour smeared across his left cheek. I have no idea where he found the hat, but he's worn it every time he's been in charge of dinner for the past month.

"Meredith," he calls, waving the wooden spoon in his hand. "Would you mind chopping those vegetables?" He points to the cutting board already set up across the island.

Why did he need my help when Harper's right here?

I glance in her direction and she flips the textbook open, revealing a large diagram of a man's...erm, *parts*, and quickly covers the page with her worksheet, eyes flashing to Papa.

Her cheeks redden when she notices me watching. "What?" she snaps.

I quirk an eyebrow. I recognize the textbook—everyone has to take Health 101 freshman year, but I can't resist making her squirm a bit.

"I'm doing my homework!" she insists.

"Mm-hm," I tease and take up the vegetable-cutting station.

I'm not sure what Papa's making, but the scent of garlic fills the kitchen, and I can feel the heat of the oven from here. My eyes start watering almost immediately after I start chopping the onion, and I try to rub at them with the inside of my elbow instead of my hand so I don't get any of the food in my eyes, but they start burning just the same. "*Ugh*." I whirl around, eyes squinting, trying to feel my way toward the sink.

"Onions?" Papa asks.

"Always."

He chuckles a little. "I'll get it."

I hear the sink run, then Papa presses a wet paper towel into my hand. The water takes the edge off the burning enough that I can open my eyes again.

"Switch places?" Papa offers. "You just need to turn the potatoes over in about five minutes."

I nod, still dabbing at my eyes.

Papa nods at the now-empty roll of paper towels. "I'll go grab another."

I grab the spatula from the counter to flip the potatoes as he heads for the hall.

"*Harper!*" Papa's gasp fills the kitchen. "What is this?"

I turn to see Papa practically prying the textbook out of Harper's hands, her mouth open in a small oval of terror. His gaze shoots back and forth between me and Harper as if the two of us are conspiring on this. "What class is this for?" he demands, waving the offending textbook in the air.

Harper sends me a pleading look. I stand frozen on the opposite side of the kitchen, spatula still in hand. I'd always assumed Papa and Maman would hate the Sex Ed part of that class, which is precisely why I never talked about it or let them see my homework.

"I'm guessing it's for Health class," I say. "All freshmen have to take it."

Papa's mouth drops open in an almost cartoonish way as he snatches Harper's worksheet from the table and reads through the questions. My muscles tense, waiting for an explosion, but it never comes. Instead, Papa's body goes very still, except for the slightest shake of his head.

"You took this class too?" he finally says. It takes me a moment to realize the question is directed at me.

I try to swallow, but it feels like it gets caught in my throat. "Yeah, everyone does—"

"I *told* Colette..." he trails off, shaking his head, and hands Harper back her homework and textbook. "This is what we get for sending you to public school," he mutters.

"It's just a short section of the class," I offer. "Like two-weeks long—"

But Papa isn't listening. He's already dialing something on his phone and heading for the door. "Can you finish dinner, Mare?" he calls over his shoulder. "I need to make a call."

"Sure," I say, though he's already out the door before he can hear my response. Harper and I exchange a grimace.

"That can't be good," she says.

My mind runs through every possibility of who he

could be calling—Maman to discuss the grave mistake of letting us go to a public school, Mr. Johnson to do whatever he and his friend do—I'm assuming the male equivalent of me and Jo bitching about our lives—or, the worst case scenario, he's calling the school to complain.

"No," I agree. "This is not going to be good."

4

HERE'S THE THING ABOUT MY FRIENDSHIP WITH Johanna: she's my best friend, and I'm hers. But she also has plenty of other friends. And like most outgoing, charismatic people, she's easy to like. But for me, Jo is one of my *only* friends. I don't know why making friends has always been so easy for her; when we were five on the playground, she'd just walk up to any kid and start talking to them, even if she'd never seen them before. For me, it's always seemed so much more complicated. No one is interested in being friends with the quiet girl because she doesn't seem that interesting. It's all too easy to not notice her at all.

It's not until the next day at school, when Jo decides she's giving me the cold shoulder until I support her on her Mr. Graham endeavors, that I realize how serious she is.

In the halls, she walks right past me like everyone else does; during lunch, I have to sit at a table all by myself in the corner while she sits with her friends from the yearbook staff; I wait for her by her locker, but when she sees me, she turns and walks the other way. She hasn't ignored me like this since a stupid fight we had sophomore year, and that time it lasted *weeks*.

The only words we exchange during the entire day are when I lean over during fourth period and tap her with my pencil. Mr. Graham is busy writing something on the board, and Jo is pretending to take notes, but I can see she's really just doodling.

"Jo," I whisper.

She hesitates a few seconds before glancing my way. "What?" she mouths.

"How long are you going to keep this up?" I ask.

She raises her eyebrows, glances at Mr. Graham, then back to me.

My expression is apparently not what she wants to see, because she turns back to doodling butterflies that look like crooked hearts. A few minutes later when I try to get her attention again, she pretends like she doesn't notice.

And that's how the rest of the day goes.

Suddenly it feels like there's this barrier between us, this slowly growing distance, and I'm terrified she's not going to stop pushing me away until I support her on this. And all I know is there's just about nothing I wouldn't do to keep her, and I refuse to waste our last few weeks of high school with this pointless radio silence.

So after the final bell, I make my way back toward the west part of campus. Mr. Graham agreed to tutor her for an hour after school every other day, and today is their first session. I peek through the window of his classroom. He's standing at the front of the room writing something on the board, and she's seated in the first row, chin propped on her hand, an empty notebook on the desk in front of her. There's something cat-like about the way she watches him, eyes slit and flickering back and forth, following his every movement. When he turns around and says something, gesturing with his hands, Johanna nods seriously, twirling her pencil around her fingers.

The hallway is quiet and empty, with everyone else already heading home for the day. My footsteps seem twice as loud as I pace back and forth in front of the door, trying to figure out what I should say to Jo when I see her. *I'm sorry? I can't support you, but please stop ignoring me?* I don't know if I can make it through the rest of the year like this. Maybe my face will look pathetic enough that she'll take pity on me.

I sigh and wander to the lockers across the hall, press my back against their cool surface, and slide down until I reach the floor. I'm about to pull out some homework to work on when the faint sound of approaching footsteps breaks the silence. I see the shoes first—shiny and black but worn enough to leave permanent wrinkles in the leather. A familiar pang twists in my gut before I even see his face.

"What are you doing here?" I ask, suddenly feeling very small sitting on the floor.

Papa looks around the empty hallway, confusion pinching his eyebrows together. "What are *you* doing out here?" he counters.

I point at the classroom in front of me. "I'm waiting for Jo. You didn't answer my question."

Papa straightens his already straight tie. "I have a meeting with your principal in," he checks his watch, "five minutes."

If your entire body could groan, that's the sensation that fills me. "Why?" I ask, even though I'm pretty sure I know the answer. *Damn it, Harper.* Why couldn't she just do her homework in her room like every other angsty teenager?

"Just to have a chat," Papa assures me, as if sensing my unease.

"This isn't about Harper's homework—"

"I'll see you at home," he cuts me off and continues down the hall. "I don't want to be late."

With that, he disappears in the direction of the admin building, perfectly comfortable finding his way from the many meetings he's had there before.

An hour later, Jo slips out of the classroom. She's all dolled up today, more so than usual. But it's Jo, so she made sure it wasn't too obvious. She's wearing a casual black T-shirt dress with riding boots, her hair loose and wavy. Her cheekbones are perfectly bronzed and shimmery. I notice the long, gold necklace dangling from her neck and smile a little. I gave that to her for her sixteenth birthday.

When she sees me sitting against the lockers, she

frowns, but she doesn't turn around and walk away, so I guess that's progress. I rise to my feet and pull my bag onto my shoulder.

"What are you doing here?" she asks and crosses her arms over her chest.

"It's Tuesday." I shrug. "You always come over on Tuesdays."

Her frown lessens, just a shade, but her eyes are narrowed now, flickering back and forth across my face, watching me the way she was watching Mr. Graham.

Maybe if I act like everything is normal, things will actually go back to normal. "So are you coming or not?" I ask with a nod to the side.

Her eyes are still narrowed, but she takes a step toward me. "Only if we stop and get milkshakes first."

I PULL LITTLE RED STEW UP TO THE MENU IN THE farthest parking spot from the door at the drive-in, noticing for the first time the large chip in the black nail polish on my right thumb, even though I just painted them yesterday. I make sure to pull my car close enough to the machine this time so I don't have to climb out to slide my card. The metal speaker is rusted, the yellow button faded and stained with age. The glossy board behind it advertises half-off milkshakes after 2:00 p.m. with enlarged, over-saturated pictures of fried food so cheap I don't like to think about what it's really made of.

The drive-in is packed with cars and kids from our

school, a shiny new car in every spot. I love my little Stew, but at times like this, it's impossible not to notice his chipping paint, his cracked leather seats, the way his passenger door only opens if you lift the handle *just right*...

The great thing about drive-ins, however, is we don't have to get out of the car, so we don't have to deal with the people. Johanna leans across my lap to shout her Oreo cheesecake milkshake order out my window.

"Gross," I comment before ordering my own, vanilla.

"Boring," she observes with a grunt of disapproval.

We sit in silence while we wait for the shakes, watching our classmates laugh and lounge together on the picnic tables surrounding the restaurant. A dozen or so are all trying to squeeze into a table built for half that much, leaving some standing behind seats and others perched on the edge.

Bracing myself, I take a deep breath and decide to go for it. If we're going to talk about this, we might as well do it now when she's dependent on me for a ride so she can't get away.

"How'd your tutoring session go?" I ask, trying to keep my voice casual.

She props her feet on the dash and leans back, eyeing me sideways. "Was this all a ruse to get me alone so you could lecture me?"

"Of course not. We've done Milkshake Tuesdays every week since I got my license."

She still looks suspicious. "It went well."

"Did anything...happen?"

Now she rolls her eyes. "Nothing *happened*, so you can

stop looking like someone shoved a porcupine up your ass. I'm not an idiot. I can't just throw myself at him right away. It needs to be subtle. Today was just planting the seed."

"So you've got it all planned out, then?"

"Look, Mare, if you're just going to judge me—"

"I'm not judging you, Jo." I sigh and grip the steering wheel with both hands. I focus on how soft and warm the leather feels against my palms. "Okay, look. I don't like what you're doing—you *know* I don't like this at all—but I'm not willing to risk our friendship over this. I don't want to spend the last weeks of our senior year fighting."

She sits up in her seat, cautious excitement prodding her face. "So…"

"So you better be really freaking careful if you're going to do this. And not just about not getting caught, but also, what if Mr. Graham turns out to be a perv or something? And you have to tell me *everything*."

Her entire face breaks into a grin. "You want the dirty details, do you?"

"No. I want to be able to cover for you if you get yourself into trouble."

She nods. "Okay, deal."

A carhop in roller skates pulls up to the car with our milkshakes. When I roll down my window and exchange a couple of dollars for the drinks, our classmates' laughter seeps in. As he skates away, a large, white SUV pulls into the spot beside me, the music so loud it's shaking the car.

Ashley.

I quickly roll up the window.

She either hasn't noticed us or doesn't care. Every seat

in her car is packed with other members of the Pretty Committee. Johanna notices a moment later and sits up straighter.

"Don't leave," she says.

I was already reaching for the ignition. "Why not?"

"Because then it'll look like we let them chase us off!"

"Or it'll look like we already got our food, which we have." I emphasize this with a sip of my milkshake.

"*No*, it'll look like she scared us off. No way." She reaches over and plucks the keys from the ignition before I can stop her. "We're staying."

"You can't be serious." I try to snatch the keys back, but she stashes them in her pocket. "Jo. This is ridiculous. It's not going to look like anything. She hasn't even noticed that we're here, and if she does, she's not going to care."

"She hasn't noticed us, huh?" Jo points through the windshield. The Pretty Committee is now standing amid the picnic tables with the jocks, laughing and talking to each other, looking straight at us.

I have a bad feeling about this. "Maybe we should just go..."

"Oh, hell no. Especially not now. Hold your ground, Mare." Jo stares pointedly back at them.

And then the first packet of ketchup is thrown. It makes contact with the windshield and explodes in a small burst of red. There's not even enough time to react before more start pounding against the car, covering the windshield. It gets to the point where there's so much ketchup that I can't see through the glass enough to see who's throwing. Judging by the quantity, it's everyone. I briefly wonder how they're managing to make them explode, unless they're opening the packets before throwing them.

After the initial jump of surprise, Jo and I sit silently in the car, waiting for it to stop. Jo, however, looks like her head is about to blow up. Her hands are clenched into fists in her lap, her teeth locked together. I'm more annoyed than anything, thinking about how I'm going to have to clean my car later.

Once the windshield looks like a crime scene, the pounding stops, replaced by a chorus of laughter. I'm too consumed by my thoughts, wondering if turning on the windshield wipers will just make it worse, to stop Jo when she throws the door open and jumps out.

Oh no.

I hurry out of the car as she stomps toward the crowd of students. They're literally caught red-handed, what with the ketchup dripping down their fingers, but they don't look the least bit concerned. If anything, they seem thrilled that Johanna is engaging.

I'm terrified of what will happen a moment before it does: Jo marches right up to Ashley and slaps her.

Silence falls over the crowd. For a moment, nobody moves. The rest of the Pretty Committee looks outraged. The guys look thrilled at the prospect of a fight. Ashley brings a hand to her cheek, where a distinct red mark in the shape of Jo's hand is beginning to form.

The moment doesn't last long.

"You crazy bitch!" Ashley shrills and lunges forward as if to seize Johanna's hair.

I surge forward, grab Johanna by the crook of her arm,

and yank her out of Ashley's reach. Ashley stumbles forward, her hands catching air, and her eyes shoot to me. The look she gives me is so cold, I actually shiver. She's undeterred. She, along with a couple of her friends, step toward us, wanting a fight. Johanna clenches her hands into fists—if this *does* turn into a fight, Johanna isn't going to be doing any more bitch-slapping or hair-pulling. It'll be the real thing.

I yank her back again and shove her toward the passenger seat. "Get in the car," I order.

She doesn't look happy about it, but she complies. As soon as I slam the door shut, Ashley bangs her fist against the window.

"Get back out here and face us, you cowards."

Johanna's entire body tenses at the word. Snatching the keys from her, I throw the car into reverse before she can jump back out, and run the windshield wipers at the fastest possible speed. The ketchup smears across the windshield, but I don't stop. I just keep driving.

"I can't believe you stopped me. Do you have any idea how long I've wanted to kick Ashley Miller's ass?"

Johanna and I are sitting in my basement, finishing off our milkshakes, catching up on some trashy reality TV shows on Netflix. Every couple of minutes, Jo brings the fight back up, shaking her head and clenching her jaw as if just thinking about it is pissing her off all over again.

"Honestly," I say around a spoonful of my milkshake's

dregs, "If it had been *just* Ashley, I might have let you. But you were outnumbered one to, like, twenty. You're badass, Jo, but you're not that badass."

"I would have had you for backup." She can't even say it with a straight face.

I snort and accidentally spit some of my milkshake, which just makes Jo and me crack up harder. I have my talents, but none of them include any sort of physical activity. My mother tried putting me in ballet as a kid because I was so uncoordinated, but took me out of the class after two weeks to save me the embarrassment and the other dancers the hazard.

I shake my head, wiping the milkshake from my chin. "I can't believe you slapped her."

"It felt so good." Johanna rolls so she's hanging upside down from the couch's arm. "Sorry about your car, though."

I shrug and set my milkshake on the coffee table. "I'll take it to the carwash later, but I bet it'll still smell like ketchup for another week or so."

Jo scrunches her nose. "At least none of it got inside."

"True."

"So..." Jo grins. "Sunday is just a mere five days away."

I snort, fishing my spoon around the bottom of my cup for the remaining frozen chunks. "So?"

"*So*, that means you'll see Sam at church. You have to talk to him. And don't give me anymore of that, *Gee, Johanna, I don't know*, bullshit. You're doing this. *This* Sunday. You signed a contract."

I roll my eyes. "You realize that isn't a real contract, right?"

"That's irrelevant." She's been hanging upside down for so long now that her face is nearly as red as her hair. "You agreed to this. Now it's time for you to start following through."

I don't argue, because as much as the idea terrifies me, a small part feels a kind of exhilaration. I *do* want to do this. And on Sunday, I will.

5

On Sunday morning I quickly realize how much easier it is to be brave with Johanna in my basement than it is standing on a curb outside of the church, alone, my entire body jittering like I've had three too many shots of espresso. My family arrives early, as usual, but I trail behind them as we cross the parking lot so they can't see the nervous energy thrumming through me. Suddenly I'm afraid I'll lose my nerve. Harper shoots me a narrow-eyed look over her shoulder, scrutinizing my face as if my guilt is written there.

A black car pulls into the lot.

"Where's Johanna today?" Papa asks as we near the front doors.

Sleeping in, probably wanting to leave me alone for what I'm about to do. I trail the car with my gaze, willing my parents to hurry up and get inside. "She's not feeling well," I lie.

"Oh *no*," Harper mock pouts.

We just ignore her.

"I'll add her to my prayers," Maman says.

The car finishes its leisurely stroll through the empty rows, parking just a few yards away. When its passengers emerge onto the blacktop, my heart speeds up and pounds painfully against my ribs.

"I'll meet you guys inside," I tell them. Harper shoots me another suspicious look, but disappears into the church without a word.

I am hyperaware of how damp the fabric beneath my armpits feels and make a mental note to keep my arms down at my sides so no one else will see. I should have worn a looser shirt. Or something black. Anything but yellow. *Of course* sweat would be obvious in yellow. The blouse was a little too small, too—an extra-small from my early high school years before my boobs came in. I definitely should've picked something less form-fitting so I wouldn't constantly have to remind myself to suck my stomach in.

Mr. Johnson's wearing the same black suit—or at least one that looks similar enough to last week's that I can't tell the difference; Sam's in a pair of khaki shorts and a white collared shirt, the shirtsleeves pushed up to his elbows, his dark hair disheveled. I'm beginning to think that's how it always looks. Mr. Johnson laughs at something Sam said as they cross the lot. I don't think either of them have noticed me yet. This just reminds me that they will, in fact, notice me at some point.

My hands start sweating. I wipe my palms on the back of my jeans—I managed to talk Maman into allowing me to wear them as long as I wore a nice blouse on top, hence the ugly yellow monstrosity—and force a smile as they approach.

I should really invest in some of that lotion that makes your hands stop sweating I keep seeing on infomercials.

"*Bonjour*, Meredith!" Mr. Johnson calls, looking all too pleased at his attempt at French. It comes out as "bun-juer."

My fight-or-flight response is in full gear, and I'm about two seconds away from bolting and forgetting the whole thing. I need to get him out of here before I lose my nerve.

"*Salut*, Monsieur Johnson. Sam."

"Hey," Sam responds, takes the sunglasses from his face, and hangs them from the neckline of his shirt. When he meets my eyes, a soft smile pulls at the corner of his mouth, and I have to look away.

"No friend today?" Mr. Johnson asks.

This is it. Now or never.

Oh my God, my entire body is trembling.

Get ahold of yourself.

"Yeah, she's not feeling well. I was hoping maybe Sam could keep me company instead until the service starts?" My voice steadily rises with each word, ending in a shrill, shaky peak.

Sam blinks, his eyebrows rising in surprise. Mr. Johnson just grins. "Of course, of course. Your father and I have been talking about how the two of you should spend more time together. In fact, feel free to sit with them during the service, Sam." Mr. Johnson's practically bouncing with excitement as he nudges Sam toward me and hurries into the church.

Now we're alone, and there's a fifty-fifty chance I'll throw up.

A corner of Sam's mouth quirks. "I think you just made his life."

"He and my dad, both."

His expression shifts just a notch, like a record skipping. "Did your dad ask you to hang out with me?"

Is that disappointment on his face? I can't ignore the small thrill the thought gives me. "No, not at all." I take a deep breath, trying to steady my voice. "I was actually wondering if you wanted to get out of here."

Full-on shock blooms across his face. "Right now?"

I fold my arms behind my back, hooking each hand around the opposite elbow. I don't trust my voice not to get all high-pitched again, so I just say, "Mm-hm."

"We'd miss your dad's service," he says slowly. His eyebrows lower over his eyes—and now I can't get Jo's comment about flirty eyebrows out of my head.

"Oh, right." I rock back on my heels. *Abort, abort, abort.* I wave my hands like the whole thing was no big deal and I'm definitely not having a heart attack right now. "Of course, if you want to stay—"

Sam shoves his hands in his pockets, intimidatingly calm. I can't read his face at all. "I mean, if you want to, I'm totally fine with ditching it. I just wasn't sure if you'd want to miss it."

I nod at the plaza across the road. "How about we go get some coffee instead?"

I HAVE NEVER IN MY EIGHTEEN YEARS OF LIFE MISSED one of my dad's sermons. It's not even a rule in our house—it's just assumed to be understood. But instead of guilt, this small act of deviance is giving me a sort of...thrill.

Sam and I make our way across the street, occasionally filling the silence with meaningless small talk—most of which he has to supply because I'm too socially inept to think of the proper things to say. He's polite, but reserved. We both are. Although our dads have been best friends all our lives, I don't think either of us knows much about the other. We grew up together, but once we reached our teens, we went separate ways. I think the last time we had a conversation was middle school. We were never *close*, but we spoke. An acquaintances-by-default kind of thing. But it was a lot easier to talk to him on a swing set back when we both had braces. Now he looks like an underwear model, and I'm shaking so badly I probably look like a Chihuahua.

This unspoken mystery of where we now stand draws a line between us, and I don't think either of us knows how to cross it.

When we reach the coffee shop, he holds the door open for me, and I blush for no apparent reason. Inside, the lights are dim and the small wooden tables are empty. Light jazz music plays in the background. The woman behind the counter has a half-shaved head and nearly a dozen piercings distributed throughout different regions of her face. She glances at us with a bored expression.

"You, uh, want to grab us a table and I'll get the drinks?" Sam offers.

"Black iced coffee," I say by way of response, and he looks relieved that I didn't make a big deal out of him paying. Truthfully, I just now realized I forgot my wallet and he saved me from a mortifying moment at the cashier.

It isn't until I'm sitting at the table in the corner waiting for him to return with the drinks that it hits me. Coffee, him paying—this looks suspiciously like a date. Which means I'm actually doing this. Which means he's going to sit down across from me any second now and I'm going to have to hold an actual conversation with him. What do we talk about? I doubt he's still into dinosaurs and Disney movies. Am I supposed to bring up our extinct friendship, or am I supposed to be flirty? How do you even *be* flirty? Does he like funny girls? God, I don't even know what he likes anymore.

Now I'm blushing all over again. This was such a stupid idea. No matter how badly I want to be this girl, I'm not. I'm not confident and cool. I'm just *not*. I'm so consumed by my own panic that I don't even notice him approach until he's sitting across from me and there's a coffee cup in my hand.

"Wow. You look like you're trying to solve some kind of differential equation or something."

I blink at him. "Huh?"

"I just mean—" He clears his throat. "You looked really concentrated on whatever you were thinking about, is all."

"Oh." I laugh. It comes out horribly hysterical and cackle-like. I slam my mouth shut. Oh, God, he's going to think I'm crazy. *Think of something funny to say back.* The only thing I can think of is, *You looked like you were constipated when you showed up to church with your dad, with your scowling and everything,* but oh my God I can't say that. That's not even funny! It's just gross. And now that it's in my head, I can't think of anything else.

And now we're sitting in uncomfortable silence.

"So, um, you go to Northfield now, right?" he offers as he folds his sunglasses and sets them on the table.

I leap in. Easy enough topic. "Yeah. You go to Madison Prep?"

Northfield is the main public school, and Madison prep is the all-boys private school across town. There's a separate branch of Madison for girls—but the entire school is ridiculously expensive and difficult to get into if you're not a legacy. It's for the smartest and the richest—and as Jo commonly corrects, the snobbiest. Northfield is sort of the dumping ground for everyone else.

Sam's dad is a Madison Prep alum.

"Yeah," he frowns.

"You don't like it there?" I ask, grateful the conversation is leaning toward him.

He shrugs and sips his coffee. "It's fine. I guess I can't complain, because I know I'm getting a good education, but I swear everyone there just takes themselves too seriously. You'd think they were curing cancer or something with the way they strut around. Some classes just feel like our only purpose is to sit there to give the teacher an audience for him to talk about how awesome he is. Or give him an opportunity to require us to buy his book."

I nod, but not because I understand or agree. Honestly, I only processed about half of what he said. I'm trying to listen, but it's like my anxiety is muffling everything around me and I can't hear anything over my own pounding heart. But then realize I need to say something in reply, and a cold moment of terror seizes me. Do I reply seriously, or make a joke?

Mon Dieu, why is this so hard?

He saves me again and asks, "Do you like Northfield?"

He must feel like he's having this conversation with himself.

"Uhh..." I trail off and stare intently at my coffee. "There's nothing wrong with the school. It's just...well...yeah."

He's leaning toward me, elbows propped on the table. He's close enough to me that I can see the dark blue outline of his eyes, the freckles on the bridge of his nose. Suddenly the table doesn't feel like enough distance between us. I can smell the mint from his toothpaste. "It's what?" he asks.

I lean back in my chair in an attempt to put more space between us, but it does little to calm my nerves. "I guess it's more my fault than the school's that I haven't liked high school."

"How do you mean?" he asks, his brow furrowing a bit. The way his gaze never wavers from my face makes me feel like I'm standing center-stage, sweating beneath a spotlight.

I hesitate, licking my lips. There's no good way to explain this without sounding like a complete loser. "I guess I just feel like I never really put myself out there, so I've missed a lot of opportunities."

Finally, he relaxes back into his chair, one arm propped on the table, the other holding his coffee. My feet drum against the floor, tapping out a steady rhythm—*one-two-three, one-two-three, one-two-three.*

"So if you're not super involved with school," he asks, "what do you like to do for fun?"

I cross my legs beneath the table in an attempt to appear more casual. I don't think it helps. "I volunteer at an animal shelter, so that takes up a lot of my time."

"That sounds cool."

"Yeah, I love it. My dad's allergic to practically everything, so it's the closest thing I've got to having a pet."

"Ugh, I know what you mean." He leans forward again, bracing both of his arms against the table, coffee cup seemingly forgotten at the edge. "Well, my dad's not allergic to animals, he just doesn't want all of the responsibility. You probably don't remember this, but when we were like eight I begged him for a dog, I even wrote him this long, detailed note on how I would take care of it, and sell my toys to pay for its food."

"Aw," I say, because *Mon Dieu* that is adorable.

He shakes his head. "He didn't go for it. I was crushed."

I laugh and gesture toward him. "And clearly you still haven't recovered."

He nods with a mock-serious expression. "It was a scarring experience. I guess being an only child, I was just lonely, and thought a dog would help. Once I realized he'd never go for the dog, I tried to convince him to let me at least have a hamster."

"No luck?"

He lets out a wistful sigh. "None."

"What would you have named it?" I ask. "If you had gotten the dog?"

"Rex, obviously."

I scoff.

"What?" His voice gets higher in mock offense.

"It's just so *common*. We've had at least six Rex's come through the shelter this year alone. Surely you could come up with something better than that."

"Oh, really?" he laughs. "If you're so creative, then what would you have named it?"

"What kind of dog are we talking?"

He takes a moment to consider. "Something big. Manly."

"Easy. Name him Queso."

"*Queso?*"

"Yeah. Why not?" I shrug. "I like nachos."

A grin takes over his face, and he leans back in his chair, draping one arm over the back. He somehow manages to look calm in whatever he does, like nothing makes him nervous. Everything about him is easy, relaxed. I would *kill* to feel like that.

"You have any dogs at the shelter named Queso?" he asks.

"No, but we do have this little terrier, Banjo, who is probably the cutest thing you'll ever see. And there's this ten-year-old German Shepard, Pluto," I say, numbering them off on my fingers. "He's such a sweetheart. But my favorite is probably Squirt. She's this little Maltese. I would adopt her in a second if my parents would let me. She has so much energy, so it kills me that she sits in that little cage all day. I try to let her out every time I go, but that's only a couple hours a week. It's so sad."

"What is it you like so much about her?"

"She is just the cutest. She does this thing when she gets excited—you know, I can't even explain it." I wave my hand and realize I'm grinning so hard my cheeks hurt. "You'd have to see it."

"I'd like to."

The grin freezes on my face. I look up to see him watching me with a quiet intensity, though his smile is soft. I open my mouth to speak, and quickly shove the words out into the open before I lose my nerve. "I work there from five to seven on Tuesday, if you want to see her."

The smile stretches further up his cheeks. "Yeah? But only if it's not any trouble. I don't want to be in the way or anything."

"You wouldn't be in the way! And the dogs *love* when people come in and play with them."

"So they're good with strangers?"

"There are a couple who are a little shy, but the way most of them behave, you'd think they'd known their visitors their whole lives. It's adorable."

"Do you remember that time when we were kids—we must have been nine, maybe ten—when we saw that rabbit in your backyard and spent like three hours trying to catch it?"

Vividly. It was during my tomboy phase when I wore nothing but basketball shorts and insisted on wearing my hair in two braids every day.

"And we tried to make a cage out of twigs so we could keep it as a pet without our parents finding out," I add.

"You named that one, too. What was it?" He raises a single eyebrow knowingly.

I hang my head in shame. "Cuddles."

"Hm. How...*common*."

"Hey. We were *nine*—at least my naming capabilities have improved. Yours have stagnated."

"Are you implying I have the naming capability of a nine-year-old?"

"That's exactly what I'm implying."

"But you've had more practice working at the shelter," he says, pointing a finger at me. "Unfair advantage."

I roll my eyes. "Excuses, excuses."

He pauses and gestures between us. "This is kind of weird, right? It's been, what? Seven years since we've hung out?"

Wow. I knew it had been a long time, but hearing the number makes it feel even longer. I say as much aloud.

He finishes his coffee and sets it aside. "At risk of sounding unbearably cheesy, it kind of feels like we never stopped being friends. I don't know, I guess you're just easy to talk to."

"Be honest. It's because I still look like I'm eleven." I'm only half-joking.

He laughs, his whole face lighting up as he does so. Some people have attractive laughs, where they just look really good. Sam's isn't like that. His nose crinkles, his eyes squint, and his whole face kind of contorts, but it's still inexplicably beautiful, even if just for the sake of knowing for certain that it's genuine.

"You, on the other hand," I continue, "grew like a tree. What are you now, like six-foot?"

"Six-one, to be exact. And you're, what? Five-foot?" he teases.

I am short, but I'm not *that* short. "Three. Five-*three*."

A flash from my phone in my periphery snags my attention and I glance down. A text from Johanna pops onto the screen, asking for an update. My eyes shoot to the time. "Oh, no."

His gaze snaps to me. "What?"

"The service ends soon."

Thankfully, Sam seems to understand the situation without having to ask. We scramble to our feet, push in the wiry chairs, and hurry out the door. A couple of cars whiz past before we can jog across the road to the church. We're about to reach the front doors when Sam grabs my wrist and pulls me aside. My entire body jolts to life at the contact, but I try not to let it show on my face.

"Wait," he says. "I want to make sure we get to do this again."

"Do you want to give me your number? Then I can text you the address for the animal shelter in case you want to drop by some time." Stupidly, I blush, and then wave my hand to try and disguise it. "You know, to see the dogs. But if you don't want to, I totally understand. You're probably busy—"

He cuts me off by taking the phone from my hand and punching in his number. Handing it back to me, he smiles. "I took the liberty of texting myself so I'd have your number, too."

It takes everything in me to stop my face from breaking into a stupid smile. I slip the phone into my back pocket as people start filtering into the parking lot around us. I should really head inside to find Maman and Harper and do some damage control.

"Okay, so, maybe I'll see you Tuesday then?" I say, taking a step away.

He shoves his hands in his pockets and smiles. "Don't forget to text me that address."

Despite my best efforts, the stupid smile breaks out. "I won't."

Handling my family afterwards turns out to be much easier than I expected. I just tell them that Sam and I decided to sit together in the back, and Papa looks so thrilled that he lets the subject drop at that, never mind their usual *united front* lectures.

I should probably feel bad about lying to them.

But I don't.

6

A COLD FIST OF PANIC SEIZES ME AS MR. GRAHAM'S EYES scan the class, probably seeking out the most guilt-ridden face, trying to determine who didn't do the reading.

I did the reading. But that doesn't stop my face from flaring, my hands from suddenly producing too much moisture, and my heartbeat from rising to a painful gallop against my ribs. Because, inevitably, if he calls on me, heads will turn in my direction. Eyes will zero in on my red cheeks and the beads of sweat in my hairline. I'll try to speak. My blood will thunder so loudly in my ears I'll barely even hear my own voice as it comes out thin and shaky—a dead indicator to everyone around me of just how nervous I am over something completely simple and stupid like getting called on in class. And they'll all know. They'll all know I'm a panicked, shaky mess. God forbid I get the answer *wrong*, because then I'll look like a panicked, shaky, *stupid* mess.

The longer he waits to call on someone, the higher my stress amplifies, like someone is slowly turning up the volume, until my entire body is strung so tight I start looking for escape routes just to make the chaos inside of my body *stop*.

He calls on a redhead named Max on the other side of the room.

My entire body releases, the pent-up nervous stress washing out of me in waves. My hands shake as the energy leaves my body, and I almost feel out of breath, like I just stopped jogging.

I feel like I need to lie down.

The bell rings as Max starts to answer, cutting off his words.

In most classes, the second the bell rings, it's a stampede for the door. Not Mr. Graham's class. Students, mostly of the female variety, linger around, slowly packing their belongings and chatting with Mr. Graham, trying to get his attention. How these girls don't realize how painfully obvious their efforts are, I'm not sure. Ashley Miller, always the ringleader, stands at the front of the room, leaning against Mr. Graham's desk, effectively blocking his path to his briefcase, daring him to lean over her. The other members of the Pretty Committee linger, waiting to see how this plays out.

As Johanna and I are heading out, Jo pauses by the door and calls, "Ashley!"

Mr. Graham glances over at us, but Ashley ignores Jo, twirling her hair around her finger.

"*Ashleyyyyy,*" Johanna sings.

Finally, Ashley glances over and narrows her eyes to slits. "*What?*" she mouths.

"Don't forget, we're having a group meeting at my house after school." Johanna flashes her sweetest smile. "Don't be late!"

"Whatever," Ashley replies.

Johanna looks like she could keep doing this all day, but I grab her by the elbow and not-so-subtly lead her from the room.

"So," she says as we turn down the hall toward the cafeteria. "On a scale of one to ten, what are the odds Ashley bribed someone to dump their lunch on us today?"

"It really just depends on how fast she'd be able to find someone to do it...I say a solid seven." I hook my elbow through hers. "So maybe we should eat outside."

"Are you kidding?" she laughs. "I hope she does it. Because if *she's* the one to start it, that gives me an excuse to dump my chocolate pudding down her shirt. That's my *dream*."

"These are the things you dream about, Jo?"

"These are the things I *live* for." She grins and taps her temple. "It's all chocolate pudding and sexy world history teachers up here. Though I imagine up here," she reaches over and messes up my hair, "is all coffee shops and Sexy Samuel."

We're nearly to the cafeteria when a pack of underclassmen girls comes screaming around the corner, running as fast as they can. Some of them are half-dressed and clutching their clothes to their chests as they run. Jo and I freeze and flatten ourselves against the lockers to avoid getting trampled, and exchange a wide-eyed glance.

"She's a dyke!" the short brunette at the head of the pack shrills as they all continue to barrel down the hall.

"Don't let her near you! You might get infected!" screams another.

"You guys, she had a camera! I saw it! She was *filming* us!"

This sends another wave of screams among the group.

"What a freak!"

Once they pass, I poke my head around the corner. It looks like they came from the girls' locker room, and a couple of kids are still standing around, laughing. I have half a mind to go ask them what the hell is going on, but then the locker room's door swings open, and the last girl steps out.

Her face is streaked with tears, her complexion blotchy and red.

"Harper?" I ask.

Sniffling, she pushes past me. "Leave me alone."

"Harper!" I call after her, but she just keeps walking, head ducked between her shoulders, and hurries down the hall.

Unsurprisingly, Ashley shows up to Jo's house that afternoon half an hour late. What is surprising, however, is how prepared she is. The moment she steps through the door, blond curls tied back in an *I mean business* ponytail, heeled oxfords clicking against the hardwood, she struts to the kitchen island and dumps the class textbook, a spiral notebook, and half a dozen scholarly sources, printed and neatly stapled.

She looks at the two of us, currently lounging on the barstools with an impressive platter of nachos half-devoured between us, and raises her eyebrows.

Jo pushes a bottle of mustard toward her.

Ashley scrunches her nose. "What's this for?"

Johanna shrugs. "In case you wanted to throw this, too." When Ashley doesn't move, Jo picks the bottle back up and twirls it in her hands. "Or do you discriminate against condiments?"

For a moment, Ashley and Johanna just stare at each other, and it occurs to me that I'm the only one here to get in the middle if they start slapping each other again. Ashley crosses her arms over her chest and flicks her gaze between the two of us. Her cheeks almost look a bit flushed.

"Do you guys mind?" she snaps, though the words have less bite than usual. "I'd like to get started on this so I can get out of here as soon as possible."

Eyes still narrowed, Johanna nods her chin at the pile of papers. "What are those?"

Ashley huffs and plops herself in the barstool farthest away from us. "So I made the executive decision for our topic and already did some research on gender dynamics during the Mongol Empire, and I thought we could tie it back to our current political climate and ongoing equality debates." She shoves the stack of papers toward us. "I picked out some sources that look promising, but we'll probably need a few more."

Johanna stares at Ashley, mouth slightly open, and it takes me a moment before I finally reach forward to grab the papers.

Ashley crosses her arms over her chest and glances between the two of us. Her eyebrows have returned to their normal position, and there's a hint of uncertainty in the way her eyes flicker back and forth. "Will that work for you two or what?"

"That's actually a good idea," I say, flipping through the sources, all of which are totally legit. I'm not sure why I expected them not to be, but damn.

Johanna just keeps staring at her, mustard still in hand, as if daring Ashley to give her a reason to use it.

"What?" Ashley snaps and throws her arms up. "If you're going to make another dig at my intelligence you might as well do it now to get it out of the way."

Johanna finally closes her mouth and sets down the mustard. "Alright, Commander Miller. Where do we start?"

AS ASHLEY ASSIGNS JOBS, NOW PACING AROUND THE kitchen like a true drill sergeant, I check my phone for the tenth time that afternoon. I haven't seen Harper since that moment in the hallway when she'd ducked her head between her shoulders and shoved past me without a word, but I've left her a couple of texts. No matter how many times I check, there's still no response.

"Are we boring you?"

I glance up to see Ashley's face very close to mine, her bright-peach manicured hands braced on the island between us. I quickly set down my phone. Every time she looks at me with those calculating eyes, a cold flash of fear washes over me. "I'm finding contemporary sources. Got it."

"Good." She leans back, tightens her ponytail, and surveys our materials spread across the island for a second. "I'm going to the bathroom."

Her gaze darts to Johanna, waiting.

Johanna points up. "Upstairs, first door on the left."

Wordlessly, she twirls, her ponytail whipping around in a wide arc, and struts out of sight. We wait until her footsteps disappear upstairs before risking a word.

"I don't know about you, but I'm completely mind-fucked right now," Johanna murmurs.

I mutely nod my agreement.

Jo's gaze darts to my phone. "Has Harper responded?"

A sigh is my only response.

"Damn," Johanna mutters. "Maybe try when you get home? She might just need some time to think, you know?"

"Let's talk about something else," I say. "You never told me how it went with Mr. Graham the other day."

Her face twists into a mischievous smile. "It went well."

I resist the urge to groan. I was hoping after a while the situation might grow on me—or Jo would drop it—but it isn't any less weird than when she first suggested it. I glance over my shoulder to make sure Ashley hasn't returned and lower my voice. "What does that mean? Did something... *happen?*"

Smile diming, she waves her hand in front of her face like she's swatting away a fly. "Nothing happened. Yet. *But*, when he was showing me something in the notes, I was standing all close to him so our legs were touching, and I touched his hand while I was pointing to something, and he didn't pull away. So that's a good sign, right?"

I cringe internally.

Jo must see it on my face because she huffs and leans back in her seat. "If you don't want to hear about it, then you shouldn't have asked."

"I'm just worried about you, is all."

"You always worry, and I love you for it, but it's not necessary."

Her words just make the weight in my stomach increase tenfold. No matter how I picture it, this situation can't end well, and it's utterly baffling to me that Jo can't see that. If he rejects her, she'll get hurt. If something *does* happen and it gets out, he'll get in trouble, and who knows how much social backlash she'll get. And even if it doesn't get out, there's no way it'll turn into anything more than a one-night stand or some short-lived fling, and when it ends, it'll be torture for her to sit in his class. However this plays out, Jo will be the one to get burned, and I don't want to see that.

She raises her eyebrows as if daring me to fight her on this again. She must know how this is going to turn out, and she doesn't care. To her, it's worth the risk. And even though I don't understand that, not for a second, I know I can't stop her.

"Okay." I raise my palms in surrender. "Okay."

Johanna reaches over and lays her hand on my arm. Her nails are midnight black, her fingers lost under an assortment of rings. "Even though I hate you for it sometimes, thanks for worrying about me."

"I wish you'd stop giving me so many things to worry about."

She rolls her eyes. "No. Then you wouldn't even want to be friends with me anymore because I'd be *boring*."

"Or sane," I counter.

"Eh." She hops up from her seat and opens the fridge. "Overrated." She holds up a bottle of champagne. "Is it too early for this?"

"Not sure our commanding officer would approve."

She purses her lips and glances in the direction Ashley disappeared. "She's kind of been gone for a long time, right?"

"Maybe she's putting bleach in your shampoo bottles," I say helpfully.

Jo snorts, returns the bottle to the fridge, and pulls out a green juice instead.

When we hear Ashley's footsteps making their way back down the stairs, Johanna launches herself into her barstool, raises one of the printed sources, and tilts her head to the side as if deep in thought. I yank my laptop closer and squint at the screen, pretending to search for new articles.

"Well." Ashley reappears and claps her hands, pausing

by the refrigerator. Her lips tuck in and press together as if she's suppressing a grin. "I think we all know what our tasks are. How about we reconvene in a couple of days to see how much progress we've made?"

Jo and I exchange a glance.

"You don't want to get started on it now?" I ask.

"No need." She shrugs, and I notice she's already retrieved her purse from the front of the house, the bag slung over her shoulder and secured neatly to her side. "I'll leave those here." She waves at the printed sources. "I have copies. You two can get working now if you want. I'm personally just more productive working alone."

This was more of what I was expecting when Ashley showed up today. Of course she doesn't want to stay and be forced to hang out with us. She just wanted to boss everyone around and leave as quickly as she came.

"Uh—" I start.

"Great! We can talk about when to meet next in class tomorrow." And with that, she turns and heads for the door, her heels clicking furiously against the floor.

When we hear the front door close and the vague sound of her car engine starting out front, Jo and I look at each other again.

"So does that mean I can break out that bottle of champagne or what?"

The first thing I do when I get home is head for Harper's bedroom. Maman and Papa aren't home yet, and the house is eerily silent. I pause outside her door, listening. I'm not sure what I'm expecting, but there's just silence. Maybe she's not in there, but I have no idea where else she'd be. I rap my knuckles softly against the surface.

"Harp?" I call.

I hear a rustling sound, and then, "I'm busy!"

Her voice sounds weird. Thick. Like she's been crying. "Harper, can I come in?"

There's a pause. "Are Maman and Papa home yet?"

"No."

Another pause. "Okay."

I nudge the door open and peek inside. All the lights are off, the light from the window cutting a line down the center of the room, and she's sitting on her bed in the corner, her feet curled beneath her, a mess of discarded tissues surrounding her in a ring.

Usually, her art supplies take up the majority of her room—her easel in the center, newspapers scattered across the ground, her hundreds of paints lined up on the windowsills, bookshelves, and the edge of her desk. But today, everything is cast out of focus—her old paintings carelessly piled atop one another on her desk, her sketchbooks shoved in her closet. The usual pile of sweaty workout clothes that accumulates in the corner for *weeks* before I have to beg her to do laundry because of the smell is nowhere to be found.

I slowly approach the bed. With Harper, especially when she's upset, you have to treat her like a wild animal—slow and cautious—or you risk spooking her. Or having her attack you.

But today she just lets me sit next to her. Sniffling, she looks away and wipes her cheeks.

"So, I guess you saw what happened at school," she mumbles.

"A little," I admit. "Are you—?" I was about to ask *are you okay,* but realize how stupid of a question that is and stop myself. "Do you want to talk about it?" I try instead.

"Like you care," she mumbles. She doesn't even look at me.

That hurts. I press my lips together, trying to think of the right things to say. Harper and I have never exactly been *close,* but I always figured we'd be there if we ever really needed each other. She, apparently, doesn't feel the same way. And I can't help but feel that's my fault.

"That's not true," I say quietly.

She blows her nose and tosses the tissue into the growing pile before her. "It was just these girls at school. It's stupid."

"It's not stupid if you're upset about it."

She shakes her head and clenches her jaw as if trying to fight the tears, but more roll down her cheeks all the same. "It was after gym class in the locker room. We were all getting changed, same as every day, and then all of a sudden Rachel Miller whips around and starts screaming that I was a dyke and I was checking the other girls out while they were changing and filming them. So then everyone in the locker room started freaking out and trying to put clothes on as fast as they could. Then everyone started running away. For the rest of the day, every time one of them saw me, they called me a dyke, and then it started spreading around and..." she trails off and wipes her face again. "I just don't understand why Rachel did it. I never did anything to her."

Of course it was Ashley's younger sister. My hands clench into fists. I don't understand why they do it either, and I don't have any comforting words for Harper. Because I know all too well that you can wait and wait for a mean girl to get bored of terrorizing you, but sometimes they just never do.

"Did you tell anyone?" I ask.

She sniffles again. "Huh?"

"You know, like a teacher or someone. Tell them what Rachel did."

Harper scoffs. "Like that'll help. It won't change anything. Then everyone will just say I'm a dyke *and* a snitch."

"You want me to beat Rachel up? 'Cause I'll do it." I'm only half-joking.

"You couldn't beat anyone up if you tried," Harper mumbles.

Unfortunately, she's right. "It *would* be pretty embarrassing if I got my ass kicked by a freshman, wouldn't it?"

I nudge her with my elbow, but she doesn't laugh. She doesn't even smile.

A try for a different angle. "You know it'll blow over. Give it a few days until the next scandal blows up and everyone will forget about it."

Harper is silent for a long time. At first, I think she's going to shut down and push me away the way she usually does whenever things get slightly emotional, but then I realize she's crying again.

"But what if it's true?" Her voice comes out so quietly, I can barely hear it. "I never *did* any of that, but—"

That was the last thing I was expecting her to say. And for a minute, I can't formulate a response. All I know is I've *never* heard her voice sound like that before, and I'd do anything in my power to make sure it never sounds like that again.

When I finally manage to string together a response, the words come out small and breathy. "It doesn't matter. No, that's not what I mean. I mean, of course it *matters*. But it doesn't change anything, you know?" My neck feels hot as I fumble for words. "It doesn't change anything for me. Or anyone else who cares about you."

Her laugh comes out hard. "It's not that simple."

"No," I agree quietly. "It's not simple." That didn't come out the way I wanted it to, either. I wince and silently curse myself, desperately trying to think of the right thing to say.

"I don't know what the right thing to say is," I admit. "But I love you." I put my hand on her shoulder, and to my surprise, she doesn't pull away. She just closes her eyes and folds her hands in her lap.

"Does God hate me?" she whispers.

I swallow hard, biting back every angry word I want to say right now. "No, Harper," I say firmly. "He doesn't."

She shakes her head again. "Maman and Papa—they'd never be okay with this. They'd never understand."

I am the last person who should be giving her religious

advice, but I don't think telling her that now is going to help. We've never talked about it, but I've always gotten the sense that Harper believes a lot more than I do. Instead, I just say, "Harper, listen to me. There is nothing wrong with you, and you have nothing to apologize for."

Her head whips up, eyes wide. She grabs my arms with a crushing intensity. "You can't tell Maman and Papa. Promise you won't tell them. Promise, Mare."

"Harper—" I try to pull my arms away, but her fingers dig in.

The tears are running down her cheeks again. "Please. I just need more time to figure things out, and I don't want them to freak out. They'll be so angry."

I stare at her pile of tissues on the floor for several moments, my eyebrows pulled together. I want to comfort her. I want to tell her our parents will love her no matter what, that this won't change anything, that it won't prompt a frantic overreaction full of Bible verses and whatever else they think will "fix" this. But I think she and I both know the truth, as ugly and unfair and hypocritical as it is.

"I won't say anything," I whisper.

7

I SHOW UP TO THE ANIMAL SHELTER THAT EVENING IN MY usual bright red T-shirt, the word *volunteer* printed in large, white block letters across the back. Jada, the shelter's manager, greets me as I step through the front door and the bells announce my entrance. She asks about my health, the health of my family, and how school's going, as she does every time she sees me. She's a tall, thin woman in her early thirties with some of the darkest, most beautiful skin I've ever seen. Her family moved to America from Nigeria when she was ten years old, and when she speaks, you can still pick out distinct hints of her Nigerian accent. It makes everything she says sound warm. Honestly, her letter of recommendation is probably the one thing I have going for me in my college apps.

I look away when she asks about my family today, my stomach still tight with guilt and anger about what happened with Harper. I'd been so nauseous I skipped dinner. Though I still don't have an appetite, my stomach keeps growling to remind me of the neglect.

"Hey, Jada." I smile and join her behind the counter, depositing my cell phone and car keys into my little cubby under the desk. It's not required or anything, but I like to have no distractions when I'm with the dogs. If I can only give them a few hours of my time, I'm going to make sure they have my complete attention.

"Have they already been fed?" I ask.

"No, you can go ahead and do that. Nick picked up some new bags of food—it's supposed to make their coats shinier or something. He thinks it'll make people more likely to adopt." She shrugs like she doesn't believe it but she's willing to humor him. Nick is the shelter's owner; it seems like every day he comes up with The Next Big Idea that's going to get all of the dogs adopted. I can't give him too much grief about it, though, because he genuinely does care about the animals and just wants to find them homes. "They're under those boxes in the back."

"Okay, I'm on it." The storage room is the very last door in the back hallway, and you have to pass the kennels to reach it. The sound of my nearing footsteps is enough to send a couple of the dogs into an excited tizzy.

"I'll be right back, I promise," I call to them as I pass. The door to the storage room is broken, so I have to prop it open with a loose brick, which Jada's daughter has painted to look like a ladybug. As I dig through the boxes in the back, my mind starts spiraling. Every inch of my body is very much aware of what day it is, but I'm trying not to think about it. It's just another Tuesday.

It doesn't matter if Sam shows up today. I don't care either way.

Really, I don't.

Finally, I reach the boxes of dog food at the bottom of the pile. Just as I manage to move the last one, the bells above the front door announce someone's arrival.

A weird mixture of excitement and anxiety jolts through me. I glance at the clock on the wall. It's only 5:15. I take a deep breath, forcing myself to remain calm. *Count five things you can see, four things you can touch, three things you can hear, two things you can taste, one thing you can smell.* That could just as likely be someone coming to look at the dogs as it could be Sam.

I haul the heavy bag into my arms, supporting the weight with a knee until I can get a good grip, and hurry back into the hall. When I reach the lobby, I see Sam standing in front of the counter, chatting with Jada. He's wearing a pair of shorts that are almost purple, a white T-shirt, and matching Vans, his dark hair rumpled. Judging by the way Jada's grinning and openly looking him up and down, she approves.

I pause beside the desk, using my knee to nudge the dog food back up into my hands when it starts to slip.

"Hey, Sam," I say. Somehow, my voice doesn't shake. I'd really rather not have to do this in front of Jada, though. Being awkward in front of Sam alone is bad enough.

He turns, sees me with the bag that's half my size, and grins. "Hey. Need some help with that?"

"No, it's fine, I've got it." At least it gives me something to do with my hands. "Jada, is it okay if he comes to the back with me?"

Jada looks up from her paperwork, a bemused smile curling her lips, and nods. "Mmm-hmm."

The moment we enter the room with the dogs, my eyes fall on Squirt's cage, and I am immediately grateful for the distraction. She jumps up at the sight of us, balances on her hind legs, and begins scratching her front paws against the cage. In Squirt language this means, "Take me out and pick me up!"

She's a small puffball of a dog, her white fur fuzzy and all-consuming. Sometimes it's hard to believe there's actually dog under all of that fluff. When I don't go straight to her cage and instead head to the table in the center of the room to deposit the bag of dog food, she starts scratching harder like she can dig through the bars. She barks once in her eerily human-like way to get my attention.

Sam beelines for her cage. "Is this her? Is this Squirt?"

Squirt falls back onto all fours as Sam approaches, her tail whipping back and forth. She leans back on her haunches, barks again, and does a little playful jump that screams *come catch me*, even though she has nowhere to run. It's hilarious to watch her do it on the ground, when she actually *does* have some place to run, and take off, her itty bitty legs propelling her as fast as she can go. She usually just does figure-eights around the room, occasionally stopping to make sure people are paying attention.

The longer Sam looks at her, the more excited she gets, until she's wiggling around so much, she looks like she's going to jump out of her skin.

Sam laughs and pokes his fingers into the cage; Squirt eagerly licks them. "Is this the excited thing she does you were talking about?"

"You should see her do it when she's out of the cage."

I grab the food scoop from the table and start filling the little plastic bowls stacked on the corner.

"Need some help?" Sam offers.

I slide him one of the full bowls and nod at the cages. "There's a little slot at the bottom. You can just slide it in. Watch out for Rooty there on the end. She loves her food so much, she might accidentally take your hand off."

Sam takes the bowls as I finish filling them and deposits them into the cages one by one. Once we finish, the room is filled with the happy sounds of the dogs inhaling their dinner and licking the bowls clean for good measure.

"Now's the fun part," I say as I recollect the bowls and stack them beside the counter. I point to the leashes hanging on a peg nailed beside the door. "You wanna help me get them out back so they can get some fresh air?"

Sam already has the leashes in hand. "Do you take them all at the same time?"

"There are only ten of them right now, so yeah. And especially with two of us, that shouldn't be a problem."

I start with Squirt's cage because she's the easiest to get on a leash. Also, she's my favorite. She starts doing her weird jumping thing again until I finally slide the cage's door up, and she jumps right into my arms. As I try to wrestle the leash onto her squirming body, she lands a couple of kisses just below my chin.

Once I get the leash secured and set Squirt on the floor, she starts jumping up and down in excitement.

Sam laughs aloud. "She's like a little jumping bean."

"Right? I actually wanted to name her Bean," I say as I open Banjo's cage. "But Nick, the owner, gets final say, and he liked Squirt better."

As I get the rest of the dogs out, I attach their leashes one-by-one to the counter in the center of the room until they're all out and staring at me, tongues hanging out of their mouths, tails wagging.

"This is their favorite time of day," I tell Sam and give him half of the leashes. The dogs take off, yanking him forward. "They'll show you the way," I call after him, laughing as he runs with them instead of yanking on the leashes and forcing them to walk, as most people would do.

My five dogs take off after them, and I let them yank me along until we reach the backdoor. The moment I open the door, they all try to break through, one yanking the leash right from Sam's hand. His eyes go wide as it falls to the floor and the dog takes off.

"Don't worry about it," I say before he can take off after the dog. "The back is fenced in."

We follow the dogs out and close the door behind us. The back is really just a big patch of grass, with a couple of toys and bones scattered throughout. We're only required to take them out for twenty minutes or so after dinner to see if they'll go to the bathroom outside, but I usually keep them out longer if the weather permits. Even if it is fenced in and they don't have a lot of space to run, it's better than those cages, and they seem to like the sun and fresh air.

Sam helps me release the dogs from the leashes, and they take off. The younger ones immediately jump into a wrestling match, as if picking up where they left off from a previous day, whereas some of the older dogs just like to go lie in the grass and soak up the sun. Squirt and Banjo start a chasing game, one sprinting across the yard, then waiting for the other to catch up before taking off again.

"Do they always have so much energy?" Sam asks.

I sink into a seated position in the grass, and Pluto, our old German Shepard, comes and plops his head in my lap. "Squirt does." I smile, my eyes tracing her progress across the lawn. Just looking at her makes my chest feel warm.

Sam joins me in the grass and scratches Pluto's head.

As if she can sense we're talking about her, Squirt bolts over to where we're sitting, jumps up, and licks Sam from one corner of his mouth to the opposite ear. He flails back, wiping at his mouth.

"Could you at least buy me dinner first?" he says.

Squirt barks in response and circles us before finally plopping herself into my lap, forcing Pluto to move. He doesn't look too upset about the change. He just slumps against my side and licks my hand to remind me of his presence, or rather, remind me to pet him. I use one hand for Pluto and one for Squirt, and hope none of the other dogs look over and notice, or they'll all come bounding over in jealousy.

The second I start petting Squirt, she rolls onto her back to give me better access to her belly. "You're such a little flirt, Squirt." I nuzzle her nose.

I glance over to see Sam watching me, his head cocked in that way of his.

"You're so good with them," he says.

I'm the first to break the eye contact. "It's because I'm so bad with people. Gotta make up for it somehow."

Sam laughs, leans over, and scratches Squirt behind her ears. "So, how often do you volunteer here?"

"At least four days a week, sometimes more if they need me."

"That's quite the commitment."

I shrug, my gaze still trained on Squirt. "I like it here."

We fall into silence, and my mind immediately starts spinning in frantic circles, searching for something to say. I glance at him out of the corner of my eye, but he doesn't seem to mind the lull in conversation. He's just watching the dogs play, a slight smile on his face. The breeze picks up and rustles his hair.

"So I actually have an ulterior motive for coming today," he says. "Though I did want to meet this one." He scratches Squirt's belly and she rolls her head to the side to look at him.

"Ulterior motive?" I ask.

"Well." He pulls out a few blades of grass and twirls them through his fingers, then trains his calm and unwavering gaze on me. I can feel my cheeks burning, and it takes every ounce of my willpower not to look away. "I'm here so I can formally ask you on a date."

Okay, so that was not what I was expecting. My face is definitely hot now, and no matter how much I try to fight a smile, the corners of my mouth curve without my permission. "Exactly what did you have in mind?"

"Nope." He shakes his head and leans back on his hands. "Trade secrets. You'll just have to wait and see. How's Friday night sound?"

My throat goes dry, making it difficult to swallow. This is happening. This is actually happening.

A very large and loud part of me wants to say no. To say no and get out of here and *run* and just forget about this whole thing. And not because I don't like Sam. Not because I don't want to go. But every nerve in my body is burning and shaking, and there's so much turmoil inside of my veins that I think I might be sick with it.

But more than that, I'm sick of *this*. I am sick of this feeling. I'm sick of *listening* to it and letting it control everything I do.

So, I take a deep breath, stretch my mouth into a smile that probably looks forced, and say, "Friday night sounds perfect."

8

Around two o'clock on Friday afternoon, I get a text from Maman. Buried beneath a dozen emojis and unnecessary exclamation marks is a plea for me to drop off food on my way home from school since she's been so busy at work and hasn't taken a lunch break.

I immediately find this odd, unless her employees didn't show up for work today. Her boutique is doing well and always turns a generous profit at the end of the month, but it rarely has more than a handful of customers inside at a time. Definitely not enough to keep her from running next door to the sandwich shop at the very least.

Still, I go. If nothing else, it'll distract me for a bit so I can't obsess and over-think about my date with Sam tonight. I stop at Panera on the way back for a soup and salad and pull into the parking lot outside of her boutique. The moment I pull in, I can tell she has some ulterior motive, because the only other car in the lot is *hers*.

I grab the bag of food and head inside. The layout of the store has been the same for as long as I can remember. The first thing you see when you walk in the door is the big round table full of jewelry made by local women, most of whom are stay-at-home moms trying to make some extra cash. Racks of clothes span out from there, organized by color and season. Floor-to-ceiling mirrors with golden decorative frames are propped in every corner, making the shop appear much bigger than it actually is.

I used to love coming here when I was younger. Harper and I would run through the aisles, spinning around in front of the mirrors, swallowed by dresses three times our size. I think Maman has a photobook full of pictures from our visits and impromptu fashion shows, all blurry and crooked, taken by budding-photographer Johanna on a disposable camera.

I can't even remember the last time I was in here.

The checkout counter—really just a glorified desk—is tucked away in the corner, so I weave my way through the clothes in that direction. When I reach the back, however, there's no one else in sight.

"Maman?" I call.

"*Mon Cœur!*" She scurries out from the back room in gray skinny jeans, chucky black ankle boots, and a stylish black sweater with flared sleeves. Her hair is done up in an elaborate twist, exposing the large silver hoops dangling from her ears.

I'm wearing an over-sized T-shirt that says *Adopt Don't Shop* and plain black workout leggings that I'm pretty sure I've already worn twice this week.

"I brought your favorite." I hand her the bag.

"*Thank you.*" She pulls me in for a hug and promptly sets the bag on the desk, clearly not as hungry as she'd led me to believe.

"Well." I shrug and start to turn for the door. "See you—"

"Wait! Wait! While you're here..." She grabs my arm and starts pulling me toward the storage room.

And now, the moment of truth.

The storage room is usually just a couple of rows of shelves with various boxes full of things like the supplies needed for tagging clothes, sewing kits, and extra inventory. Today, Maman has hung a dress from every available surface like some sort of art gallery.

She grins as she pulls me inside and starts gesturing around. "Now, don't think too much about it; which one catches your eye first?"

The dresses range from full-blown prom dresses with shiny gemstones and puffy skirts to cocktail dresses with slits and open backs. It's a sea of black, cream, hot pink, neon green, and every color in between. I blink a few times.

"What am I looking at?" I ask, my voice flat.

"Well." She scampers over to a white minidress with lace sleeves and floral embellishments. She takes its skirt in both hands and stretches it out as if I hadn't been able to see it well enough before. "I know you have your date with Sam tonight...and I just thought..."

"*Maman,*" I groan.

"What?" she whines. "Can you blame me for wanting to be included? It's your *first date*. This is so exciting!"

I take a deep breath before responding, urging myself not to be frustrated, because the look on her face is so excited and genuine, and I really don't want to hurt her feelings. "I just don't think it's that kind of date, Maman," I say.

Her entire face scrunches up in confusion. "What do you mean?"

"I mean it's a lot more casual. I'll probably just wear jeans."

"*Jeans?*" she gasps, scandalized.

"I don't want to be overdressed! Then I'll just look silly."

Her entire body deflates in disappointment. "You're sure?"

"Pretty sure."

She sighs and runs her hand down the full-length red dress closest to her. "I didn't even get to pick out your *prom* dress." She sounds on the verge of tears.

This is correct, because I didn't even *go* to junior prom, and I don't plan on going this year, either. But even if I did, I don't think she realizes pretty much no moms get to pick out their daughters' prom dresses. Pointing this out now will win me no points, though.

"You want to go eat your salad?" I offer.

She waves a hand and sniffles. "I'm not hungry. I already ate."

I hold back my scowl. I can't even be mad that she sent me on a pointless errand and made my entire car smell like clam chowder for nothing. She just looks so crestfallen and *pitiful*. And as misguided as it was, she was just trying to do something nice.

"So, I was thinking," I say before I can talk myself out of it. "Since I'm about to graduate and head off to college, before I go, maybe we should have, like, a girls' day?"

The last two words are almost physically painful as they come out of my mouth, because I already have a good idea of what such a thing is going to entail, but the peace-offering clearly works, because Maman stops sniffling.

"Girls' day?" she asks.

I shove my hands in the side pockets of my leggings and shrug. "Yeah, like, you, me, and Harper could go do something. Maybe see a movie…"

Her eyes widen, and I can practically see her thoughts erratically cartwheeling behind her eyes. "We could make a whole day of it! Nails, massages, shopping—"

I open my mouth, but she keeps talking.

"You'll have to talk Harper into it, though." She paces as she talks, probably already planning every second of the day in her head. "She'll never agree if she thinks it's my idea."

I gape at her. "And what makes you think we'd have any more luck if she thought it was my idea?"

Maman rolls her eyes. "Of course she will."

"Harper hates me!"

Maman opens and closes her mouth a few times, like she can't decide on what to say, which would be a first for her. She settles with tilting her head to the side, a small smile teasing at her lips.

"Meredith," she says. "Harper worships you."

"Yeah, right," I snort.

Maman's small smile has turned into a full-on smirk. "*Mon Coeur*, you have much to learn. So, will you tell Harper?"

"What day do you want to do it?"

"How about Sunday, after church?"

"Okay."

Maman grins and shuffles toward me, flapping her hands, which is her way of showing she's about to hug me. I don't even complain when she plants a wet kiss to the side of my face, surely leaving behind bright red lipstick prints.

The bell above the door rings as someone enters the shop.

"Oh!" Maman squeezes my arm, then hurries toward the front. "*Bonjour!* Welcome in!" she calls.

I wind around the racks of clothes, heading for the exit, but freeze by the navy dresses when I see who Maman's latest customers are. Ashley Miller is standing by the jewelry table, arms folded over her chest, looking like she's been dragged here against her will. An older woman in head-to-toe bright-white Lululemon and platform black flip flops (they still make those?) is standing next to her, sifting through the rack of white dresses. Her blonde hair is yanked back in a severe bun, almost as severe as her thick cat eyeliner. She glances up as Maman heads toward them, asking if they need any help, and I immediately see the resemblance.

Same puckered facial expression, like she just swallowed something sour. Same cutting gaze, like she's judging everyone around her. Oh yes, Ashley is definitely the spawn of this woman.

"We're looking for a dress for my daughter," the woman tells Maman, turning away from her. "Something not...*trashy.*" She flicks away the dress she'd been holding as if it left something gross on her hand and paces back toward her daughter.

Maman doesn't respond at first, probably also trying to figure out if the woman just insulted her store.

"What's the occasion?" Maman finally asks.

"A wedding." The woman glances down at the jewelry table and purses her lips.

"Oh! I have some great dresses for that." Maman crosses over to the dresses on the opposing wall. "I think this would look nice on you!"

Maman holds out a dusty-rose lace dress to show Ashley. My body tenses, waiting for her reaction. If she treats Maman the way she usually treats me at school, I'm not sure what I'll do.

Ashley looks at the dress, her eyebrows raising. The expression isn't entirely...unpleasant. She reaches out to feel the fabric.

"Oh, no." Her mother comes over, examines the dress, and then examines her daughter. "Absolutely not." She takes the dress out of Maman's hands and puts it back on the rack.

"I kind of—" Ashley starts.

Her mom cuts her a look. "It'll make you look fat," she says.

Ashley's mouth tightens, but she doesn't respond.

Maman stares at Mrs. Miller, who just whips back around and starts shuffling through the remaining dresses, before turning her gaze on me with a *can you believe this?* expression. Unfortunately, yes, I absolutely can.

The moment I start edging toward the door, Ashley's gaze cuts to me. She looks startled for a moment; she clearly hadn't noticed me standing there before. Her expression quickly shifts to the all too familiar look of disdain.

"What are you doing here?" she snaps, but there's less weight behind it than usual.

I don't even bother responding. "See you at home." I wave to Maman and skirt around Ashley to the door. I almost feel bad about leaving Maman alone with them, but I don't have the mental capacity to worry about the Millers right now. I have a date to get ready for.

9

I'M NOT SURE WHO IS MORE EXCITED ABOUT THIS DATE, me or my parents. At 6:55 p.m., I'm sitting in the living room waiting for Sam to pick me up when they both come shuffling into the room, grinning like someone just came on the television and announced we've finally achieved world peace. Maman eyes my jeans-and-black-tank-top ensemble. The grin fades.

"Are you sure you don't want to wear a dress?" she asks.

"You look *magnifique*, my love," says Papa, squeezing me to his side. As far as he's concerned, the less skin showing, the better.

When Sam pulls up in his black SUV—exactly on time—I'm relieved to see him step out in dark jeans and a gray T-shirt. Being underdressed would have been equally as embarrassing as showing up in a sparkly prom dress. I'm still jittery with nerves, but they're not necessarily the bad kind.

He stands on the porch with a small bouquet of peach and white flowers, and Maman grins like *she's* the one going on the date.

"Nice to see you, Sam," says Papa.

"Likewise, Mr. Beaumont." He reaches out to shake his hand. Papa's grin widens to match Maman's. "Mare won't be out too late. I'll have her home by ten."

Papa nods his approval as I slip past Maman, hook my hand through Sam's elbow, and try to escape out the door.

"Wait! Hold on!" Maman hurries forward. I swear if she whips out a camera and asks us to pose, I will drop dead. Mercifully, she just takes the flowers from Sam. "We need to put these in some water. And where are you kids headed?"

"He isn't telling me. It's a surprise, Maman." I widen my eyes and tilt my head to the side. "You don't want to ruin the surprise, do you?"

She doesn't take the hint. "Well, he can tell *me*." She leans her ear conspiratorially towards Sam.

"We're leaving," I announce and pull Sam out the door.

He glances at them over his shoulder and issues a polite goodbye before turning to me, unable to suppress his grin. "Your parents—"

"Don't even say it."

He opens the passenger door for me before hurrying around to his side and starting the car.

"You really won't tell me where we're going?" I ask.

"Nope," he says cheerfully, pats his jean pockets as if checking to see if he forgot anything, and pulls out of the neighborhood.

We catch the tail-end of the sunset as we drive, the last few tendrils of burnt orange slowly fading behind the mountains. Sam turns the radio on at a soft volume, and for several highway exits, neither of us says a word. Usually, this would ignite a furious anxious cycle in my head as I desperately searched for something to say, but it's actually sort of comfortable. And there's something about not feeling the pressure to fill the silence that makes the muscles in my shoulders relax, just a bit.

Eventually, Sam pulls off the highway, and several turns later, we end up on a bumpy dirt road that jostles the car so much, I have to brace a hand against the door.

I try to peer out the window, but there isn't much to see, just empty land and darkness. "Are you sure this is the way…?"

"I promise I'm not taking you out into the middle of nowhere to kill you."

I throw my hands up. "Well, I hadn't even thought of that until you said it."

He winks. "Don't worry. We're almost there."

The road leads to a gigantic plot of land, mostly dirt with clusters of weeds, where a dozen or so cars are already parked. Thick green trees line the perimeter, and at the front hangs a large white tarp. A small booth covered in string lights sits at the opposite side of the lot, and I press my face against the glass, trying to get a better view, when Sam pulls up to a small booth sitting to the left of the entrance and rolls down his window.

The man inside is wearing a bright red hat, and he leans forward with a toothy smile when we pull up. "Two?"

"Already got them." Sam digs in his pocket and offers the man two crumpled ticket stubs.

The man tips his hat. "Welcome! Just make sure you actually park in one of the spots." He grins again and waves us in.

Sam pulls up near the front, but a decent distance away from the rest of the cars. As he backs into the spot, he glances over at me. "So, what do you think?"

I turn around to see the people in the car diagonally in front of us hop out and make their way across the lot to the concession stand. The sun is tucked beneath the mountains in front of us now, the smallest hints of orange still lingering in the sky. When the breeze picks up, the white tarp sways a bit.

My cheeks ache with the force of my smile. I can't help but feel like I'm in some sixties romcom. "I love it," I say. "I've never been to one of these before."

"This one is a little more rundown than the places closer to town, but it's a lot better."

I hadn't thought it seemed run down in the first place, but it's not like I had anything to compare it to. "Why is it better?"

He just winks and hops out of the car. "You'll see."

I stare at him in confusion. "Isn't the point of a drive-in to stay in the car?"

He rolls his eyes and nods his head to the side. "Come on."

I get out and follow him around to the back of the car, where he pops the trunk. The SUV's backseat is flattened out, exposing an array of blankets and mismatched pillows.

A small battery-operated lantern sits in the center beside a picnic basket.

I look at him, surely wide-eyed. "*Damn.* You went all out."

He gestures forward and bows his head with a sideways smirk. "After you, my lady."

I curtsey—I actually freaking *curtsey*—and hop up. Sam climbs in after me as I crawl to the back and prop myself up on the pillows and throw a blanket over my lap.

"I hope you're hungry." He wedges the picnic basket between us and pulls out a bag of tortilla chips and a container of queso. "I believe someone here said she likes nachos."

I laugh and cover my face with my hands. "I can't believe you remembered that."

As we set up our plates and get situated among the blankets and pillows, the lot begins to fill with cars and the sky finally shifts to black. I smile as the stars begin to poke through the darkness. I can see now why Sam chose this drive-in. It's so far removed from the city that the light pollution doesn't reach us, and you can see—I mean *really* see—the stars.

When I finally look away, I catch Sam staring at me.

"Worth the drive?" he asks.

I blush for no apparent reason. Hopefully it's too dark for him to notice. "Definitely."

I am hyperaware that the following silence is not as comfortable as it was in the car. I keep staring straight ahead at the screen, even though nothing is being projected on it yet, and nibble quietly on my chips. I accidentally swallow too large of a chunk, and the chip's pointy edge stabs the inside of my throat. Now I can feel all of my usual tells starting to creep up on me: the clammy palms, dry mouth, heart thudding dramatically against my ribs no matter how calm my mind is and how rationally I try to reason with my body to *calm the fuck down*. I need to start talking or this is only going to get worse.

"So, I have a question," I blurt.

Sam props a pillow against the side of the car so he can lean against it and face me. He sets his plate off to the side. "Fire away."

"At the coffee shop, we only really talked about me," I venture. "I didn't have the chance to ask what you've been up to the past seven years."

Sam raises his eyebrows and blows the air out of his cheeks. "Well. When I was eleven, I ran for student council. And lost. It was rigged. When I was twelve, my father made me join a soccer league, and there were three other Sams on the team, and since my hair was rather long back then, they all took to calling me Samantha—"

I nudge his leg with mine. "I'm serious."

"So am I! The nickname stuck until I was *fifteen*—"

"Sam."

"Fine," he sighs and leans his head back against the window. "What do you want to know?"

I shrug. "I don't know? What are your hobbies?"

"I like to write," he says matter-of-factly.

"Writing?" I ask, surprised. "What kind of writing?"

"Anything, really. Short stories, that kind of thing. I was thinking about maybe going to college for writing, but my dad wants me to do something else. Anything else." He laughs humorlessly. "All he cares about is me finding a job that pays well."

"Do you ever let anyone read your stuff?"

"Not yet. I want to make sure it's good first." He sighs and rakes his hand through his hair. He stares off toward the still-blank screen, sucking the corners of his mouth in. "I just get so frustrated with myself, like maybe I'm trying too hard, and that's why my writing doesn't come out the way I want it to sound. It's like..." He turns back to me, gesturing widely with his hands as he talks. "Have you ever read a really good book, and it's like magic? It's so well-written that reading it feels like listening to your favorite song?"

I nod, because I actually have no idea what he's talking about, but I want him to keep talking.

"That's the frustrating part. I've been trying so hard to achieve that. I just want my writing to be great and unique, to find something worthwhile to say. Sometimes, it feels like my own passion for it is eating away at me—like it's in this cage in my chest, rattling the bars, desperate to get out." He leans back against the window and shakes his head. "The problem is, I've been trying to dissect and recreate magic, and you just can't. You can't *make* magic. It's like when you're looking for magic, it disappears. I don't know. It just feels like I *could* be a good writer, but exactly what I want to say is out of reach."

"Do you know anything about physics?" I ask.

"Physics?"

"Yeah." I shrug, suddenly self-conscious. "What you're

describing sounds like this energy principle—that energy cannot be created or destroyed, only transformed. And there's this other one, where if you try to observe electrons, their behavior changes. The very act of trying to observe it changes what you're looking for."

"That's exactly it!" He grins and shakes his head once. "Wow. Yeah. I'm totally stealing that comparison." He laughs and fishes some more queso out of the container. "It just feels like the more I try to breathe life into it, the more it falls flat. Sorry, didn't mean for that to turn into a Ted Talk."

"I think if you write as well as you just explained that to me, then it's probably a *lot* better than you think, Sam."

He cracks half a smile. "Don't mistake my psycho babbling for actual talent."

I laugh. "Spoken like a true tortured artist."

"Tortured because the art is *le garbage.*" He winces. "That didn't sound French."

"*Des ordures,*" I correct. "And it sounds to me like the only way to know if it's actually *le garbage* is to let me read it."

"You'd want to?" he asks.

I can feel the blush creeping back. "I'd love to."

"Well," he says, his expression suddenly serious. "You'll have to prove your trustworthiness first."

My jaw drops open. "You don't think I'm *trustworthy?*"

He just twists his mouth to the side and shakes his head.

I throw a pillow at him. "I'm still not sure you haven't brought me all the way out here just to murder me yet."

He props the pillow behind his head. "Well, I guess if that's the case you'll find out soon enough, won't you?"

When the movie starts, we move the picnic basket and lantern to the front seats to get them out of the way and position ourselves so we're facing the screen. Now that it's getting later, the temperature is noticeably dipping. A chilly night breeze drifts through the open trunk, so Sam and I sit side-by-side, propped up with pillows, and share the two blankets. They're plaid and warm, and have the distinct scent of his aftershave.

Our legs are pressed against each other beneath the blanket.

I am hyperaware of this fact, even long into the film. My entire body is tense with nerves no matter how many times I order it to relax. It's like my body is betraying me, like it's determined to sabotage this situation.

"Are you cold?" Sam asks.

"Just a little. I'm fine."

"Here." He wraps his arm around my shoulders and pulls me against his side. Immediately his body heat relieves the wind's bite, and he leaves his arm around me. I feel the stupid urge to grin and try to relax against his side.

"Since you got your question, does that mean I'm allowed one?" he asks.

I consider this. "One."

"You wanted to skip your dad's service last week."

I can feel him looking at me, but I keep my gaze trained on the screen. "That doesn't sound like a question."

"I'm not going to lie, I was really surprised. I don't think it's any secret that the only reason I go is because of my dad, but you...I don't know. I always thought you were really into that kind of stuff."

"My family is," I concede.

"And you're...not?"

I finally risk a look in his direction. His expression is curious, if a little serious, but there doesn't seem to be any judgement in his eyes. "You want to talk religion on the first date?" I ask with a laugh.

He shrugs, smiles a little. "I'm just trying to understand you. You're really different from the girl I used to know—and don't get me wrong, there's nothing wrong with that. I'm definitely not the guy I used to be. I just want to know who you are *now*. And I'm guessing this is probably a big part of it. We don't have to talk about it if you don't want to."

How he managed to nail me in so little time together, I have no idea. "If you really wanna know, I was twelve when I started having doubts," I find myself saying—it almost feels like an out-of-body experience, like someone else is saying the words that I've never managed to speak aloud. I start talking faster, trying to rid myself of the words before I can talk myself out of it. "And by the time I reached high school, I didn't just doubt what I'd been taught; I disagreed with it. And I guess now that I'm older, and I've started to see religion in the context of the outside world, I just have more and more contempt for it. I hate how narrow-minded it can make people. How it breeds judgement and hatred and superiority complexes."

I pause, gauging his reaction. There's no disgust in his expression, so I guess that's a good sign. He just waits for me to continue, his head cocked in that oddly endearing way of his.

More than anything, I'm surprised he's listening. Not just listening as a courtesy, but actually *listening*, listening. And it's unnerving, knowing I could just keep talking and no one would stop me. No one would interrupt me or talk over me.

Because when you're quiet, you learn to speak in short, fast sentences, because you're not sure how long people will listen to you. You get the words out as quickly as you can—sometimes so quickly, they start to slur and trip over each other, just so you won't have to be the center of attention for too long.

But this isn't like that. I have the floor. And I have a boy looking at me like he wants to hear what I have to say, no matter how long it takes me to say it.

It's equally terrifying and thrilling.

"Whenever people quote scripture at me," I continue. "I feel like they're trying to shove religion down my throat. Honestly, it makes me feel like I'm suffocating. Like everyone is always trying to force these beliefs on me that I just don't have. All my life, everyone has acted like what they believe is the only right thing to believe. But I've never understood why their beliefs are automatically more correct than mine. Why do I *have* to believe the way they want me to? Why am I going to hell just because I believe differently? For all the reasons Christians don't believe in the gods of other religions, why can't those be the reasons I don't believe in their god? There's no *proof*, and I guess I'm just not the kind of person who can believe on faith alone. And whenever I asked questions in Sunday school, my teachers would look at me like there was something wrong with me for not believing blindly."

I take a deep breath. The more I say, the more words seem to bubble up in my stomach, desperate to break the surface. I've suppressed them for so long, it's like they're jumping at their opportunity for freedom. That all too familiar self-consciousness comes crashing back, and the silence suddenly feels much heavier in the wake of my words. "Sorry," I say, staring at my hands in my lap. "I'm ranting."

"No," Sam shakes his head, a thoughtful expression on his face. "It's okay. I get what you're saying. Completely."

"I've never been able to talk about this with anyone before," I say quietly.

"You've never talked to anyone about it?"

Shrugging, I look away. "Johanna, my best friend, she kind of knows. She knows I don't believe like my parents do, but that's pretty much it. It's just not something we really talk about, you know?"

"And your parents? Do you think you'd ever tell them?"

"I don't know," I admit. "I'd like to think that someday they'll be willing to hear it, but they're just so far into their religion, like it's some kind of hole in the ground, and they can't see anything outside of it anymore. I think I'm just better off not telling them. If I do, I'll get exactly what I'm trying to avoid."

"So, you don't believe in it?" Sam asks. "Any of it?"

"I believe in science," is all I say.

He nods a few times, gaze trained on the screen, mouth

set in a way that tells me he's thinking pretty hard about something.

"What about you?" I ask, suddenly self-conscious for talking so much.

He nods his head thoughtfully and takes a deep breath. "A part of me wants to. I can see the appeal of there being a greater plan, a purpose. Of there being someone watching over me."

I wait.

He shrugs. "But I don't know. I just can't get the logical part of my brain to shut off. I go to church for my dad's sake. He needs that faith. It's what gets him through the day. My mom left more than ten years ago, but he's still not over it. And even though I don't agree with him, I have nothing against him believing in God, if it helps him. He has every right to believe whatever he wants to believe."

Sam twists so he's sitting next to me again, his arm pressed against mine. "So, is this the most dysfunctional first date you've ever been on, or what?" he laughs. "*Grease* and religious discussions in the trunk of a car."

I let out a long, shaky breath that sort of sounds like a laugh. "I wouldn't know, actually. I don't really have anything to compare it to."

His eyebrows shoot up. "Really? None?"

I shrug, my cheeks flooding with heat. "Nope."

He considers this for a second. "Well, I should probably try to redeem it for you then, shouldn't I?"

Before I can respond, he leans over and takes my face with both hands. He pauses, our noses almost touching, his eyes searching mine. When I don't pull away, he closes the rest of the distance between us.

For the first time in eighteen years, a boy is *kissing* me, but there are no fireworks. I suddenly realize I have no idea what to do, so I open my mouth and sit there. And it feels...weird. For a moment all I can focus on is how weird someone else's lips feel—soft and kind of squishy—how inconvenient is it to have teeth in this situation, how weird your tongue feels in your mouth when you don't know where to put it. It's nothing like in middle-school slumber parties when everyone kissed their hands for practice.

Sam, on the other hand, clearly knows what to do, so I follow his lead. He keeps one hand cradled around the side of my face and traces the other down my back.

I start to get a sense of the way to move my mouth with his, and then suddenly it doesn't feel so weird anymore. It feels *good*. The blood rushing through my body runs hot, but not the nervous kind. It's like electricity is buzzing along my skin and the air between us is on fire. He pulls me closer, and I wind my hands around the back of his neck and into his hair because I've seen people do that in movies.

But then he starts to lay me down, and the heat that floods my system is *not* the electricity kind. My entire body tenses and I pull back. He immediately backs off, his hands resting on my arms.

"Sorry, I shouldn't have—"

"It's okay," I say at the same time.

For a second, we just stare at each other in the darkness, a little out of breath. His cheeks are flushed, his lips slightly swollen, and I blush furiously when I realize *I* did that. He reaches up and tucks my hair behind my ear, but neither of us says anything.

"Um." I scoot away from him a little. "We should probably—" I nod my head toward the movie screen.

"Yeah." He slides back into place at my side. For a moment, a a cold wave of terror washes through me that I'd done something wrong, and now things will be awkward between us. But then he holds out his arm, an offering, and I settle back against his chest, listening to the pounding of his heart starting to slow.

I feel that stupid urge to grin again, but I can't fight it this time. Because I think I finally understand why these are the kinds of kisses parents worry about.

10

When I show up to the library late Saturday morning to meet Johanna and Ashley, I'm still buzzing from the night before. I keep catching myself smiling, and even when I pinch my lips together to stop, the smile pops back out a few minutes later. I can't help but marvel that I'd actually *done* it. I'd made it through a date without freaking out, or breaking down, or scaring Sam off by being too awkward and weird. We'd actually *talked*. Let alone the other things we did. It was probably incredibly tame by anyone else's standards, but just thinking about it makes my cheeks burn.

"So, I take it the date with Sexy Sam went well."

I startle. I must have been lost in thought again, because I didn't even see Johanna come into the library, but now she's standing across the table from me, arms crossed over her chest, a wide smirk on her purple lips.

I wipe the grin from my face, but my lips tremble with the effort. "I have no idea what you're talking about."

"Oh my God!" Johanna slides into the seat next to me and throws her bag on the table. "You can't stop smiling! And you're blushing!" She pokes my cheek.

"Stop!" I laugh, swatting her hand away. "It went well, okay?"

Johanna's jaw drops open. "He kissed you."

"I didn't say that!"

"I can *tell!*"

"Tell what?"

Ashley is standing on the other side of the table, eyebrows raised expectantly. She's in an all-black tracksuit with some designer's name stamped down the side of the leg. Her blonde hair is pulled back in a messy high ponytail, and judging by how smeared her eye make-up is, it's leftover from the night before.

I wonder how long she's been standing there.

But if she'd heard anything important, she wouldn't be asking.

"I can tell that we're almost done with the project," I say. It sounds even dumber out loud than it did in my head.

Ashley narrows her eyes like she, too, thinks I'm an idiot before lowering herself into the seat across from us. "So, did you guys do your part, or what?"

She pulls out her laptop and a stack of papers from her bag and sets them on the table. We divided up the paper based on the type of research, and decided we'd all just edit together the chunks we'd written later on. Johanna tosses her own pages into the center of the table. I set mine down in front of me.

"Well, does someone want to start editing it together, and the other two can start making the PowerPoint for the presentation?" I offer.

"And by that, you mean I edit the paper and you two go off and make the slides," Ashley says, deadpan.

"Do you *want* to make the slides?" Johanna asks.

"I'm just *saying*," Ashley huffs and swipes the pages from the center of the table.

What she's *saying*, honestly, I'm not entirely sure.

"Do you have something to say?" Johanna snaps.

"Jo," I warn under my breath.

Ashley's gaze slides between the two of us slowly, like a snake sizing up a mouse.

"We could all edit the paper and then all work on the PowerPoint," I offer.

"And have to spend my entire Saturday stuck here with you two?" Ashley mutters, shuffling the papers in her hands until they all line up.

Johanna folds her hands on the table and leans forward, smiling. "Then what would you like to do, Ashley?" Her voice is so sweet, it makes my teeth hurt.

I kick Jo under the table, but when I glance back up at Ashley, it seems like she didn't even hear us. Her gaze is trained somewhere over our heads, her eyebrows pinched together, tension lining her mouth. Her hands are starting to crumple the papers she's holding. I try to follow her gaze, but all I see are the library stacks.

"Ashley?" I ask. "Are you okay?"

She immediately snaps out of it and sets the papers down a little too loudly. "I'll start editing the paper."

"Are you sure?" Johanna asks slowly.

"It's fine," she snaps and whips open her laptop.

"Well, if you want to switch off halfway through or something, let us know," I offer, taking out my own computer.

She ignores me and stuffs headphones into her ears.

I glance over my shoulder again, but all I see is a girl in the stacks by the windows. She's crouched down, her face turned away from me. I'm about to turn back around when I notice a second girl, half hidden by the shelves, bent over next to her, a hand rubbing circles on the first girl's back.

"You want to start with the text and I'll look for images?" Johanna asks. "Mare?" She pokes my arm.

I turn around. Now *my* eyebrows are pulled together. It was weird, sure. But what's weirder is why it interested Ashley so much.

"Sure," I mumble to Johanna, though my gaze is focused on Ashley, who is scowling at her laptop screen, the music from her headphones loud enough to hear from here. Oddly enough, it sounds like she's listening to jazz. She glances up and catches me staring at her, but she just glares at me for a few seconds before returning to her work, nails tapping furiously against the keyboard.

WE WORK MOSTLY IN SILENCE. THE PROJECT ONLY TAKES an hour or so to finish, and the second we print out the final paper, Ashley *bolts*. Seriously, I don't think I've ever seen someone move that fast without actually running, blonde ponytail whipping behind her.

Jo and I linger for a bit, packing up our things and chatting in hushed voices, until we head out to our cars. My phone *dings* with a text from Sam, a video of a Maltese puppy, which looks a lot like Squirt, fast asleep with its head inside of its owner's tennis shoe.

"Why are you grinning like an idiot?" Jo teases.

"No reason." I shove the phone in my back pocket as we reach the parking lot.

Johanna eyes me for a second, nodding slowly. "Mmm-hmm. Don't think I don't know it wasn't lover boy."

"Want to come over?" I offer, pausing outside my car. Jo's is a little further down the lot.

"Ugh, I wish." She fishes her phone out of her bag and frowns at the screen. "My parents are flying back in today and I told them I'd pick them up from the airport."

"Damn. How long are they staying this time?" I wince as I say it. The Palmers aren't exactly an off-limits topic, but we somehow always manage to avoid it. If her parents' persisting absence bothers her, she doesn't show it. She says she's used to it—*that's the life of a pilot and flight attendant's daughter*—but I know it can't be easy. Johanna just shrugs.

"Who knows. How about tomorrow?" she offers.

"I can't. I promised Maman and Harper a *girl's day*."

Johanna pops her eyebrows. "Yikes."

We stand there for a beat, and I twist my car keys around in my palm. We used to hang out almost every weekend and drop by each other's houses constantly during the week. And I know it's just because we're both busy, but I can't help but notice as graduation gets closer we see each other less and less.

Johanna must see it on my face, because she throws her arm over my shoulder and squeezes me tightly against her side. "Don't worry about it, Mare Bear. We'll just do it next week. Text me about any updates with *Samuel*." She jostles my shoulders.

Laughing, I pull away. "Tell your parents I say hi."

She rolls her eyes and waves as she starts walking backwards to her car. "Yeah. If I can get a word in."

I watch as she climbs into her Jeep and cuts out of the parking lot, swerving around cars so she can weave through the rows instead of going over the speed bumps. It isn't until her break lights disappear around the corner that I turn back to my car and get inside.

11

FOR THE FIRST TIME IN YEARS, I WAKE UP SUNDAY morning feeling something other than dread. In fact, I'm so excited to see Sam that when my parents start praising Jesus and listening to some Christian radio station at the breakfast table, I manage to sit peacefully in my seat instead of bristling in discomfort.

Harper, on the other hand, sits across the table from me, staring at her pancakes as if the sight nauseates her. We haven't really talked since Tuesday, at least not about anything of real substance. I want to have another conversation with her, but I don't know what to say that will make her feel better, and I don't know how to approach it. All I know is I refuse to leave her alone in this any longer.

She glances up and catches me staring at her, but instead of responding with her usual scowl, she just looks away.

Since it's another overcast day and it's still pretty

chilly out, Maman lets me and Harper wear pants, but not even this small victory is enough to lift Harper's spirits. And now that I'm paying attention, I realize she's been acting like this for a while now, as if she's trying to disappear into a shell. What I'd thought had been her usual moodiness and general unpleasant attitude was fear. Shame.

I have never felt like a more horrible human being than I do right now.

We're some of the first people to the church that morning, as usual. As I start to break off from the family to wait for Sam, I pause.

"Harper?" I call.

She glances at me over her shoulder.

"Do you want to sit with me and Sam today?" I offer.

Maman and Papa freeze in the doorway, and at first I think they're going to explode about destroying our *united front*, but when they turn, they're both beaming.

"What a wonderful idea!" Papa exclaims.

"*Magnifique!*"

"Um, okay." Harper joins me by the tables, looking half-relieved, half-confused, as Maman and Papa disappear inside.

As Mr. Johnson's car pulls into the lot, I grab Harper's arm. "I'm about to tell you a really big secret, so I need to know that I can trust you. That you won't tell Maman and Papa."

Harper narrows her eyes. "Okayyy."

"We're ditching the service and going to the coffee shop across the road instead."

Harper's jaw actually drops. "Is that what you guys did last time? I *knew* I didn't see you anywhere in the back!"

I raise an eyebrow. "Do you want to come with us or not?"

Harper shoots a look at the church over her shoulder, and when she turns back to me, she lowers her eyebrows and crosses her arms over her chest. Usually, the motion would look standoffish, but there's something about the way she hunches her shoulders in, like she's trying to make herself smaller, that hurts my heart. "We won't get in trouble?" she asks.

The service doesn't start for another half-hour or so, and the early arrivals are mingling in the lobby, occupied with their conversations and pastries from the coffee cart.

"No one will notice," I say. "And even if they do, it's still early enough that we could say we just ran to get better coffee before the service." I nudge her. "Besides, what's the harm in missing it just one time?"

Harper still looks unsure. "But what if—"

"*Shh!*" I hiss as Sam and his dad approach.

"*Bonjour*, Meredith and Harper!" Mr. Johnson waves. His pronunciation is a little better than last time. "I'll leave you to it then." He pats Sam on the back and heads inside. "*Au revoir!*" he calls over his shoulder. It comes out as *aww vah*.

Sam scrunches his nose at the sound. "He totally butchered that, didn't he?"

"Yeah." I smile at him. I can't stop smiling at him, which would be completely embarrassing, but he's grinning right back at me.

Harper looks at me, then at Sam, her face scrunched together. "What is the matter with you two?"

I snap out of it, ordering myself not to blush. "I invited Harper to come with us. I hope that's okay."

"Of course!" Sam's grin returns, and he really does look happy and not like he's just trying to be polite. "I've been wanting to talk to the little sis anyway. Get some dirt."

Harper's usual stoic mask cracks, just a little. "If it's dirt you want, I've got plenty of that."

I swat her lightly on the arm. "You do not."

"Come on, Harper, let's walk." Sam hooks his arm through hers and begins to lead her toward the coffee shop.

"I'll just leave you two to it, then," I call after them.

"Aw, don't feel left out. Hop on." Sam motions to his back.

"You are not giving me a piggyback ride."

"No? I'm sorry, Harper, hold on one second." He releases her, turns to me, and in one fluid motion, he sweeps me over his shoulder so he's clutching my legs with one hand (thank God for the pants) and I'm dangling against his back.

"Sam!" I squeal. Yes, I actually *squeal*.

He calmly walks to where Harper waits, re-hooks his other arm through hers, and resumes walking.

"You two are disgustingly adorable," she says. I can't see her face from this angle, but I imagine it's a mixture of a smile and a look of disgust—the two usually go hand-in-hand with her.

Sam doesn't release me even after we reach the coffee shop. When we walk in the door, the barista makes a squeak of surprise, but Sam just carries me to the same table we sat at last time, deposits me in a seat, asks Harper for her order, and then heads to the counter for the drinks.

Unfortunately, the shop isn't empty like last time. There's a middle-aged man sitting in the corner with a laptop and gigantic headphones, staring at us with his lip curled back.

Harper takes the seat beside me and rests her hands on the table. Her gaze flickers from her hands to my face a few times before she finally says, "Thanks for letting me come with you guys. I know you'd probably rather be alone—"

"Harper," I cut her off. I consider reaching out and taking her hand, but that might be a bit much. "I'm glad you're here. Really."

She smiles, and it's a real one. I honestly can't remember the last time she smiled like that, and at *me*. Over the past few years, our entire relationship has been reduced to snarky comments, eye rolls, and curt replies.

"So, are you two, like, a thing now?" she asks.

"Yes." Sam appears with the drinks and sets them on the table. As he takes his seat, he looks me directly in the eye and says, "Totally a thing."

"So, Sam," Harper cuts in before I can respond, but that doesn't stop the violent burning rushing to my cheeks, or the way my lips quirk up into a stupid smile at Sam's words. How casually he'd thrown them out, as if it were obvious. "What are your plans for after high school?" She clasps her hands together on the table and raises her eyebrows at him like an interviewer. Like she's *scoping him out* for me.

Sam seems completely unfazed. "I'm planning on majoring in journalism," he tells her. "Not as impressive as your sister's fancy veterinarian endeavors, but at least I'll get one of those cool notepads. Or are those for detectives? You know what, it doesn't matter." He waves a hand. "I'm getting one anyway."

Harper nods slowly—it's apparently an acceptable answer—and takes a sip of the drink Sam brought her. She has to suck in the corners of her mouth to hide her disgust as she sets it back down. Why she asked for a black coffee when she can't drink anything unless it contains half her weight in sugar, I have no idea.

"I've heard you're quite the artist." Sam tilts his cup to her.

Harper's head whips toward me.

I shrug innocently.

"Must have been a pretty boring date if you guys had to talk about me," she jokes.

Sam meets my eyes, and I can't stop my mind from flashing back to the way his mouth felt, to sitting so close I could feel the heat from his skin and the beat of his heart through his shirt. The smell of his aftershave. The rough feel of the stubble beneath his jaw. There's something behind his eyes that tells me he's thinking about the same thing. His gaze erases everything else around me, and it's just me and him, my vision tunneling and blocking out everything else.

"So, what do you like to draw?" Sam asks, but his gaze

lingers on me just a moment longer. When he looks away, the trance breaks, and the noise around us suddenly seems louder—the tapping of keys on a laptop in the back, the rumbling of the coffee machine, the whirl of a ceiling fan. My heart hammering embarrassingly hard in my chest.

Harper tells him about the difference between using watercolors and acrylics, and which paintbrushes look the best with different types of paper. Sam never looks away from her. He leans forward on the table, nodding as she talks, the left corner of his mouth lightly curled up, encouraging her to keep going. I can tell by the way Harper keeps touching her hair that she's self-conscious, but the more she talks, the stronger her voice comes out, and I can guess exactly how she's feeling. How having Sam look at you like that can light a match in your chest, igniting a confidence you didn't know was there.

I watch Sam as he scratches the stubble beneath his jaw —fuller now than it was on our date—how he tilts his head to the side when he listens.

He glances up and catches me staring.

"The two of you should totally collaborate," I blurt out. "Sam writes the story; Harper does the drawings. You guys could become a famous picture-book writing team."

"You write fiction, too?" Harper asks.

Now it's Sam's turn to look slightly abashed. "A little." He meets my eyes again. "We'd have to only write books about animals so Mare can do our fact-checking, though. You know how to draw a Maltese?"

When we meet back up with Maman after the service, Sam gives me a quick kiss to the side of my head like it's the most normal thing in the world before heading off with his dad. It leaves my entire body feeling hot and tingly. Harper and I linger outside of the church, pretending like we've just come from the service, when Maman rushes toward us, eyes and lips stretched wide.

"Girls' Day!" she squeals.

Harper and I both widen our eyes, but probably for different reasons.

Maman crushes us in a hug as if she hadn't just seen us an hour ago, but when she pulls away, I notice two rather awkward-looking people lingering behind her.

"Oh!" Maman pulls back and steps aside, flapping her arms at the two women to come closer. "How rude of me. I invited Ramona and her daughter Silvia to join us. I hope that's okay." Maman looks to me and Harper, eyebrows drawn together, like we might actually be upset by this.

I can't stop myself from staring at Silvia. She's in a floral maxi-dress, a cream cardigan on top, her dirty-blonde hair chopped into a bob that barely skims her chin. She's staring at her feet, tucked inside yellow sandals, her toenails painted light pink.

The last time I saw her, she was in ripped black jeans, chipping black nail polish, a *Grateful Dead* T-shirt, and her hair was down to her lower back—she was constantly braiding it and pining it into cool styles that looked like they belonged on *Game of Thrones*. Harper, beside me, also seems to be ogling her former friend.

"Silvia just got back from visiting her grandparents

yesterday," Maman is saying, "so I thought it could be fun for us all to go out shopping! Harper, Meredith, you know Silvia, of course."

Silvia finally glances up, but even when her eyes meet mine, she doesn't seem to see me.

Ramona, her mother, is standing beside her in a hot-pink pencil skirt and black and white polka dot blouse. She wraps her arm around Silvia, who immediately flinches at the contact.

I glance behind them, but there's still one noticeably absent figure. "Where's Papa?" I ask.

"Oh." Maman waves her hand dismissively. "He's staying late today to meet with some other parents from your school. He said he'd find a ride home."

"Meeting about what—?" I start to ask, but Maman's already resumed flapping her arms and directing us to her car across the lot. Harper glances back at Silvia, who trails behind us with her mom, then shoots me a look. I wonder if she heard the rumors, too. I can't exactly ask her now, though.

We file into the car, everyone silent but Maman, who keeps tittering on obliviously about which stores we should hit at the mall and the coupons she got in the mail. Ramona joins her in the front seat, praising Papa's sermon about loving everyone today. Even I can admit that Papa's good at his job, but considering the restrictions on who *everyone* entails, it sounds like a load of B.S.

Harper squishes into the middle between me and Silvia, who scoots to the very end of her seat, practically flattening herself against the door to put more distance between herself and my sister. She stares out the window wordlessly.

"It was a long drive back from Montana yesterday," Ramona says, turning around in her seat to look at us. "Silvia's a bit tired." She reaches over and squeezes her daughter's knee.

Silvia stares at her mother's hand until it releases her, then glances at Harper and me. "Yeah, sorry. I just haven't gotten much sleep."

Judging by the deep purple circles beneath her eyes, there's probably a lot more truth to that than Ramona's story implies.

Maman fills the car with some gospel music on the radio as we drive, saving us from trying to fill the time with awkward conversation. As soon as we head into the first department store, Harper grabs my hand and slows until we fall to the back of the group. I watch as Maman takes off toward a rack of frilly blouses and eagerly starts collecting them into her arms.

"You've heard the rumors, right?" Harper whispers.

I nod.

Her gaze darts to Silvia, who is standing beside her mother at the jewelry counter. Ramona's chatting with a woman behind the counter, who's nearly a foot taller than she is, with ruby-studded earrings that go all the way down to her shoulders. Silvia's just standing off to the side, fidgeting with her cardigan and scanning the space around her.

"They did something to her." Harper's eyebrows draw

together as she watches her friend. "That's not...that's just not Silvia."

"Meredith, Harper!" Maman calls, holding up a burnt orange tank top. She waves it around like a flag to signal us over.

"I have an idea," Harper murmurs as we head over to where Maman is stockpiling clothes. She already has too many to carry, so she's pushed aside the clothes on a nearby rack to hang her finds.

"Hey, Maman?" Harper says. "Do you mind if Mare, Silvia, and I head to the food court real quick to grab smoothies? We can meet you and Ramona at whatever store you go to next."

I hold my breath, waiting for Maman to offer to join. She surveys her pile of clothes, clearly not finished here yet.

"We'll be quick!" Harper adds.

"Okay," Maman concedes. "I think we're just going next door after this. But don't take too long!"

Silvia joins us wordlessly as we head out into the mall. I let Harper take the lead on this one, partly because the two of them used to be friends, and also because I straight-up have no idea what to say.

The halls are flooded with shoppers, their arms decked out in various shiny bags. A group of giggling middle school girls cuts us off as soon as we step out of the store, hurrying to the other side where some bright pink store has the word *sale* in the window.

Silvia stares after them with a blank expression.

"We're glad you're back," Harper offers, nudging her

friend with her elbow as we start toward the food court.

Some form of a smile flashes on Silvia's face. It looks painful. "It's nice to be back."

"I like your haircut," I offer.

Silvia's hand flies up, smoothing down the back of her hair. The smile is gone from her face.

Okay, so clearly I just shouldn't talk.

"Can I just be straight with you?" Harper bursts, grabbing Silvia's wrist and pulling her to a stop. A family with half a dozen kids and two strollers tries to edge around us, and we step to the side of the walkway.

Silvia pulls her wrist away and cradles it in her other hand. She sighs. "I know what you're going to—"

"There have been rumors going around ever since you left," Harper says.

"There are always rumors going around." Silvia rolls her eyes, but she's clearly avoiding eye contact with Harper. "What else are bored church ladies supposed to fill their boring lives with?"

"So, you're saying there's no truth to them?" Harper pushes.

Silvia doesn't respond at first, shooting a glance over her shoulder. "I should probably get back to my mom."

"Silvia, I know we haven't talked in a while, but—"

"Don't you get it?" Silvia hisses, taking a step toward Harper. For the first time since I saw her standing there, I recognize that old fierceness in her eyes. "I can't talk about this."

Harper opens her mouth to respond, but Silvia has already whipped around and started rushing back the way we came. I stare after her, noticing the line of her hair is uneven in the back.

Harper may not have gotten the answers she wanted, but I think I just did.

12

The school day on Monday passes as can be expected: tediously and in a haze. The only thing that keeps me semi-awake enough to shuffle from class to class is the quad-shot espresso I grabbed on my drive to school. From the drive-through, obviously. I don't need the stress of face-to-face interactions that early in the morning.

My classes pass in yawns and desperate looks at the clock until three o'clock finally rolls around, and freedom has never felt so good.

But even then, my mind keeps wandering back to Silvia. The uneven line of her hair swaying back and forth.

She didn't speak another word to me or Harper the rest of the afternoon, and no matter how many shopping bags Maman accumulated, or how many blindingly bright articles of clothing she showed us, the negative energy surrounding the whole trip wouldn't fade. Enough so that even Maman picked up on it and called it quits after a mere two hours of wandering through the mall. No pleas to prolong the day with facials or a movie or anything.

When I pull up to the house, Sam's SUV is already sitting by the curb. I park in the driveway and notice him waiting on the front porch, his backpack at his feet, a white paper bag in his hands. When he notices me, he shoots to his feet, tossing the strap of his backpack over his shoulder, and beams.

"Hey," is all he says, like it's completely normal for him to be here. Is that what people do when they're dating? Just show up whenever they want to see the other person? I'm happy to see him, of course, but my anxiety could do without the lack of planning.

"Hey?"

He raises the bag and his shoulder simultaneously. "I thought we could hang out. I know you probably have a ton of homework, but I thought maybe we could study together or something." His smile falters, just for a second, like he's doubting showing up here.

"What's in the bag?" I ask.

"I know they're not *technically* French, but I figure everyone likes fries, right? And I don't know about you, but I'm starving."

I laugh and take the bag as he offers it to me. Inside, there are two large orders of fries, both of which, if I'm being honest, I could totally devour on my own. "You figured right." I nod my head toward the house and unlock the door. "Come on in."

We both kick off our shoes by the door and I lead him to my room on the second level. Even though Maman and

Papa aren't home, I leave the door open, if only to avoid a lecture on the off chance they somehow found out. We've never actually had to flesh out the *no boys alone with you* rule since Harper and I have never brought boys home before, but I'm definitely willing to bet closing the door is off limits.

Sam pauses in the doorway, taking it all in. I do a quick scan on the ground to make sure I didn't leave any dirty underwear or something equally embarrassing laying around, but everything's in place; my bed is neatly made, the lavender comforter tightly tucked into the bed frame; the twinkle lights strung around the perimeter of the room are glowing softly, except for that batch in the corner with the broken bulbs; my textbooks are stacked in a neat little tower beside my bed with an old AP Chem one proudly standing on top, because I'd been reading from it for fun last night. I'd even vacuumed the cream shag carpet the other day.

There used to be a small glass desk in the corner, but I let Harper take it when she started high school since it made my room feel a little too crowded, and I like doing my homework on my bed anyway. There's a small cream butterfly chair in its place now, occupied with a couple throw pillows that match the bedspread perfectly.

"You painted the walls," Sam finally says and follows me inside. I plop my backpack on my bed and situate my pillows against the headboard to assume my usual homework position.

I guess he's right; the last time he would have been in here was probably eight years ago, back when the walls were bright green and pink. Around freshman year, Papa helped me paint them a neutral beige again, save for the dark brown accent wall across from my bed, where photos of all the dogs we've had come through the shelter are strung on a piece of twine held up by little clips.

He paces over to the wall, looking at the pictures, and points. "Squirt!"

Her picture is the farthest to the right, and it's the perfect candid shot of her outside, head twisted over her shoulder, tongue hanging out the side of her mouth.

I chuckle a little. "I think that's my favorite picture of her. Jo took it."

He inspects it a second longer. "She's a great photographer."

I smile like a proud mom.

He points to another picture, this one closer to the center. A chubby six-year-old me stands center frame on a porch with a bright blue sky behind my pigtails. In it, I'm proudly holding up some starter microscope kit in a bright yellow box above my head, smiling so wide you can see all of my missing teeth. Grand-mère and Grand-père, who gave me the gift, are squatting beside me, both donning goofy grins and thumbs-ups. Large black sunglasses take up most of Grand-mère's face, but Grand-père just squints against the sun, his face a deep tan from all those hours working in the garden.

My chest twinges a bit at the sight. When Harper and I were younger, the whole family made yearly trips to France to visit them, but as we got older and everyone's schedules got busier, those trips started happening less and less. I think the last time we went, I was in middle school. I used to love hiking through the French countryside with Grand-père as he pointed out all the different kinds of plants, or visiting the city with Papa, hearing about his study-abroad adventures in college and seeing the coffee shop where he and Maman met.

"Weren't they...?" he trails off, pressing his lips together like he's second guessing his question. He points to the picture of Grand-mère and Grand-père again. "I thought I remembered talk of them moving here, way back when."

The twinge returns. I nod. When I was twelve, they started the papers to immigrate here, but even with family in the United States, the process is still unbelievably outdated and slow. I shrug. "They're still waiting. Some people wait *decades* before they make it to the front of the line. So all they can do is wait."

"Wow." Sam takes a step away from the wall. "I had no idea it took that long. Is it like a quota thing?"

"Yes and no. Quotas, and also just an overwhelmed system that hasn't been updated since the nineties."

"Yikes. I'm sorry."

I shrug again. "It is what it is, I guess. I just feel horrible for them. They've already been waiting for over six years. It feels like so much lost time."

"Yeah. Sorry. I didn't mean to dig all of that up for you."

"It's okay." I give him a wide smile, trying to lighten the mood again as he comes over to join me, stretching out along the foot of the bed. His tall frame is way too much for my queen mattress to handle, so his feet dangle off the end. He pulls a book out of his bag and reaches a hand toward me. I stare at it, confused.

He peers at me over the book. "Fry?"

I laugh and set the greasy bag between us—I usually refrain from eating in my bed because I hate all of the crumbs, but today, strangely, I couldn't care less—and hand him a few of the fries. He dips his head in thanks as I pull out The Binder.

There's something about being told *no* or *you can't* that has never sat well with me. So naturally, upon hearing from everyone around me that college—at least any colleges I'm actually interested in—was out of the question, I'd taken it upon myself to find a way to work around that. The Binder is so full everything is practically bursting out of it. Printed-out copies of all the college applications I submitted, old essay drafts, financial aid applications, private scholarship applications, separate essays for each scholarship, work-study applications, advice columns for scholarship essay writing—everything I could possibly need is in here.

Sam stops what he's doing when I pull it out and stares.

"What is *that*?" he asks.

"My golden ticket out of here," I reply, flipping it open and pulling out an old draft of my UC Davis essay for motivation, along with my dozens of current scholarship applications. It's my ultimate dream school, and they have an amazing vet program for post-grad. I worked doubly hard on that application, but it won't mean much if I get in and can't afford it.

Tuition is forty grand.

A year.

I'm both anticipating and dreading my acceptance decision showing up in the mail this month.

He scoots closer and cocks his head, trying to read. "College apps?"

I sigh. "It's a never-ending process."

"Need any help?" he offers.

I smile at his discarded book at the foot of the bed, something about writing craft. He follows my gaze and waves a hand. "I'm just reading that for fun."

"I could use some help with my essay," I admit. "It's for a pretty competitive scholarship, so I really need it to stand out."

"Say no more." He glances at The Binder.

"Here." It takes me a minute to dig through everything and find the right essay, and it's kind of crumpled and stained with what appears to be ketchup in the top right corner. I wince. "I was working on it at lunch."

He laughs, takes the essay, smooths it over his lap, and pulls a red pen out of his bag. "What's the word limit?"

"500."

While he dives in, stretching out at the foot of my bed and holding the paper over his face as he reads, I focus on my other application for a small private scholarship. Well, I try to. We work in silence for a while, but my eyes keep darting in his direction every time I hear that red pen scrawl against the page. I'm already on the fifth draft of that essay, but writing has never been my strong suit. I haven't even seen Sam's feedback yet, but I can already feel a wave of embarrassed nausea percolating in the pit of my stomach. Writing is to Sam what science is to me, and now he's going to think I'm an illiterate idiot.

I've finally managed to stop looking over at Sam every three seconds and focus on my own work when I feel him reach over and squeeze one of my feet.

He holds up the essay.

"You're done?" I ask.

"Do you want my feedback now or after you're finished?"

His expression is unreadable. It makes me want to throw up.

I straighten and clutch my application to my chest protectively. "Just get it over with."

"It's not bad!" he laughs.

I groan and cover my face with my paper. "'Not bad' is basically synonymous with 'not good.'"

He jostles my foot. "It's *not bad*. It's well written, and you do a great job of explaining why working at the shelter has meant so much to you, but..."

I close my eyes, bracing myself. "But what?"

It takes him a few seconds to respond. "Have you ever thought about writing about something else?"

My forehead scrunches together. "Like what?" There's pretty much nothing else interesting about my life.

He shrugs a shoulder and looks away before saying, "Well, how about your family?"

"My family," I say flatly.

Sensing my defensiveness, he pushes himself up to a seated position and raises him palms. "I just think you have an interesting story that you could use to your advantage.

It would definitely help you stand out. The way you were brought up and your own beliefs has given you an interesting perspective, especially given the field you want to go in. I don't know." He lays the essay down gently beside me. "It seems like a natural angle to work to me. Just something to think about."

I stare at the essay and Sam's neat, tight handwriting scrawled in red ink in the margins.

"I'm sorry, I didn't mean—"

"No! No." I grab the paper and add it to the stack in my lap. "I asked for your opinion. Thank you. I'll...think about it."

He reaches out and grabs my foot again, shaking it playfully. "The essay is good as is. Definitely good enough to get you that scholarship, if those people have any sense. You don't have to listen to me."

He doesn't remove his hand, which is momentarily enough to distract me from the overwhelming exhaustion and dread at the idea of starting that essay from scratch all over again. Of staring at a blank screen.

His hand tightens, just a bit. He meets my eyes, and a slow smile plays at his lips.

I realize what he's going to do half a second before he does.

"No—!"

The second he starts tickling my foot, I squeal, and The Binder hits the floor with a loud *thump*. I try to pull away from him, but he just tightens his grip, laughing. "Ticklish?"

"Sam!" I try to squirm away, laughing so hard, my ribs

begin to ache. When that doesn't work, I resort to kicking him repeatedly with my other foot until he lets go. For a second, I think that'll be the end of it, but then he leaps toward me, pinning me to the mattress, and starts tickling my ribs. I'm laughing so hard, I can't breathe. I swat at him and try to roll away, and now he's laughing as hard as I am.

"Stop, stop, stop! *Sam!*"

He finally stops, and it dawns on me that he's on top of me, his face inches from mine. We're both breathless, our chests heaving. He glances down, locks eyes with mine. A heartbeat passes.

Two.

Three.

I can smell the fries on his breath. His aftershave. Feel the heat of his skin.

"*Ugh.* What are you guys *doing?*"

We jerk apart so fast, Sam practically hurtles himself off the bed. I quickly sit up, covering my chest with my arms even though I am one-hundred percent clothed. Harper is standing in the door, arms crossed, her upper lip curled back.

"Hey, Harp." My voice comes out rough, and my cheeks warm at the sound of it.

"Want a fry?" Sam offers. He's standing beside the bed, one hand behind his neck, swaying awkwardly on his feet.

Harper eyes the greasy bag, only for a moment, before her scrutinizing gaze darts back to us. "Do Maman and Papa know he's over?"

She crosses her arms, but she's not wearing her usual smug expression that screams blackmail—or worse, telling our parents just because it seems to bring her joy when they're disappointed in me. Maybe now that I know a secret of hers, she's worried I'd retaliate; not that I would ever sink that low, and she must know that, too. So maybe this truce is actually...*friendly?*

"I'm not going to tell on you," Harper continues. "I'm just saying. You should probably be more careful since they'll be home in, like, five minutes and Papa would *kill* you."

The heat in my cheeks intensifies. I can't even look at Sam, but out of my peripheral, I can see that his face is as red as mine feels. Honestly, it had been completely innocent—we don't have anything to feel guilty about. We didn't *do* anything. But if Harper hadn't walked in, would we have? That unspoken possibility leaves the air thick between us.

"It was nothing, Harp," I say. "We were just kidding around."

She arches her eyebrows. "Mmm-hmm."

"So, Harper," Sam jumps in as he sits on the edge of the bed. "You still up for helping me with that book? If I get you a rough draft in the next couple of days, do you think you'd have time to draw me some pictures?"

She hesitates, looking a little thrown by the change in subject. A hint of pink rises to her cheeks. "You were serious about that?"

"Hell yeah, I'm serious." As soon as the words exit his mouth, he winces. "Sorry—"

A corner of my mouth quirks at Sam's apology, as if Harper of all people, who gets in trouble with our parents on a daily basis for her language, would be offended by the word "hell." It's adorable that he cares enough to not want to offend her, though.

Harper leans against the doorframe, arms still crossed. "I guess I could give it a shot. What kind of illustrations did you want? I could do paint, or colored pencil, or—"

Sam holds up his hands. "I'm giving you complete artistic freedom. Do whatever you'd like."

Harper grins a full-on Harper Grin. The kind that looks like it should be in some sort of pageant. "Okay." She clears her throat and retreats a step into the hall. "I guess I'll just, uh, leave you two to it, then." She waves her hands once and disappears down the hall.

My face drops into my hands as Sam's soft laughter fills the silence.

"That was so embarrassing," I mumble.

"At least it wasn't your parents," Sam offers.

"True. If it had been my dad, there might have been a rifle involved."

Sam just chuckles and scoots over until he's sitting beside me. "I'm distracting you from your work," he says, glancing down at my application. "Sorry."

So far, the only thing I've written is my name. I've already filled out the simple parts, but all of the short-answer sections are blank. I've drafted them each about a dozen times, but like the essay, I just can't seem to get it right. How are you supposed to sum up not only who you are, but also why you're good enough for the money, in a measly hundred words?

"Don't be." I tuck the sheet back into The Binder and

fish around for the application for an even smaller scholarship that I think I have a good chance of landing. It's only for two-hundred dollars, but I'll take what I can get. "I've been procrastinating that application for so long; it doesn't take much to distract me."

"So, you're saying I'm nothing special?" He pushes his bottom lip out in mock-pout.

I pat his leg. "We can't all be winners."

The sound of the garage doors opening cuts off his response. Since my room is directly above the garage, the doors make my entire room vibrate.

"Ah, that'll be *les parents, oui?*" says Sam.

I smirk at his French attempt, finding it much more endearing than when his father does it, and hop up from the bed. Taking his hand, I pull him toward the door. "*Les parents* will be pissed if I don't let them fawn all over you."

He quirks an eyebrow. "Fawn?"

"Oh, you couldn't tell from the night you picked me up? They *adore* you. I think they like you more than me, to be honest."

Sam links his fingers through mine as we head down the stairs, and I don't even worry about whether my palm is sweaty or not. As we reach the bottom, the door to the garage swings open and my parents step through, chatting animatedly in French. The moment they catch sight of Sam, the chatter cuts off.

"*Samuel!*" Maman squeals, steps forward, and kisses him on the cheek. "So nice to see you. *Ça va?* How are you?"

Papa looks like he'd like to join in, but can't get around Maman, so he stands behind her, smiling.

"It's nice to see you, too, Mrs. Beaumont. I'm doing well. Mare and I were just studying together."

"Oh, how wonderful." She smiles at me, and suddenly her eyes go wide as if the most brilliant idea in the world just occurred to her. "Oh! You must stay for dinner, Sam. We would love to have you!"

"As much as I'd love to, I really should get home to the old man. If left to his own devices, he'll probably end up eating some TV dinner."

"Tomorrow, then," Maman offers. "You and your *Papa* should join us for dinner. Wouldn't that be lovely?" She turns to Papa.

"Of course, of course," he agrees.

Sam bobs his head. "I'd love to. I'll see if I can get him out of the house." Sam gives my hand a small pulse as if asking if this is okay with me, and I squeeze back.

Maman claps her hands once. "Tomorrow night?"

Sam smiles and nods. "Tomorrow sounds great."

13

The next day, Jo makes the announcement. She's far more dressed up than usual, her hair curled, half of it pulled back in a messy top-knot. She's wearing her usual distressed skinny jeans, a gold and shimmery tank tucked in the front, and a leather jacket thrown on top. She even bothered to wing her eyeliner and gloss her lips. Though she probably went a little overboard with the strawberry perfume. If I get too close, I can *taste* it. We're sitting in Mr. Graham's fourth period when she twists around in her desk and whispers to me, "Today is the day!"

I glance at her sideways. "*The day?*"

She bobs her head enthusiastically. "You know," she says out of the corner of her mouth. "*The day* I finally make a move."

Some optimistic part of me had been hoping she'd been talking about *anything* else, but I guess by now I should know better.

"Jo—"

She whips up a manicured hand to stop me. "We've already been over this, so don't try to talk me out of it. We have a tutoring session after school, and I'm gonna go for it. I've planted the seed, and I've definitely detected some interest. Now is the time."

"You're going to do it *here?*" I hiss. "At the school?"

She rolls her eyes and glances around to ensure no one's listening. Everyone else is busy with their own side conversations and note-taking. "It's not like we're going to do it on the desks—though, to be perfectly honest, I wouldn't really mind that—"

"*Johanna,*" I groan.

She holds up her hand again. "*But* I'll settle for just a kiss today. Preferably a passionate one with lots of touching."

"Can you not?" I lean away and shiver at the mental image. "I really don't want these pictures in my head."

"Hey, from what you told me about your date with Sam, it was just as hot and heavy with you two, so no judgements."

I open my mouth to say *at least Sam's our age*, but stop myself. That'll accomplish nothing. "Just be careful."

She flips her hair over her shoulder and blows me an air kiss. "Worry not, little duckling. I'm wearing my big-girl panties. I can take care of myself."

Ashley whips around in her seat. "Would you two shut up? Some of us are trying to *learn.*"

Ashley, surprisingly, is not all dressed-up today. Instead of her usual dress-and-wedges-ensemble, she's wearing black leggings and an oversized sweatshirt, her hair thrown back in a messy ponytail. Even like this, she looks like a rock star, but *still*. I don't even think she's wearing any makeup besides some concealer under her eyes.

Jo glances around the room, taking in the guys in the corner making paper airplanes, the various individuals staring at cell phones under their desks, and the cluster of friends at the front of the room whispering to each other. "I don't see it," she says.

"Maybe *I'm* trying to take notes," Ashley snaps.

Jo raises her eyebrows at the magazine half-hidden beneath Ashley's notebook. "Sure."

"Would you two just give it a rest?" I mumble.

Ashley's eyes cut to mine. "I think you have something on your face." She runs a thumb along her cheek. "Is that...*ketchup*?" And with that, she whips back around, flipping her hair into my face.

Johanna and I exchange a look.

"What's with her?" Jo mouths.

I shrug.

We'd turned in our group paper as we walked in for class today. The moment that paper hit Mr. Graham's desk, Ashley had retreated to her seat, pretending as if she'd never associated with us, probably already trying to purge the experience from her memory.

"Sam's having dinner with the parental figures tonight, right?" Jo whispers.

I grimace and nod. "And his dad's coming."

Jo shivers. "That man has always given me the creeps."

"You and everyone else."

There was nothing *wrong* with Mr. Johnson, *per se*, but there was a notable difference in the way he treated Papa, his friend, and everyone else, his inferiors.

A moment later, Ashley sneezes so forcefully, she knocks her pencil off her desk. It's a remarkably powerful sneeze, but the sound she makes is little more than a high-pitched squeak. The pencil rolls and tumbles until it lands against Johanna's shoe.

"Jesus," Johanna mumbles.

"I believe you're supposed to say 'bless you,'" says Ashley. She raises her eyebrows at Johanna. "Well? Can you hand me my pencil?"

Johanna doesn't blink. "Nope. I'm busy, trying to take notes and all."

"Is everything all right back there, ladies?" Mr. Graham calls from across the room. I glance up to see several students turned around, staring.

"Yep. Everything's great," Ashley says, getting up from her desk. "Just dropped something." As she scooches through the aisle to retrieve the pencil, I realize a moment too late that my feet are propped out. Ashley notices a moment too late, too, because the next thing we know, she's tripping over them and sprawling onto her hands and knees over Johanna's backpack. Her head snaps up to glare at me, murder in her eyes, as if I intentionally tripped her.

I stare open-mouthed in silence for several beats before finally managing to stutter out, "I am so sorry—"

"Save it," she snarls and wrestles herself back into her seat. Sans pencil. She turns around to face Mr. Graham, and I can practically see the steam rising from her shoulders.

Johanna widens her eyes in mock-terror and mouths, "You'd better sleep with one eye open."

I cover my mouth with my hand so Ashley doesn't hear me laugh.

THAT AFTERNOON, SAM SHOWS UP HALFWAY THROUGH MY shift at the shelter, and we take the dogs outside to play like before. He's still in his Madison Prep uniform—gray slacks, white button-up, loosely knotted navy tie—though it appears he ditched the jacket.

Johanna had begged to come with me today, wanting to finally spend some time with Sam—and probably ask him a million embarrassing and inappropriate questions—but got a phone call from a client about their engagement photos, asking at the last minute to move up their photo session to this afternoon. They'd offered her extra, not that Johanna really needed the money, but she *did* need the pictures for her portfolio, and they were going to cancel on her if she couldn't do it today. Some of the art schools she applied to apparently look at portfolios late in the game, but they're a big factor in admissions. I've always thought Jo's portfolio looked amazing, but she's been convinced lately there's not enough variety and has been booking new clients like crazy.

But as much as I love her, I'm kind of glad I get to keep Sam to myself for at least a little while longer.

The sky is a bruise, and the wind has a bite today. It's been overcast for the past week straight, and at this point I think everyone's just waiting for the snow. But knowing Colorado, it could just as easily be ninety degrees tomorrow as it could be storming. Only time will tell.

Sam and I sit on the grass, Squirt in my lap, Pluto's head in his, and we watch as the rest of the dogs wrestle each other.

"So, I brought you something." He pulls out a small stack of paper from his bag but hesitates before handing it to me. "It's only a rough draft, so I'm still working on it, but I thought I should give it to Harper so she could start working on the pictures."

"You did it? You actually wrote the picture book?" I take the pages from him eagerly. "Can I read it?"

"It's just the rough draft. It still needs a lot of work."

"Will you tell me what it's about then, and I'll wait to read it until you feel like it's ready?"

"Okay." He looks relieved as I set the pages down in front of me. "So, the main character's name is Marty, and he's a mouse—not a rat—but no one seems to understand the difference. And no one wants to be friends with a rat, because they all think rats are mean and dirty and whatnot. So Marty starts disguising himself as other animals to try to find a friend."

As he talks, his words come out progressively faster, as if he can't wait to get them out in the open. His eyes are alit with excitement, and he talks with his hands, as if his words alone wouldn't hold enough power to convey the story. I can't look away.

"He dresses up like a cat," Sam continues, "But the cat in the house just tries to eat him; he dresses up like a dog, but the dog just sits on him; he dresses up like a person, but the humans just chase him out of the kitchen with a broom. So he ends up going back to his hole in the wall, kind of defeated, and he finds a rat inside. And the rat ends up being really nice and cool, so I'm thinking of ending it with some cheesy line like, *Maybe being friends with a rat wouldn't be so bad after all.* Then having the title being *Not a Rat*, or something."

When he finishes, he glances up at me, his face slightly flushed. "It's a work in progress, but—"

"Sam, I love it."

"Yeah?"

"Yeah." I laugh and squeeze his arm. "I really, *really* love it. I'll give these pages to Harper as soon as I get home. She's going to be so excited. It's been all she can talk about. Thank you."

He cocks his head. "For what?"

I shrug. "I don't know. For being so nice to her. She... she really needs it right now." I glance down at Squirt in my lap and run my fingers through her fur. "She's just been having a really hard time lately."

"Is she okay?"

I sigh, debating whether to tell him. Ultimately, I decide against it. It's not my secret to tell, and if Harper found out, she'd be equally pissed and humiliated. "She's just going through some stuff, and these girls are bullying her at school. It's a mess, really."

He leans over and squeezes my knee. "Anything I can do to help?"

I pick up the stack of papers. "Actually, I think this will help. She needs to get her mind off everything. And she hasn't been doing her art lately, probably because of everything that's going on, so maybe this'll help get her out of her funk."

The door to the shelter swings open with a *screech* and Jada pokes her head out. "Mare, there's a man here to see one of the dogs."

"Should I bring them back inside then?" I ask.

"No, that's okay, I think it will be best if he sees them outside of the cages anyway." She steps out to the lawn and holds the door open behind her. A tall man follows her. He stops beside the door, hands in the pockets of his dark suit, eyes shielded by tinted sunglasses. He doesn't say anything.

I gently roll Squirt off my lap—who promptly darts away to play with her friends—and rise to my feet. Sam does the same.

"Mare, this is Ryan. This is Mare," Jada tells the man. "She can help you with whatever you need. I'll be at the front desk if you need me."

"So you're here to see one of the dogs?" I ask after Jada slips back inside.

He nods, lips pursed, and removes his sunglasses. His eyes are trained on the dogs. "The Maltese," he says.

My heart drops into my stomach, but I try not to let it show. This shouldn't be surprising to me; I've always known that Squirt could get adopted at any time, that I should be *hoping* for it for her sake. I guess I'd always kind of hoped my parents would come around and let me adopt Squirt, because in my mind, she was already my dog.

"Squirt," I call, and she trots dutifully to my side and gazes up at me with a wide-eyed expression. "Is she the one you were thinking about?"

Ryan eyes her in almost a hungry way, but says nothing, and doesn't move forward.

I glance at Sam, but he looks just as confused as I feel.

"She's the only Maltese we have right now," I add, the hairs on my arms beginning to prickle.

"Oh, yes. She's the one," he says and continues to stand there.

Usually, Squirt runs and greets every visitor, almost as if she understands the process and desperately wants to make a good impression, but she stays beside me, quiet and still.

"If you get down on the ground so you're more at her level, she'll probably come over and say hi to you," I offer.

He narrows his eyes as if studying her before finally glancing at me. There isn't anything technically wrong with his face, but maybe that's what strikes me. It isn't that he's expressionless. It's that he's *trying* to be expressionless.

Squirt retreats a little behind my legs.

"That's quite all right," he says and pulls a phone from his pocket. "She'll do just fine. I can pick her up tomorrow."

"You'll need to fill out the paperwork and everything with Jada at the front desk."

He nods, no longer facing us, brings his phone to his ear, and disappears back inside.

I glance down at Squirt, who looks like she's trembling.

I squat down and scoop her up, and she tucks her face into the crook of my arm. Sam meets my eyes, his forehead creased.

"That was weird, right?" I ask.

He nods. "That was weird."

14

AFTER LEAVING THE SHELTER, SAM AND I GO SEPARATE ways. I need to get some homework done and he needs to grab his dad and get ready to come over for dinner later. The drive passes in a blur of trees, streetlights, and rain reflecting off the road. My body goes into autopilot the second I get behind the wheel. I can't stop worrying about Squirt and the bad vibe I got from the guy who wants to adopt her. And when I try to think of the night ahead to distract me, it does nothing but amplify my nerves. Everything's been going so well between me and Sam, and I can't remember the last time I was this comfortable around anyone but Johanna. And it's not that I'm worried my parents won't like him, because they've both made it abundantly clear that they adore Sam.

I'm worried they're going to scare him away.

My parents can be a little intense, to say the least. And if their religious lectures and quoting scriptures don't scare him off, I wouldn't put it past my mom to start daydreaming about our future wedding and children aloud over the potatoes. We've barely been seeing each other a week, but I know she's already thinking about it.

I smell the mushroom bourguignon the second I walk through the door. Maman knows it's my favorite, and it's been months since we had it. The smell brings me back to Grand-mère's kitchen, eight-year-old me standing tippy-toe on a stool to watch Grand-père dice the carrots and onions while Maman helped prepare the mushrooms for the stew, Grand-mère and Papa bickering at the table. I remember being shocked when they added the red wine, and Harper and I thought we were hilarious, acting like we were drunk after having it for the first time.

I should call Grand-mère later. She'd probably love to hear about how tonight goes.

I call out to Maman as I head for the stairs to let her know that I'm home.

"How were the puppies?" she asks.

I wince a little, picturing Squirt's quivering body again, but that's really not something I want to get into right now. "Great. I'm just going to try to get some homework done before Sam and his dad show up."

She steps around the corner, and I pause on the stairs at the sight of her. She's in a sleek black dress that I recognize from her boutique, a slit inching up her right leg, and matching pumps, her hair slightly curled with half of it twisted atop her head. The highlight on her cheekbones is blinding.

"What is *that*?" I demand, pointing at the dress.

She glances down at herself and does a little spin. "How do I look?"

Like she's trying to look like my hot older sister, but I'm assuming that's exactly what she's going for.

"Maman, we're just having dinner here. Why so fancy?"

This is, of course, a stupid question. Every occasion is a formal event to Maman.

"You should always look your best, Meredith," she says.

"Please tell me you're not making Harper and Papa dress up, too."

She lifts her chin a little. "Of course they are. And I expect you to look nice, too. How about that wonderful white dress I bought you? The one with the lace?"

The one that looks like it should be on a seven-year-old flower girl? Yeah, I'll pass.

"Maman, you're going to make Sam and his dad uncomfortable." Not to mention *me*. "They're going to show up in, like, jeans or something and then feel underdressed."

She waves her hand as if the thought is completely ridiculous and heads back into the kitchen, her heels clicking against the wooden floor. "I expect you to be down here and ready in an hour!" she calls over her shoulder.

I make a sort of growling noise under my breath and ascend the rest of the stairs. When I make it to my room, I dump my bag on my bed and turn to face my closet. I am *not* going to wear that white dress, but that means I'm going to have to find something else that Maman will deem acceptable. So pants are probably a no-go.

Plus, the night is going to be stressful, so I need something that won't show my sweat.

My eyes skate over the dresses at the end of the rack—all chosen by Maman, so definitely out of the question—and sift through the ones I picked out myself. Once I rule out swimsuit cover-ups, old school dance dresses that probably wouldn't even fit my boobs anymore, and a terrifyingly risqué little black dress that Johanna gave me when it didn't fit her, there's not much left to choose from.

Eventually, I settle on a navy strapless dress that cuts off just above my knees. Usually Maman makes me wear a sweater over it to church, but tonight I find a small gold necklace that lands an inch below my collarbone and leave it at that. I can't bring myself to put on heels like Maman, but I know she'll yell at me if I go downstairs barefoot, so I slip on a pair of simple ballet flats. My hair is wavy from being in a bun all day, but I let it down over my shoulders and run my fingers through it until it looks somewhat presentable.

I try to fill the anxious waiting time with reading a few chapters of my AP Bio book, but can't force my mind to concentrate. Every time I get to the bottom of a page, I completely forget what I just read and have to go back and read it again. After several painful minutes of this, I toss the book aside in frustration and promise myself I'll do it later. I pull up the Closet Atheists webpage and occupy my time scrolling through the different discussion threads instead.

All too soon, the doorbell rings, and suddenly every nerve in my body shoots to life. I squeeze my hands into fists at my sides over and over again to calm myself. *Squeeze, release; squeeze, release; squeeze, release.* I shouldn't be this nervous. There's nothing to worry about.

Really.

It'll be fine.

Harper's head appears in my doorway. "Sam's here." She hesitates when she sees my face and straightens. "You okay?"

"Yeah," I say too quickly, smoothing my hands over my dress.

Harper's wearing a red scalloped dress with short-sleeves and a murderous expression. I smirk a little at her black Converse.

"If you give me grief for my shoes—"

"You look great, Harp. And if it were up to me, we'd both be wearing jeans right now."

Her face relaxes a shade. "Maman's really blowing this out of proportion, isn't she?" She fusses with her hair, done in a loose side braid, and tucks the escaped strands behind her ears.

I join her in the doorway. "Just let her have her fun, I guess."

Sam and his dad are standing in the foyer when Harper and I descend the stairs. Papa stands with his arm around Mr. Johnson's shoulders, grinning at something his friend said. Sam meets my eyes. He looks nice. Okay, more than nice. He's in gray fitted slacks and a white button-down, slightly unbuttoned at the collar, shirtsleeves rolled up to his elbows, his dark hair perfectly pushed back and styled. When he looks at me, he doesn't quite smile, but his lips part like he wants to. I raise my eyebrows and roll my eyes as if to say, *Yes, this entire situation is completely ridiculous.* This time, he does smile, and gives me a wink as I reach the bottom of the stairs.

The sound of clacking heels announces Maman's approach before she appears, still wearing bright pink oven mitts on both hands. I don't smell any smoke, so that's a good sign. "Ah, *parfait!* We're all here. Come in, come in! Everyone have a seat!"

I sit between Sam and Harper on one side of the table as Maman, Papa, and Mr. Johnson take their places across from us. Sam seeks out my hand under the table, and I squeeze his fingers, cringing at how damp I'm sure mine are.

"Smells amazing, Colette," Mr. Johnson says.

"Oh." Maman waves her hand and places her napkin on her lap. "It's nothing."

Yeah, she only spent four hours cooking it today.

"Meredith," Papa says. "Why don't you say Grace for us?"

How about I just stab myself with a fork instead?

I shift in my chair, skin prickling. It isn't the first time I've been asked, of course. But a blanket of anxiety settles over me like a second skin all the same. It's not about the words themselves—I've heard it so many times that I know exactly what to say to make them happy. It's that I don't *want* to say them, but it doesn't feel like I have much of a choice. That tiny reminder of how trapped I am is enough to coax my claustrophobia into a slithering vice around my throat.

My mind darts to that post I saw on Closet Atheists, and __Oblivion__'s suggestion about calmly explaining how I won't participate, but I'll respect if they want to continue. I could do it. Right now. I could tell them.

One look at their expectant faces reminds me that, no, I absolutely cannot.

"If you don't mind, Mr. Beaumont, I can do it," Sam offers.

Surprised, I glance sideways at him. Surely, the thought makes him just as uncomfortable as it does me, and then I realize he's doing it so I don't have to. As we join hands and bow our heads, Sam clears his throat and begins.

"Lord, we thank you for this wonderful meal and even better company." He pauses, probably scrambling for something else to say, and I squeeze his hand for reassurance. "So, um, please bless this food that we're about to eat and, uh, keep us on our right paths. In Jesus' name. Amen."

"Amen," the three adults echo.

"Thank you," I mouth to Sam. He winks at me.

"So, how's the petition going, Andrew?" Mr. Johnson asks.

Papa lets out a long sigh as he fishes his spoon around his bowl. "Not as well as we'd hoped. Another group of parents have teamed together to argue *against* us, if you believe that." Papa shakes his head as if he actually cannot fathom such a thing. "We have another meeting with the principal and the other group this week. Hopefully we can make them see reason."

"Petition?" I ask, gaze shooting back and forth between the two of them. "A petition for what?"

Papa shifts in his seat, not quite meeting my eyes. "Yes. I, along with several others parents, were alarmed by your core health curriculum and decided we should do something about it. Honestly, I'm appalled that no one spoke up before now."

Other parents from school. When Maman had said Papa was meeting with some other parents after church the other day, I'd thought nothing of it. He meets with other parents to chat or pray all the time—in the Christian community, he's kind of suburban royalty, and everyone is always lobbying for a few minutes of his time. It hadn't even occurred to me she'd meant a formal meeting. And about *this?* It had been stupidly optimistic of me to think he'd drop it.

My fingers tighten around my fork until the metal bites into my skin.

"I don't know how they live with themselves, honestly," adds Mr. Johnson, generously topping off his glass of wine. He pours until it reaches a precarious height just shy of the top, so he has to slowly bring the glass to his face, lips out stretched, to prevent any from spilling. "Actively fighting for their children to be having premarital sex—having it taught in schools?" He shakes his head. "Who lets these people be parents?"

My hand stings so much, I think the metal might be drawing blood. Sam lightly touches my arm, and the trance breaks. I take a long, slow breath in through my nose, and release my hold on the fork.

This whole situation leaves such a sour taste in my mouth. Papa wants my entire personal life to bow to his religious agenda? Fine. I've grown to live with that. But now he wants to come in and start slashing health and science classes from my school because they don't align with his beliefs? He's not even just trying to pull Harper out of the class—he doesn't want *anyone* taking it. And the fact that so many other parents are following him, so many agree with him. Has no one ever heard of separation of church and state? Teaching abstinence only doesn't stop teenagers from having sex—it just creates an entire generation of uneducated people who don't understand anything about safe sex, STIs, and how their own bodies work.

A rage so heavy and violent fills my chest that I don't think I could speak right now even if I wanted to. And the fact that he actually thinks this is okay, that what he's doing is *right?* It's unfathomable. It's deluded. It's arrogant, is what it is. Thinking he knows better than everyone else; that everyone else needs to follow what he believes with no exceptions. That no place is safe from his uninvited tampering.

Sam touches my arm again, but this time, the rage doesn't leave. It's a living, writhing thing inside of my chest.

Our side of the table is silent for several minutes as we shovel the food into our mouths. I can't take my eyes off Papa's slightly smug face. I can't even taste the food.

And for a moment, just a small, quiet moment, I think in the very corner of my mind, *I hate him.* Guilt overwhelms me as soon as I think the words, and I know they're not true. I could never hate him. But this? I do hate *this.*

Finally, the subject shifts. As Papa starts talking about this week's service, I force down three long, deep breaths and finally pry my eyes away from him. I lean over to nudge Harper's foot beneath the table to distract myself. "I forgot to tell you," I whisper. "Sam gave me a rough draft of his story today so you could get started on the illustrations."

"Really?" Harper perks up and leans around me to see Sam.

"Yeah, I'll grab it for you after dinner."

"And there's no rush on the pictures," Sam tells her. "I'm still revising the story—what Mare gives you is just a rough draft—so it'll probably take me awhile. Just get them to me whenever you can."

"What's this about a book?" Maman asks.

I try not to flinch. I'd kind of hoped our parents would be too invested in their own conversation to hear ours.

"Sam's writing a children's book, and I'm going to illustrate it for him," Harper says, her voice hesitant, as if she's not sure whether she's supposed to share this information.

"I think that's a wonderful idea!" Maman beams.

I glance over at Sam to make sure it's okay to talk about this. The lines around his eyes are tight, but he smiles back at Maman and nods. "Yeah, I thought it'd be a fun project."

"What is it about?" Papa asks.

Sam looks away and sips his water. "It's still a work in progress."

"It's amazing." I lay a hand on his leg beneath the table. "Really. He has it all planned out—"

Mr. Johnson makes a *humph* noise across the table. Sam tenses beneath my hand, his eyes shooting to his father.

"Sounds cute and all," Mr. Johnson says. There's a twinge of something I don't like in his voice. "But do you really think that's the best use of your time, son? You're going to be graduating soon, and then you'll be off to college, and before you know it you'll be working toward a career in the real world. Don't you think it's time to start dedicating your time to what you're going to do with your life?"

A tense silence settles over the table.

Sam and his father exchange a silent look. I can't see Sam's face, but judging by the hard line of his jaw, it isn't pleased.

"It is hard to believe that they're both about to graduate, isn't it?" Maman offers, clearly trying to shift the subject. "Time flies. It seems like just yesterday, the two of you were playing out in the sandbox—"

Mr. Johnson clearly does not take the bait.

"Don't give me that look," he cuts Maman off, his eyes on his son. "We've had this discussion many times. I thought we agreed you'd stop wasting your time with all this writing and start being serious about your future."

I glance from the empty wine glass in front of Mr. Johnson to Sam.

Sam clears his throat and shoots an uncomfortable smile at my parents. "Maybe this isn't the best time to have this conversation, Dad," he says quietly.

Oblivious or uncaring about making a scene, Mr. Johnson reaches across the table, grabs the wine bottle, refills his glass, and takes a gulp. I've lost count whether that's already his second or third. "Tell me when we should then. Since it seems no matter how much we talk about it, it ain't sinking in."

Sam takes a slow, steadying breath, his eyes trained on his plate. Besides his clenched fists beneath the table, he still manages to look calm. That makes one of us. My own hands are shaking, my pulse panicking in my veins.

For a moment, no one says anything. I try desperately to come up with a way to shift the conversation, but as usual, my mind supplies me with nothing useful.

Finally, Papa clears his throat. "So, how was school, Harper?" he asks. "Didn't you have a presentation today?"

Harper shifts a little in her seat as all heads swivel in her direction. "Um, yeah. It went well. I filled up my time slot, which was what I'd been most worried about, so that was a relief. And my teacher seemed to like it."

"What was the presentation on?" I ask. My voice comes out slightly strangled.

Every nerve in my body is on edge. Sam is still tense beneath my hand.

"It was for my business class. I just talked about managing money, and how to plan for life after college, and stuff like that."

"See." Mr. Johnson thumps his fist against the table, making the silverware on the table jostle. "That a girl. She knows what's worth her time. Good for you, Harper."

I should probably just stay out of it, but now my heart is in my throat, and it shoves the words from my mouth before I can stop them. "You know, if Sam were to publish this book—which I really think he should at least try to do, because it's completely brilliant—even though the picture book itself might not make him much money, it would probably look really great on his resume for future jobs and whatnot. It would show the employer that he's motivated and has a good work ethic and is creative—all things that are essential in today's job market."

Mr. Johnson doesn't look the least bit impressed, but before he can open his mouth and spew out whatever hateful words he has lined up next, Papa cuts in.

"That's a good point, Mare," Papa says. He turns to Mr. Johnson and deftly switches the topic again to the state of the economy and the ridiculous struggle for jobs right now. And for a moment, the conversation seems to distract Mr. Johnson enough for him to drop it.

Sam gives me a grateful smile and squeezes my leg. I squeeze back, the muscles in my shoulders finally daring to relax. When I glance up, I catch Maman watching us over the table, a knowing glint in her eye.

AFTER DINNER, OUR PARENTS HEAD TO THE FRONT ROOM. Harper makes an excuse about needing to write a paper, but as she heads upstairs, she asks if she can grab Sam's book from my room to start working on it.

I lead Sam out to the back patio, where we lean against the railing and stare up at the stars. The sky is clear and dark, and we leave the porch light off so as not to ruin the view. It's not nearly as good as it was at the drive-in, but it'll do.

"Thanks for saving me in there," Sam whispers.

I pause before responding, fighting my urge to pry. "Is it always like that with him?"

Sam pauses, too, and locks his hands around the railing. "More and more so, lately. He means best, I know that. I just wish..." He shakes his head. "Honestly, I don't even know."

"You just wish he'd be more supportive."

"Yeah," he says quietly. "And if not supportive, the least he could do is be a little less *against* it, you know?"

"Maybe he'll come around."

Sam laughs like he doesn't believe that's even a remote possibility.

"Thanks for stopping me from stabbing my dad with a fork."

He reaches over and takes my hand, holding it palm-up between us. There are still faint lines from the fork. His fingers are feather-light as he traces the path they carve. The touch sends a small shiver up my spine.

"So what exactly was all that about?" he asks. "He doesn't like your health class?"

I let out a long, slow breath. "I don't know how it works for you guys, but we're required freshman year to take a health class."

Sam nods.

"And there's a chapter on sex education in the class."

"Oh." Sam nods again, slower this time. "Got it. So, he wants what? Them to nix that chapter all together?"

I shrug. "I honestly don't know. He found Harper's homework the other day and freaked out, so I knew he was mad, but I had no idea he was going to these kinds of lengths. It just...it makes me mad." I laugh in an attempt to extinguish the rage starting to build in my chest again. "Anyway. Thanks for coming tonight. Even though it was kind of a disaster."

"At least the food was good," he jokes.

"God, I was so tense all night, I barely even tasted it."

"*You* were tense? What were you so tense about?"

"Honestly? I was terrified my parents were going to scare you off."

"And then my dad turned out to be the one misbehaving." He turns and leans his back against the railing so he's facing me. "So, did *he* scare *you* off?"

I roll my eyes and let him take my hands again. "You know he didn't."

He pulls me a step closer to him. "Then you should know that there's nothing your parents could do to scare me off."

"You say that now," I mumble. "But you have yet to experience the full extent of the Beaumont insanity."

He gives me a crooked smile. "Looking forward to it."

I laugh, shaking my head. The night breeze is cool as it sweeps across the patio, twisting my dress around my legs. Closing my eyes, I breathe in the scent of the damp trees and fresh air and let out a content sigh. "It's such a beautiful night," I whisper.

When I open my eyes, Sam is staring at me. His hair is

tousled and loose around his temples, his lips slightly parted.

"You're staring at me," I say. I don't mean for it to come out as a whisper, but I seem to have lost my voice.

"I can't help it," he responds, equally quiet.

I don't remember moving, but suddenly we're standing very close to each other. His back is pressed against the railing, my chest nearly pressed against him. His arms snake around my back, his fingers pressing lightly into my spine. My hands find their way to his chest.

"I really want to kiss you right now," he whispers.

I swallow hard, probably loud enough for him to hear. My cheeks flame, and my voice comes out rough when I say, "Well, it's a good thing we're out here then, isn't it?"

He leans in until there's no more space between us, until his lips find mine. The kiss starts off slowly, like it's the first time. His hands are gentle as they caress my back, and I smooth my hands over his shirt. I inhale the scent of him—fresh laundry with obvious hints of breath mint—and it does strange things to my head. This time when we kiss, I'm not thinking about what to do with my mouth, or where to put my hands. I don't worry if I'm doing it right, or if he's judging my inexperience. I just lean into him, feeling his warmth under my fingertips and this inexplicable calm that rushes over me, like the way a tight hug slows your nervous system down in the midst of an anxiety attack. And for a beautiful, blissful moment, my mind is quiet.

Our lips separate, just for a moment, our panting breaths mingling in the space between us.

"Meredith," he whispers. Something about him saying my full name, his voice rough and low, sends shivers up my spine.

Laughter sounds inside the house. Sam and I jump apart so quickly that I almost fall over. I balance myself against the railing, and Sam seems to do the same. The door is still firmly shut. Our parents are still in the front room.

We both let out sighs of relief.

My heart hammers so violently in my chest, it feels like it's bruising my insides.

"We should probably go back inside," I say, my voice hoarse.

"Probably," he agrees.

But neither of us moves.

Not for a long time.

15

On Wednesday morning, the world is purple and the rain is unrelenting. I walk into school at my normal time, surrounded by other students hurrying into the buildings, huddled beneath their rain jackets because everyone's too cool to use an umbrella.

My Converses slosh in the puddles, soaking my socks. I pull up the hood of my sweatshirt to try and deflect some of the water from my eyes, but by the time I make it inside, I'm soaked. The tile floors are slick and streaked with mud.

As I make my way to my locker, the hairs on the back of my neck begin to prickle. I glance up from my usual vantage point—the floor—and notice all of the eyes on me.

The underclassmen glance over their shoulders and look away as soon as we make eye contact, giggling. The seniors stare without shame, some whispering to friends and bursting into laughter. One of my hands flies to my face on instinct, checking to see if there's something there, but if Thomas Anderson hardly got any attention when he forgot to put his pants back on after gym class last week, I don't think some leftover toothpaste would create this much of a reaction.

Two members of the Pretty Committee approach in matching red rain boots and long black jackets, their arms linked at the elbow. As they near, they separate from each other so they can pass me on both sides. As they do, they each mutter *slut* under their breath, then hook their arms back together once they reach the other side, giggling to each other.

I whip around and watch as they keep walking. Was that directed at *me*?

I glance over to see a pod of football guys leaned against a drinking fountain across the hall, smirking. One of them presses the button, and water shoots from the faucet. "Thirsty, Meredith?" he asks.

I stare at them. Their faces are vaguely familiar, but I don't know any of their names. Which means they definitely shouldn't know mine. And why would I be thirsty? I have a water bottle—

Oh my God.

They can't be talking about—

They couldn't possibly—

I turn and speed-walk the rest of the way to my locker to escape, hyperaware of every laugh, every whisper, every word. I turn the corner and freeze. Taped to my locker is a sheet of paper, and it takes me less than two seconds to realize what it is.

The Anti-Virginity Pact is written on the top in large, neat letters, and at the bottom is my signature.

And it's a photocopy. Which means there are probably more.

Many more.

I rip the sheet from the locker, feeling like I might somehow vomit my own heart out of my chest. I want so badly to sink into myself, to fold in until I disappear altogether.

Or go home and cry. And never leave my bedroom again.

One of the two.

This cannot be happening. With shaking fingers, I manage to put in my combo and pop the locker open, if for nothing else than to hide my head behind the door. A folded piece of paper flutters to the floor. I grab it and try to unfold it, though it's difficult with how much my hands are shaking.

It reads: *James Wofford - call anytime gorgeous ;)*, followed by his phone number.

Someone slams my locker shut, and I jump back. A hockey player with long blonde hair and a black eye leans against the locker beside me, his arms crossed over his massive chest. He smiles a full-faced smile. There are a few teeth missing toward the back.

"You know," he says under his breath. "I'd be happy to help you out with that little task of yours, if you'd like."

I don't—can't—respond. I just stare at him, my mortification like fire licking its way up my entire body, before finally ordering my legs to turn and walk away as quickly as possible. I shove the two pieces of paper into my bag, tearing other copies from lockers as I go.

"I'll just leave my number in your locker in case you change your mind," he calls.

I want to die. I want to die right now.

How could this have happened? Jo kept both of the contracts, and she was the only person who knew about them. And she would never do this. Never. My mind is churning so quickly, I can hardly keep up with my own thoughts. The group meeting at Johanna's house. When Ashley went upstairs to use the bathroom. What if she'd taken the pact from Johanna's room? She *had* been acting strange once she'd come back down, but I'd dismissed the thought at the time. How could she have even known about the pact, let alone that it was in Johanna's room?

My mind whirls through all of the conversations Jo and I had in Mr. Graham's class about the pact, with Ashley *right there*. I'd thought she wasn't paying attention, but what if she'd heard *everything*?

But if it was her, does that mean she plastered both contracts around the school, or did she only manage to get her manicured claws on mine? Does she know about Jo and Mr. Graham too?

Oh my God, I have to call Jo.

The tears come, and I'm caught between trying to hold myself together so no one sees and sprinting to the bathroom to hide. The hot, bubbling panic in the pit of my stomach makes the decision for me.

I'm vaguely aware of more heads turning in my direction as I push my way down the hall, but my vision is edged with black, and all I see is a door in the distance. Calls and jeers are blotted out by the roaring in my ears.

I think I hear someone call, "Meredith!" but I'm almost to the bathroom. A few people are lingering at their lockers outside, and I can feel their heads swivel in my direction as I lurch forward and throw myself at the girls' bathroom door.

Mercifully, it's empty.

Shoving into the nearest stall, I fall on my knees before I have a chance to lock the door, crying so hard I'm hiccupping. I clutch one hand to my chest, trying to calm down, but my breaths just keep coming faster. My mind is a kaleidoscope of images.

The paper on my locker.

The hockey player's missing teeth.

The laughing gang of football players.

The Pretty Committee whispering *slut* as they passed.

Lurching forward, I empty my stomach into the toilet. My body tries to heave three more times, like it can purge the last twenty minutes straight out of my system, before finally relenting. I fall back against the toilet paper dispenser and kick the door shut, gasping for air.

The bathroom suddenly feels too quiet, the only sound my shuttering breaths.

But I don't move. I can't.

This can't actually be happening. Things like this don't actually happen.

As the first bell echoes through the bathroom, I lean my head against the door and close my eyes. I never miss class, but there's no way I'm getting myself off this floor.

And the second everyone sees my empty desk, they'll know all the rumors are true.

The flyers I'd ripped from lockers I'd passed are scattered in a heap around me. I paw through them, crumpling them into balls as I go, scanning for Johanna's name, but they all seem to be my copy of the contract. So maybe it was just me.

I send her a text, telling her to call me. When first period comes and goes, filling the bathroom with the sound of the bell for a second time, I send her another, this time telling her it's an emergency and she needs to respond to me *right now*.

I flinch as footsteps enter the bathroom and two voices fill the space with careless conversation, but remain in my spot on the floor. If they can see a pathetic lump of a human huddled on the ground beneath the stall door, so be it. Honestly, I don't see how this could get any worse.

When the end of third period rolls around and Johanna still hasn't responded, I take a few calming breaths and climb to my feet. Maybe she got her phone confiscated in one of her morning classes. All I know is, I *need* to talk to her, and the one class I know she'd never miss is Mr. Graham's fourth period. I stumble out to the sinks, bracing myself against the counter with shaking hands.

The mirror is unkind. Puffy cheeks and swollen eyes stare back at me, my mascara smeared into my hairline. After splashing cold water on my face a few times, I figure this is about as good as it's going to get.

So I grab my backpack from the floor, pop in a piece of

gum to cover the smell of vomit on my breath, and head out of the bathroom before I can talk myself out of it.

As I walk into Mr. Graham's classroom, I try to ignore the stares and whispers and head straight to my desk. The voices crawl like microscopic bugs burying deep into my skin, where I know they'll linger and bide their time, waiting to resurface and torment me all over again in the silence of my room. As I near my seat, Ashley and her friend move out of the way so I can pass without so much as a look in my direction.

There's a paper on my desk. At first, I think it's just another photocopy of the pact, but upon further inspection, I realize there's an old photo of me at the top. Probably dating back to middle school, complete with sidebangs that hang in my eyes and clumsy lines of eyeliner on my lower lash line. It's cropped awkwardly with a chunk of my face missing, probably to cut Johanna out. As if the picture itself weren't embarrassing enough, it's photoshoped onto a body that *definitely* did not belong to me when I was thirteen—heck, I still don't have those curves now.

The woman's body is scantily clad and pointing toward the camera with a propositioning finger. It looks like it was taken straight out of a porn magazine or something.

How many copies of *this* version are plastered around school?

"*You know*." Ashley twists around in her seat and smirks at me. "I'm no religious expert, but doesn't the church generally frown upon whores?"

My entire body flares with heat so intense, nausea

bubbles in my stomach. I crush the paper in my fist and keep my eyes trained on my notebook. I can feel the gazes of my classmates burning into my face, but I don't look up. I can't.

The bell rings, signaling the start of class, and I glance at Johanna's empty desk beside me. She's never late. Not to Mr. Graham's class.

My heart stutters to a stop. Between worrying about Squirt last night and all of this with the pact, I forgot about Jo's session with Mr. Graham. Yesterday was *the day*. I glance at her empty desk, then up at Mr. Graham, who is writing something on the whiteboard. Did something happen between them? Is *that* why she isn't here? But if it was something good, she would have called me straight away, eager to share the news.

If she didn't even show up today, then something must have gone very, very wrong.

I feel like I'm going to throw up again, and then suddenly I'm standing up. All heads turn toward me—at least, the ones that weren't already turned in my direction to begin with.

Mr. Graham looks up, but he won't quite meet my eyes.

Great. Even my teachers know about the pact. If I wasn't so worried about Jo, this would probably send a whole new wave of humiliation through my system.

"Is everything okay, Meredith?" he asks.

"I'm not feeling well. I need to go to the nurse." I grab my bag from the floor and hurry toward the door.

"It's probably herpes," someone mutters.

"You dropped this!" Ashley calls. I glance back to see

her waving a folded piece of paper, probably just another copy of the pact. I keep walking.

As soon as I reach the hallway, I pull out my phone and dial Jo's number. My hands are shaking so badly that it takes three tries. It rings and rings as I head for my car, but she doesn't pick up. I try again, but it goes to voicemail.

"Jo, it's Mare. Call me back. *Please.* I'm coming over."

It's still pouring when I step outside, and even with my hood, my hair is soaking wet by the time I reach my car. I turn the wipers on, but the rain is coming down so hard that they just move the water around instead of doing any good. But I drive anyway. Both because I'm worried about Johanna, but also because I need to get the hell out of here.

I ease out of the parking lot at five miles per hour, squinting and leaning over the steering wheel trying to see.

Herpes.

Slut.

What would God say about this?

I'd be more than willing to help you out...

I tighten my hands around the wheel until white splits across my knuckles.

I told Harper the rumors about her at school would blow over once the next big scandal hit, so I guess if nothing else, at least my humiliation takes away from hers. That, or it will only get worse for her when the kids start teasing her about having a slut for a sister.

I turn onto the country road that takes me out to Johanna's house, which is basically in the middle of nowhere, and flip my windshield wipers on to the highest setting. It still doesn't help. Water splashes up from the road, mingling with the heavy drops falling from the sky. The entire world outside my car is gray and dark. I can't even see the road in front of me.

The sign signaling the turnoff for Johanna's street pops up on my left earlier than I expect, and I slam on my brakes.

But the car doesn't stop.

The car swerves, and water splashes up against the windshield. I vaguely remember learning about hydroplaning in drivers ed three years ago, but I don't remember anything useful about what to do when it happens. Gripping the wheel, I try to gain control of the vehicle, but the more I try to fix it, the worse it gets.

Then the car is spinning, and water is everywhere. The car lurches, rocks forward, and then I'm falling. *Mon Dieu*, I must be going down the hill on the opposite side of the road. I pump the brakes and grip the wheel, but the car just keeps barreling downward. I squeeze my eyes closed and brace myself, envisioning all of the trees at the bottom that poor little Stew won't stand a chance against.

The car whips to the side, spins around, and stops. The rain continues to hammer on the roof, and my heart pounds in sync. I'm still gripping the wheel so tightly, my hands are beginning to cramp, but I can't force myself to let go. Tremors start in my arms and branch out to the rest of my body until I'm shaking and gasping. The wipers still whip back and forth, back and forth, back and forth. I feel tears drip down my cheeks.

With a shaking hand, I fish my phone out of my bag on the passenger seat. I have service, but just barely. I try

Johanna's number again, but it just rings and rings and rings.

"*Fuck,*" I moan, the tremors of my voice filling the car.

I stare at my contacts list. I can't call my parents. I can't deal with them right now, not after what happened at school. They'll be angry I ditched, yes, but they'll be more concerned *why*, and knowing them, they won't stop pushing until they get an answer. And they can't find out about the pact. About any of this. And they'll hear it in my voice if I call. They'll know something's wrong.

And I can't talk to—

I can't even think his name right now. Because whatever we had, I just ruined it. Completely and totally ruined it.

I don't know how long I sit there, blankly staring out the window, but the rain never lets up. If anything, it starts coming down harder. After a while, I turn off the car, and the wipers freeze halfway across the windshield.

I squint up the hill, where thick, twisting lines of mud are carved into the side from my car's descent. Before I can talk myself out of it, I throw the door open and plunge into the rain. It's freezing and heavy and the ground is sheer mud, but I just take a deep breath and start climbing.

16

Johanna opens her front door, and the moment her eyes land on me, they widen to twice their usual size. Mud covers me from head to toe since I tripped coming up the hill and face planted in the muck. I still have a gritty, sour taste in my mouth. I stand there shivering, the cold now engrained all the way down to my bones.

Johanna isn't looking much better. Her hair is greasy and thrown back in a ponytail. Her face is completely free of makeup, revealing the acne scars she never lets anyone see, and she's wearing a pair of yoga pants and a sweatshirt that hangs past her butt. She doesn't seem to be wearing a bra either, but that's not really anything new.

"I'd ask you to take off your muddy stuff before coming inside, but I'd rather not watch you strip, so come on." She nods and steps aside to let me in.

I kick off my shoes by the door, but that doesn't make much of a difference. Brown-tinted water drips from every inch of me. On the plus side, the freezing rain seemed to snap me out of it, because around halfway up the hill, I managed to stop crying.

Johanna eyes the mud dripping off me with pursed lips. "Come upstairs and I'll try to find you something to change into." She pauses, eyes flickering from me to the carpeted stairs. "On second thought, you wait there, and I'll be right back."

She disappears to the second level and returns a few minutes later, carrying an old pair of sweats and a hoodie with an eagle and *Northfield High* printed in big block letters across the front.

Once I'm dry and clothed, she leads me through the glossy hall to the kitchen. "Hungry?" she asks.

Johanna carefully avoids my gaze as I perch myself on the barstool across the counter. She busies herself, straightening a stack of papers.

"What happened, Jo?" I ask quietly.

"I think I should be asking you that," she deflects, giving the papers one final tap against the island before setting them down.

I wait.

She sighs and leans over the counter, putting her face in her hands. "You were right, as usual." She runs her hands up and fists them in her hair. "And I'm a complete idiot, also as usual."

"You're not an idiot," I say softly.

"I *threw* myself at him." She shakes her head. Her voice wobbles, but she looks away before I can see her face. "I must have looked like such a fool."

"What did he say?"

"Nothing! Fucking nothing!" She finally looks up at me, and her expression is torn between mortified and angry as hell. "I kissed him, he pulled away—actually he backed away, like several steps."

"And he didn't say anything?"

"I don't know. I bolted." She presses her fingers to her temples. "God, I can't go back and sit in his class for the rest of the year. How *humiliating*. How could I have been so *stupid?*"

"Jo." I get up and come around to her side of the counter. "You're not stupid."

She narrows her eyes at me, as if just now seeing me for the first time. "You've been crying. What happened to you?"

I rub at my cheeks, but they're dry. "It was just the rain."

"No, it's not. You're puffy, and your eyes are red. What happened?"

Now it's my turn to avoid her gaze. Sighing, I lean my back against the counter and pick at my nails. "Ashley kind of made photocopies of our pact and spread them around the school."

What little color was in Jo's face disappears.

"Just mine," I clarify. "Don't worry. I don't know how, but I don't think she got her hands on yours." As pissed as I am that she got her hands on *mine*, at least she didn't plaster Jo's everywhere. Especially not after what happened with Mr. Graham—that would just make her situation so much more awkward.

"*Don't worry?*" Jo grabs me by the shoulders. "That doesn't make it any less horrible. Mare, I'm so sorry! How bad was it?"

I just shake my head, look away, and lock my jaw. I refuse to cry about this again. "It's not even the rest of the school I'm worried about. I'm more worried about Harper. And what am I going to tell my *parents?*"

What am I going to tell Sam? is what I don't say, because I still can't even bring myself to think of what his reaction will be.

"Do they know?" Jo demands.

"Not yet, but you know it's just a matter of time."

"And Harper? Do you think she'll tell them?"

I shake my head, but a hint of doubt tickles the back of my mind. "I don't think so, but I'll try to talk to her first."

"*Ugh!*" Jo stomps to one end of the counter and whips back around. "Ashley is not going to get away with this. That bitch is not going to win. Not this time."

"Honestly, Jo, getting back at Ashley is the last thing on my mind."

"How are you not pissed at her?" she demands.

"I *am*." I'm more than pissed. Honestly, I'm shocked. Ashley has always been horrible, but this seems so low, even for her. This isn't some petty prank for a good laugh. This almost feels...vindictive. "I just have too much damage control to worry about to even *think* about Ashley."

"You know everyone at school isn't going to just move on from it," Jo says.

"Trust me," I grumble. "I know."

Johanna walks over to the living room and plops herself on the couch, facing away from me.

I pad over to the chair across from her and sink into the leather with my feet crossed beneath me. "Do your parents know? About Mr. Graham?"

She snorts. "Hell, no. I told them I had cramps so they called me out sick."

"Maybe it wasn't as bad as you think," I offer. "Sometimes when you're embarrassed, at the time you blow it up in your head to be something bigger than it was. Maybe he won't even remember it."

"I kissed him and then ran—*literally* ran—out of his classroom. I highly doubt he's going to forget that." Knees tucked to her chest, she covers her face with her hands and rests her forehead against her thighs. "I have never been this embarrassed in my life. Which is bullshit." She looks up at me. "Your problems are way worse than mine, and here I am bitching about it."

"My problems aren't worse than yours. They're just different. I don't think you can really rank shitty situations. They're just shitty."

"That would definitely be the word for it." She leans her head back and rubs absently at a scar on her cheek. "I'm really sorry about the pact. I know she must have gotten it out of my room because I was the only one with a copy. This is my fault."

"I don't blame you. There's no way you could have known she'd take it!"

She sniffles and turns away.

"Jo, I know this sucks, but are you really going to let

one guy—no matter who he may be—get to you like this? You are Johanna fucking Palmer. If he wasn't into you—and I'm guessing it was more about being afraid of getting in trouble than not being attracted to you—then screw him. Not literally, obviously."

She glances at me and smirks. "I am Johanna fucking Palmer," she agrees.

"Yes, you are."

"And I can do *way* better than a wannabe male model with a teacher's salary."

"Yes, you can."

She gets up, comes over to my chair, and folds in beside me. "You're pretty much the best best friend ever."

I lean my head against hers. "Yes, I am."

She clasps my hand in hers. "So, what are we going to do about this damage control?"

I sigh. "I have no idea."

BY THE TIME I GET HOME, I CAN ALMOST PRETEND THIS morning never happened. I can almost forget about what I've done, what everyone now knows about me. There are no whispers or giggles or narrow-eyed glances—and yet, my muscles can't quite relax, and I keep catching myself grinding my teeth.

Especially when I reach the front door, only to find a large poster board with the word *slut* smeared across the surface. I quickly tear it down and enter the house, thankful I got home before my parents. If they had been the ones to find that...

I stand in the empty foyer for a long time, slowly ripping the poster apart with my hands.

It doesn't matter.

Rip.

I don't care.

Rip.

It's not true.

Riiiip.

I don't stop until the tears clouding my eyes spill over and drip onto the paper in my hands. The house is quiet. I peer into the kitchen. Empty. The TV room, empty. I head upstairs and pause in front of Harper's door. The light's on.

Wiping the evidence of tears from my face, I knock softly. The door cracks open immediately, but just an inch. Harper's gaze is piercing through the crack. "Go. Away." She slams the door shut, and I hear the lock latch.

I'm so taken aback, I actually take a step away. "So, I guess you heard."

"Of course I heard!" she calls from the other side. "How could I not? There were a dozen of those damn flyers shoved in my locker."

I close my eyes and rest my hand against the door. "I'm so sorry, Harp. I never meant for—"

"Oh, just save it," she snaps. "You *never* 'mean for' things to happen. It's *never* your fault. It's always the world out to get Meredith, isn't it?"

It feels like she just slapped me. The tears rise again, but I bite them back. "I never said—"

"Tell it to someone who cares. This is the last thing I need right now."

My guilt and concern quickly shift into something else. Something with much more heat. "This is the last thing *you* need right now?" I demand.

"Yes!" she practically shouts. "You're the one who screwed up, so how is it fair that I'm the one getting punished for it? Do you have any idea what it was like for me at school today? Do you?"

"What it was like for you?" I echo tonelessly.

"It was *hell*," she continues as if I hadn't spoken. "Do you know what it's like to have everyone, even people you don't know, come up and make fun of you for having a slut for a sister? To have people shove your books out of your hands and write things on your locker? You were asking for it, but *me?* What did I do? Why is what *you* did *my* fault?"

Her words strike hot, leaving my skin stinging as if struck—and she may as well have hit me. But I'm not sure if the burning sensation is from shame or anger. "Would you just open the door so we can talk about it?"

"I don't want to talk about it. There's nothing to talk about."

"You know, it's probably stupid of me, but I was kind of hoping you would be the *one* person in my corner on this."

There's a pause, and then: "Maybe you should have thought about that before," followed by her footsteps retreating farther into her room.

Well. I guess that's it, then. I pretend there isn't a lump in the back of my throat, that my eyes aren't burning. That the churning in my stomach isn't the size of a wave.

You were asking for it.

My throat tightens so much, it's hard to breathe.

Halfway down the hallway, I freeze and turn back around. "Please don't tell Maman and Papa."

There's a long pause. For a moment, I think she didn't hear me, but then the words, "Maybe I won't, maybe I will," fill the space between us.

It's a few hours after sundown when I pull up to the shelter. All of the windows are dark and the parking lot is empty. Closing time was several hours ago.

I didn't technically sneak out. Maman and Papa have never had to give me a curfew since I never really do anything that requires staying out late. But I did wait until they'd retreated to their room and closed the door before I left.

I just couldn't handle their questions. Tonight might be the last night before they know. By some miracle, they haven't found out already. But I can't bank on that lasting much longer.

I fish the spare key Jada had made for me months ago out of my pocket and head for the front door. It's quiet when I step inside, and the bell above the door feels twice as loud as usual. I hear the dogs start to stir in the back, probably from hearing the bell. Just in case a concerned citizen decides to call in a break-in, I resist the urge to turn on the lights and use my phone's flashlight to guide me through the dark building instead.

The dogs go crazy when I step into the room.

"Shh. Shh." I grab a bag of treats from the table and slide one into each of their cages, coming to Squirt's last. She wiggles excitedly, pawing at the door as I approach. Instead of sliding her treat in like the rest, I open the cage. She jumps into my arms immediately, licking beneath my chin.

"Hey, little one," I whisper, press my back against the wall, and slide down until I'm sitting on the floor. Squirt curls into a ball between my legs and rests her head against my knee.

We just sit there for a while, my hand absently running through her fur. At some point, I started crying, and the tears drip silently down my cheeks, but I just stare blankly at the wall of dogs, focusing on the warmth of Squirt against my legs.

I've thought about it so many times, just taking her home. Hiding her in my room from my parents; I could probably get away with it for a solid few weeks before they found out, maybe longer if I could get Jo in on it, passing her back and forth between our houses. Just long enough until college; then I could declare her as an emotional support animal or something so I could bring her with me to school.

Squirt turns around in my lap so she's facing me and licks my arm a few times.

"You're such a good girl," I whisper, scratching behind her ears. "You're such a good girl."

She sighs happily and flops back onto my knee.

I know I should go home. Try to get some sleep. Figure

out what I'm going to say to Maman and Papa after Harper tells them, because I know she will. Figure out how the hell I'm supposed to get through the school day tomorrow.

Figure out how I'm ever going to face Sam again.

But I do none of those things.

I just scratch Squirt behind her ears, lean my head against the wall, and close my eyes.

17

It's five minutes until first bell, and I'm still sitting in my car in the parking lot. My hand has been on the door handle for the last ten minutes, but I can't bring myself to get out of the car.

I can do this.

Maybe if I repeat that to myself enough times, I'll start to believe it.

Miraculously, my car was mostly fine after flying off the road yesterday. Towing it back up the hill proved to be the difficult part—but at least Johanna finally got to test out just how much horsepower her Jeep has. And maybe some neighbors got an entertaining show of two completely clueless teenage girls standing in the middle of the road for two hours, trying to figure out how the heck to tow a car, because we sure as hell weren't calling anyone else and letting that get back to either of our parents.

Besides a few scratches and a serious coating of mud,

Stew's okay. Honestly, I was kind of hoping he wouldn't be so I'd have no way to get to school today, yet here I am.

I can do this, I can do this, I can do this.

I don't care what any of these people think of me.

They only win if I let them.

I shove the door open before I can talk myself out of it and walk into the school, head held high and eyes trained forward. Maybe everyone already forgot about it. Maybe I'm old news. Maybe—

"Hey, Mare!" A guy in a letterman's jacket bumps me with his shoulder as he passes. He's on the football team, that much I know. He's also never spoken to me before, so this can't be good.

"We've got five minutes before class. Wanna head back to my Jeep over there? I can make it quick." He winks. Two more jocks appear at his side, they exchange high fives, and all turn away laughing.

My cheeks are burning, but I refuse to stare at the ground and scurry inside as I usually would. I kind of wish I'd thrown back some witty comeback, something like, *Like you could last five minutes,* but the moment passes and they walk away, swallowed into the crowd entering the school.

I think someone else says my name as I walk, but I keep my eyes trained forward until I reach my locker, where I find a sheet of paper taped to the surface, but it's not another photocopy of the pact.

Sign up here to volunteer your services for the charity of Nail Meredith Beaumont is written neatly at the top followed by: **screw at your own risk. We are not liable for any STIs contracted during your volunteering period.*

Twenty or so names are listed below, followed by a note scrawled in black ink: *I wouldn't touch that disgusting whore if you paid me.*

Disgusting whore?

I have never in my entire life been called something so ugly.

I've always been the preacher's daughter. The goody-two-shoes. The shy girl.

But a *whore*? I've never even had sex, and suddenly I'm a *whore*?

I inhale a shaky breath, tear down the paper, and pop the door open to retrieve my French book.

It doesn't matter. It doesn't matter. It doesn't matter.

No matter how many times I tell myself that, I can't seem to swallow the feeling rising behind my eyes that feels suspiciously like tears.

I SPEND THE ENTIRE DAY WITH MUSCLES SO TENSE, MY shoulders are aching by the end of it. When the last bell finally rings, I hurry out to my car, desperately eager to get home and away from all of these people, and come out to the parking lot to find *this*.

My car is surrounded by a dozen or so members of the Pretty Committee. Literally surrounded. They stand shoulder to shoulder around its perimeter, waiting for me. Ashley stands at the head, and as she sees me approach, her peach-glossed lips break into a smirk. "There she is."

Her posse glances up, donning matching amused

expressions. They all seem to be derivatives of the same person, within a few varying shades of box-dyed hair. They're not even matching, per se, but it's in the way they hold themselves, the way their eyes follow Ashley's every movement, almost subconsciously. How every time she tilts her head or crosses her arms over her chest, the entire group's center of gravity shifts to accommodate it. There's a sharp hunger in the way they watch her, something caught between wanting to be like her and wanting to take her place.

The pair of girls directly behind Ashley, with matching dirty-blonde bobs, starts a slow clap as I approach.

This can't be good.

"Hi, Ashley," I offer and come to a stop a few paces away. I eye the door on the driver's side, but two girls are now leaning against it, arms crossed, lips curled as if daring me to try to get past. There's no way I'm getting in there without some kind of violence. Not that these girls don't deserve it, but that's not really my style. And honestly, I'd probably end up doing more damage to myself than to any of them.

"Happy long weekend!" Ashley takes a step forward and reaches her hand out to me, causing the numerous gold bracelets around her wrist to *ding*.

I stare at the oncoming hand in alarm, but she just wraps it around the top of my arm, almost in a friendly gesture, and escorts me toward the group. "We're all hanging out tonight," she informs me.

"Cool," I say noncommittally. I don't think it's any secret that the Pretty Committee hangs out practically *every* night. But that does nothing to clarify what the heck is going on here.

"No, silly." She pats my arm and releases me. "*We*. All of us. That means you, too."

My stomach knots as I meet the gaze of the girls leaning against the door again. They both show me their teeth, but I definitely wouldn't call them smiles.

"Um." My voice comes out too high. I scratch the back of my neck. "I don't think I can—"

"Nonsense." Ashley waves her hand. She's still smiling, but there's something about the look in her eye that I don't like.

"Want me to take your bag for you?"

I jump at the sudden presence of the tall girl on my right. I hadn't even seen her approach. She's at least six feet tall—easily the tallest of the group—and she's built like an athlete. Her hair is nearly as blonde as Ashley's, but it's clearly not natural. April, I think her name is. As she reaches for the strap of my backpack, I pull it tighter against me and try to take a step back. But there's another girl right behind me. I bump into her and fall forward a step toward April. "No, it's fine—" I start to say, but they're not really listening because they weren't really asking. April rips the bag from my grasp.

"Hey—"

Two other girls grab me from behind, each taking an arm, and start to pull me toward my car.

"Find her keys," Ashley instructs the tall one.

"What are you doing?" I demand.

The locks of my car click and the trunk pops open.

"Hurry," Ashley orders, glancing around the parking lot. I hadn't even bothered to notice how uncharacteristically deserted it was when I came out. That wasn't an accident.

Before I can do anything else, the two girls shove me face-first into the trunk. I barely manage to curl my legs underneath me before they slam the door down on my face. Thick darkness envelopes me. Laughter ebbs in from the other side as I feel the car rock slightly under me—other people are climbing into the car. *My* car.

I reach around blindly in the dark for my phone, and then silently curse myself as I remember it's in my backpack.

I bang my hands against the roof as the car roars to life.

"Let me out!" I shriek.

My breaths come in faster, but no matter how many times I gasp, I can't seem to get any air in my lungs.

Whoever is driving reverses so fast that my head smacks into the wall. Music starts pounding from the front as we peel out of the parking lot. I have to brace my hands on either side of the trunk just to keep myself from tumbling around.

The drive is long and bumpy, so I assume we're not on any main roads. At some point, the radio cuts out. They could've just turned it off, but I can't help but think it's because we're someplace so remote that there's no signal. I can't think of a single positive outcome of the situation—not even a decent one. I guess the worst case scenario is they're going to murder and bury me in the middle of nowhere, and then I'll end up on one of those late-night unsolved mysteries shows. So, really, we can only go up from there.

After what feels like hours, my arms aching from staying so tense and holding me up, the car slows to a stop. I can hear what sounds like gravel crunching beneath the tires, and then the hood pops open, assaulting my eyes with bright sunlight. Before my vision has a chance to adjust, someone pulls me by the arms and yanks me out of the trunk.

I hit the ground on my knees, the rocks biting in my skin. Blinking, I try to survey my surroundings. It's like I suspected: I'm in the middle of nowhere, surrounded by empty land and no signs of life. Ashley and three of her friends stand around me, looking very much pleased with themselves, and I see a white SUV sitting a little behind my car.

Dead grass and weeds surround us, extending endlessly in each direction. It almost looks like we're in the middle of New Mexico or something, but there's no way we drove that far.

"What is this?" I ask, though I know the answer. I'm getting hazed, and I didn't even join anything.

"Well." Ashley clasps her hands together like she's about to teach a room full of small children. "We threw your phone somewhere in that direction." She points to her right, a flat plane of dirt. "And your keys somewhere over there." She points to her left, another flat plane of dirt. "Have fun."

Without any more explanation, the girls take off

toward the white car. Ashley lingers behind, hands on her hips, face devoid of emotion as she stares at me.

I stare back, but before I can even think of something to say, she prowls toward me.

"Stay away from my boyfriend," she says very, very quietly.

"Your boyfriend?" I repeat stupidly.

She smiles, but there is nothing pleasant about it. "Just know, if you ever come anywhere near James again, we will do something much, much worse than this."

James? I don't even think I *know* a James.

I shake my head, slightly stunned, and glance back toward the white SUV. The other girls are standing beside it, waiting for their leader.

Ashley grabs my chin with three fingers and jerks my face to the side, forcing me to look at her. Her nails dig into my skin. "Understand?" she snarls.

"Let go out of me!" I try to pull away, but she holds fast, and sharp pain flashes up my chin. I yank a second time, this time successfully pulling my face from her grasp, and feel something hot and wet trickle down my neck.

She's crazy. She's actually crazy.

"I think you have something on your chin," she purrs, strokes my chin with her index finger, and pulls it back, proudly displaying the smear of bright red blood.

"Is this fun for you?" My voice comes out so quietly, I'm not sure she heard me, but once the words are out, I realize I really want to know the answer. I want to know how someone could consistently treat other human beings like this and still sleep at night.

"Is fucking every guy in the school fun for you?" she asks, voice sickly sweet.

"You know that's not true," I say quietly.

She shrugs. "I really don't care who you spread your legs for. But if you go after my boyfriend, I'll make your life even more of a living hell than it is right now. Or, you know what, maybe that's too obvious. Maybe I'll go after that little dyke of a sister of yours."

Whatever fear was left in my system is quickly overpowered by the pure fury surging through my veins.

"You know what?" I hear myself saying, though it's almost an out-of-body experience, because I have no control over the next words that come out of my mouth. "I feel sorry for you. Because this is it for you. After high school, you're not going to be able to push everyone around like this anymore. You won't be able to step on everyone like they're ants. You've peaked in high school, Ashley. You know what happens to the mean girl who peaks in high school? Yeah! Me, neither. Because no one gives a shit about her after graduation, and she never ends up doing anything. So live it up." I raise my arms at my sides and gesture around. "Live it up now while you can."

She stares at me in silence for several seconds. I stare right back. Then she slowly backs away to her car, and I watch them pile into the SUV. Ashley hesitates by the driver's door.

"That's it?" I call after them. "This is the best you can do?"

Ashley's mouth tightens. She hoists herself up so one foot is in the car and her body hangs out the open door.

"The sun sets in less than an hour, and I hear there are coyotes in these parts. You might want to hurry."

And with that, she slams the door, flips the car around, and takes off down the road. Dirt and gravel spit up behind her tires, and I have to turn away to shield my face from their attack.

Whatever angry bravery had taken over me in those last few minutes quickly washes out of my system as I glance in the two directions she pointed. I have no idea where I am. And she could have been lying about where she threw my stuff, for all I know. My phone and keys could be anywhere. I take a deep breath and push my hair behind my ears, ordering myself to remain calm. I just have to remain calm, and I'll find them. How far could she possibly have thrown them?

She wasn't wrong about the setting sun, though. The air is already starting to get colder. I pull on one of the door handles to see if I left a jacket inside, but it's locked. I throw my head back and take a very long, slow breath.

I've got to hand it to Ashley, she's thorough.

So I do the only thing I can: I start looking.

18

Two hours. That's how long it takes to find my things in the dirt. The cold coaxes out goosebumps along my arms as I crawl on my hands and knees, cutting my palms on the sharp rocks as I glide my hands across the ground, fingers spread wide, hoping to feel metal. I find the phone within the first hour, thankfully, so I can use the flashlight to find the keys since the sun has set completely by now.

Neither are anywhere near where Ashley said they would be.

When I get back in the car, I'm coated in a fine layer of dirt and coughing from the dust in my lungs. Both of my hands are bleeding and burning from the dirt shoved into my open wounds. My stomach growls. I dig in my backpack until I find my water bottle and chug most of it, then throw the car door open and pour the rest over my hands, wincing as they sting.

The drive—that's a whole other story. I have no idea how to get back, and there isn't enough cell service to give me directions. So I just blindly take off in the direction Ashley left earlier until I get within range so I can figure out how the hell to get home.

The longer I drive, the hotter the anger grows inside of me. My hands grip the steering wheel until my knuckles turn white. My jaw starts to ache from clenching it so tightly, and I can feel a headache thudding dully between my eyebrows.

This was too far. This has all been too far.

It's past ten o'clock by the time I make it back. There are a few missed calls from Sam, Johanna, and my parents, but I ignore them all. My eyes linger on Sam's name for a moment. Things were going so well with us. But the moment he hears about that pact...I'd be surprised if he ever spoke to me again.

When I pull up to the house, all of the lights are on. I groan internally as I shuffle to the door, exhaustion weighing down my every step. No doubt Maman and Papa are waiting up for me and have no intentions of letting me pass without an explanation. All I want is to collapse into my bed. Luckily, I've had several hours to come up with a story.

Sure enough, the moment I step into the house, Maman and Papa appear from the kitchen.

"Where have you been?" Papa asks at the same time Maman says, "Why haven't you been answering your phone?"

"I'm sorry." I try my best to sound convincing, but I'm

so exhausted that it probably just comes out monotone. "I was with a study group at the library—we have this *huge* test on Monday—and we just lost track of time. And I forgot to charge my phone last night, so the battery died."

Both of them narrow their eyes at me, as if deciding whether or not they're going to believe me. I smooth my features into what I hope is an earnest expression.

"You were studying all night at the library on a long weekend?" Papa asks, eyebrows raised.

I just raise my eyebrows back at him. "Is that really so surprising for me?"

"Why are your clothes so dirty?" Maman asks.

I'd tried to brush off my clothes as best I could before coming inside, but apparently hadn't been thorough enough.

"It was nice out this afternoon. We were sitting out on the hill behind the library before it got dark." I wince at how easily the lie rolls of my tongue, at how easily this seems to placate them. Maman huffs and crosses her arms over her chest like she's still upset, but it's clearly just a show, and Papa braces a hand on her shoulder.

"You should call next time. From a friend's phone, or the school or something. You can't worry us like that," Papa says.

His words trigger something deep in my chest, and I have to lock my jaw to hold it together. "You're right," I say, disguising my wobbling lower lip with a yawn. "I'll do better next time. I'm sorry." With that, I spin before they can see the tears rushing to my eyes, and hurry up the stairs.

It sounds like they call something after me, but the roaring in my ears blocks out everything else.

The moment I slip inside my room and close the door behind me, the tears come. Hard. And not just about Ashley and tonight. About everything. About the pact and Harper and my parents. About the people calling me a slut and the ugly things people have shoved in my locker. About the way my teachers can't meet my eyes and I can't even walk down the hall without stares or whispers. About the way Sam will look at me when he finds out. How my *parents* will look at me when they find out.

My clothes are absolutely covered in dirt and various leaves from crawling around on the ground all night, so I strip them off and toss them into my hamper. When I try to throw my backpack on my bed, it misses and crashes to the ground on its side, upending its contents all over my floor. Folders, notebooks, and pens scatter. A folded sheet of paper glides across the floor and hits my foot, landing face up, exposing part of the script on the inside: *James Wofford*.

I cock my head and pick up the paper.

James.

If you come anywhere near James again.

This is why she was so angry? *This* is the reason I just spent the last six hours of my life shoved into the truck on my own car, crawling around on my hands and knees in the dirt, shivering from the cold, blind to my surroundings and wondering if some wild animal was going to come rip me into pieces? All because of this scrap of paper that I'd never even given a second thought?

I smash it into a ball and throw it across the room, kicking the remaining pile of books on the floor. They make a satisfying *thud* as they hit my bedside table.

I haven't even done anything wrong, and they all treat me like this. I haven't done anything at all except write my name on some stupid piece of paper when I was drunk, but they're witch-hunting me all the same, just because it's fun.

How much worse could things possibly get if I actually *did* do something?

If I'm going to be treated like this regardless of what I do, then honestly, why *shouldn't* I have some fun? Why *shouldn't* I do what I set out to do? Things with Sam are done as soon as he hears about all of this. And honestly, it was only a matter of time before he figured out that I wasn't good enough for him anyway.

All this time, I've been looking at these guys offering to sleep with me as a bad thing, but honestly, maybe I had it wrong. Maybe a one-night stand is the way to go. No attachments. No drama. Just one-and-done, and then I can move on with my life.

I march over to the ball of paper and smooth it out on my bed. My hands shake around my phone as I type out the text. I keep it simple. Nonchalant. I don't want to sound desperate. The message in its entirety says: *Tonight?* –Mare

I have to close my eyes to muster up enough courage to hit send, and then I fling the phone onto the bed, my entire body vibrating with the spike of adrenaline.

My phone buzzes.

I lunge forward and inspect the illuminated screen. His reply is just as simple: an address.

MY PARENTS GO TO BED SHORTLY AFTER I GET HOME, and they both sleep like the dead, so after showering and putting on the sexiest underwear I can find under my jeans and T-shirt (and by sexy, I mean black cotton), sneaking out of the house proves much easier than TV shows and movies would lead you to believe.

As it turns out, James Wofford only lives a few neighborhoods away. Practically walking distance. After a quick internet-and-social-media search to see what he looks like, I get in my car and go. When I'm parked outside his house, which is dark except for one window on the second floor, I take a swig of the vodka I'd stashed in my purse, and then another after I text him to let him know I'm outside.

Sweet. My parents are out. I'll let you in through the front.

The house is nice—clearly upper-middle class—with various family portraits and chic décor strewn about. I glance at a photo of three boys hanging by the stairs. They're practically triplets—same dark hair, same slight freckles, same dimples, all clad in matching varsity jackets.

"My brothers," James explains when he sees me staring at it. He points to the tallest one in the middle. "That one's me, in case you couldn't tell. People get us mixed up a lot."

"And they are—"

"Also out tonight," he finishes for me and nods toward the kitchen. "Want a drink?"

I nod, almost too eagerly.

Thankfully, James' ensemble is similar to my own, so I don't feel underdressed—dark jeans and a gray T-shirt. Admittedly, it looks better on him. His shoulders are broad, muscles defined, and I can't help but notice how well he fills out that shirt as I watch him pull two beers from the fridge. Our interactions before now have been minimal, but I've definitely seen him around school before. Usually with his arm thrown around Ashley's shoulder in the cafeteria, or his tongue down her throat in the halls.

My stomach twists.

"Cheers." He clinks his beer to mine and knocks it back. I take a small sip and try not to make a face. Damn, I hate beer. But I chug it. I tip the can back and swallow as much as I can while his back is turned, fishing for something else in the fridge. He comes back out with two more beers, and hands one to me.

And then somehow we end up venturing upstairs to his room, and the door is closed, and the lights are off—except a small lamp in the corner—and terrible metal music is playing in the background. By the time we make it to his room, I've already finished the first beer.

"Just make yourself comfortable," he says, clearly indicating the bed, and heads over by the lamp. "Let me just change this music." It shifts to something much slower—almost jazzy. *Mon Dieu*, he has a sex playlist.

I perch myself on the edge of his bed, clutching the second beer with both hands for dear life. The room is small, and there's not much in it besides the bed, a desk, and a side table. There are a few posters on the walls of bands I've never heard of, and a TV set in the corner with some kind of video game console and controllers strewn about.

It's almost too dark to see, but I can definitely make out a picture of him and Ashley on the desk. I feel like she's staring at me.

He takes another large swig of his drink and slides onto the bed beside me. I take another sip of my beer.

"I was surprised when you texted," he admits. Neither of us are looking at the other.

"I was, too," I say.

We sit there for a bit just listening to the music and drinking our drinks. And I wonder if he does this often. As angry as I am with Ashley, it still leaves a sour taste in the back of my mouth. Why keep a picture of her out where he'd see it every day, but then turn around and cheat on her in the very same room? It just doesn't seem to make any sense.

Maybe this was a stupid idea—

And then his face is coming for mine, and I don't have any more time to think. It's too fast of an attack to retreat, so I just let it happen. The kiss is sloppy and tastes like beer. He pulls away just long enough to take the beer from my hands, set both cans on his desk, then come back in, his hands gripping the sides of my face as he pulls me in. He shoves his entire tongue in my mouth without warning, and I have absolutely no idea what to do with it, though he doesn't seem to notice. His hands slide down to my lower back, pull me closer.

I try to get into it. I really try. He's not a bad kisser—

there's just a fair amount of slobber, and his touch is kind of aggressive. Not scary-aggressive, but rough. And the closer I pull myself to him, and mold my mouth around his, and let him feel under my shirt, the more and more distanced I feel from the whole situation. Like I'm watching a movie.

He kisses my neck, but I barely feel it. My shirt hits the floor, but I barely notice. And all I can think about is how this is nothing like what it's supposed to be like.

It's nothing like the way it was with Sam.

No matter how hard I try to silence it, a voice in the back of my head keeps screaming, *wrong, wrong, wrong.*

Sam made me feel safe, excited, and bold all at the same time. James makes me feel...dirty. And not in a good way.

I close my eyes and try not to think about it. He rolls me onto my back and climbs on top of me, his weight pressing me into the mattress. Although he may not be Sam, at least right now, in this moment, no one's looking at me over their nose. No one's looking at me like something to scrape off their shoe. No one's calling me a whore. James is looking at me like something beautiful, like something he wants. And even if for just one night, that might be enough.

His touch is not gentle like Sam's as it trails down my body. His lips don't leave sparks where they touch my skin. And there is no affection in his eyes when he looks at me. No emotion at all, really. Just lust.

"Wait." I stop him before his pants come off.

"What's the matter?" He pulls back, just a little. His words slur slightly. I guess he had a bit more to drink than

I'd realized, but I should have guessed from the way he smells.

I shift uncomfortably beneath him. His arms are braced on either side of me like a cage.

"I don't think I can do this," I say.

His expression softens. He pushes a lock of hair behind my ear in a gesture that should feel sweet, but for some reason, it doesn't. "Everyone's nervous their first time."

"What about Ashley?" I blurt.

That causes him to pause. He leans back and lets out a long, slow breath. "You really want to talk about Ashley right now?" he finally says.

No, I suppose I don't. This is not my business, and honestly, I don't want to know any more than I already do.

But yet.

I can't stop myself from asking, "Are you two not together?"

He leans all the way back on his heels, kneeling over me, and runs a hand through his hair. "Ashley and I...we're together. But not like this, together." He points to what we're doing.

My intoxicated brain is a little slow on the uptake, so I just stare at him.

He waves his hand around as if this clarifies everything, then leans back over me, and the sudden weight of his body on mine sends a twist of nausea to the pit of my stomach. "She says she's not ready and wants to wait, but I told her I wanted these experiences before college. She didn't want to break up, though, so we have a sort of don't-ask-don't-tell policy, okay?"

"Okay." It comes out as a squeak. As his lips find my neck again, his words spiral violently in my head.

Ashley wants to wait.

Ashley won't have sex with him.

Ashley won't have sex with him, so he's looking for girls who will, and she's so desperate to keep him that she's willing to turn a blind eye.

Ashley, of all people, is a...virgin?

The nausea surges up again.

"Wait!" I say a little too loudly. "Stop. Stop."

He pulls back, his hair falling into his eyes.

"I can't do this," I say.

"Is this about the Ashley thing? I shouldn't have said anything—"

"No." *Yes.* "I just." My words come out a little shaky. "I can't do this. Not right now."

He sighs and falls onto his back beside me. For a second, we both lay there, staring at the ceiling, our breath uneven and too loud in the quiet room. I push myself up into a sitting position, hyperaware of the fact that I'm sitting here in just a bra in front of a boy I don't know, *who has a girlfriend,* and scan the ground for my shirt.

"I thought this is what you wanted," he says.

I suddenly feel so stupid. My entire body is hot, and I have to clench my jaw to stop myself from crying. The only thing that could possibly make this moment more embarrassing is if I started to cry right now.

"I thought it was," I mumble and shake my head. "I should probably just go." I move to jump off the bed, but he catches my forearm.

My gaze shoots to his hand in alarm. Is he not taking no for an answer? What if he doesn't let me leave?

"I can't let you drive home," he says. "You've been drinking. I'd drive you myself, but I've also been drinking." He releases me and gets up from the bed, re-buckling his belt. "You can stay here until you sober up." He heads over to the corner of the room to turn off the sexy-time music, still shirtless.

"Thank you," I manage.

He nods, not really looking at me. "You can sleep here. I don't mind."

After I redress and situate myself on the bed, I'm grateful he didn't let me drive. With all the adrenaline, I hadn't noticed that I have a mild case of the spins. I probably shouldn't have downed that vodka before coming inside. "Hey, James?" I say quietly.

"Yeah?" He plops down on the bed.

"Thank you."

"For...?"

I shrug even though he isn't looking at me. "For being a decent guy, I guess."

He snorts a little. "You're welcome, I guess."

JAMES FALLS ASLEEP, BUT I NEVER DO. HE PASSES OUT ON top of the covers, jeans on, shirt off, a single arm thrown over his eyes. He snores a little.

The clock on his bedside table with glowing red numbers informs me that it's just shy of 1:00 a.m.

Careful not to wake James, I sit up slowly and search my surroundings for my phone. I distinctly remember bringing it up here with me. When my eyes fall on the picture frame sitting on the nightstand, I freeze.

It's a picture of James and Ashley, arms around each other, looking very happy and couple-like. I stare at the unconscious boy in the bed beside me. He seems like a nice enough guy, and if Ashley is willing to *kidnap* for him, there has to be something special about him. But if he's dating Ashley, and proud enough of that fact to have pictures all over the place, why would he give me his phone number?

Could having sex really be that important to someone?

James stirs and rolls onto his side, facing me, but he's still fast asleep.

I stare at him for a long time. I already know what I'm going to do. Maybe I've always known what I was coming here for, but just didn't want to admit it to myself. I crawl back into bed beside him before I can talk myself out of it.

Ashley thinks we're all puppets she can use for her amusement. But I've had it. If she thinks she can walk all over me, ruin my life, ruin my relationship, and then ditch me somewhere in the middle of the desert and walk away unscathed, she's dead wrong. And all for a stupid boy who clearly doesn't care about her as much as she cares about him. Maybe Jo had it right all along. I can't let her get away with all of this. I can't.

After slipping my phone from the nightstand, I pull up the camera.

19

I SNEAK BACK INTO THE HOUSE AROUND 2:00 A.M. Despite being absolutely exhausted, I don't pass out immediately like I'd hoped. My entire body is vibrating with anticipation, and I can't turn my brain off. It just spins in the same circle, going over the same thoughts mercilessly. I spend most of the night staring at the ceiling, waiting for sleep that never comes. And then, all too soon, my alarm goes off and I roll out of bed, eyes still closed, to change into my volunteer shirt. Thankfully, I'd set a reminder on my phone about my shift today, or I would have totally forgotten. I don't usually work at the shelter on Fridays but agreed weeks ago to come in today since we have the day off school for the long weekend.

The knowledge of what's on my phone makes it feel like it weighs a million pounds in my pocket as I pull my car out and head toward the shelter. In the moment, taking the pictures had made perfect sense. They were a way to get back at Ashley, to show her that *finally* someone was giving her what she'd been dishing out for years. But now that I have the pictures, I'm not even sure what to do with them. My mind doesn't work like Ashley's. I wouldn't know how to scheme and hurt people if I tried.

For now, I do nothing with the pictures. Maybe I'll ask Johanna what to do with them later.

Besides, I have bigger problems to deal with right now. Like Ryan coming to get Squirt.

It's still sprinkling outside, and I stare out the window as I drive, my eyes barely registering the flashes of trees, damp road, and gray mist.

Maybe since the weather is so bad, Ryan won't come.

Maybe he changed his mind and doesn't want her after all.

Maybe he'll want a different dog.

Maybe he was on his way to pick her up, got caught in the storm, and crashed his car—

I freeze mid-thought, wincing. Am I really a horrible enough person that I'd wish he was in an accident solely to prevent him from adopting Squirt?

I just have a bad feeling in the pit of my stomach that keeps churning over and over until I can't pay attention to anything else. There was something *off* about that guy. Even Squirt sensed it.

When I pull into the lot, I notice Sam's car. My chest constricts. *What is he doing here?* I had four more missed calls from him last night, but I figured he'd heard by now. He *must* have heard by now. So then what is he doing here? Is he really going to dump me at my job?

The bells ring over the door as I step inside. Jada sits behind the front desk and grins when she sees me, but my eyes are trained on the waiting room, where Sam sits in the chair farthest from the door.

He stands as soon as he sees me and starts walking forward. I turn away before he can speak and focus on Jada. "Is the man who was interested in Squirt still coming today?"

Jada sighs and gives me a sympathetic smile. "He is."

"And you finished his background check?"

Her brow furrows a little. "Yes."

"And you didn't find anything?"

"Was I supposed to?" Jada's eyes flicker from me to Sam, who is now standing at my side. "I know how much you love that dog, and how difficult this must be for you, but we should be glad. That dog deserves a home. A *real* home."

"I know," I say, almost defensively. I want Squirt to have that, I do. I just want her to have it with someone other than that man. Preferably with me, but if that's not possible, at least with someone who doesn't scare her into cowering behind my legs.

She just smiles sadly at me again. "Why don't you two feed the dogs before he shows up?"

Now I have to look at Sam. I brace myself for what surely will be hatred on his face, but when I finally turn and see him, he just looks confused.

We head to the back, and the moment we round the corner, Sam gently takes my arm and pulls me to a stop.

"You've got to tell me what's going on," he says.

I don't look at him. I can't. "I've gotta get them fed before Ryan shows—"

"You've been ignoring my calls *and* Johanna's. Yeah, she called me," he says to my surprised expression. "Because she was worried about you, just like I am. Did something happen? What's going on? I haven't heard from you in *days*."

I search his face for some hint that he knows, but there's nothing. There's no anger or suspicion. It really is just concern. He doesn't know about the pact. About Ashley's *kidnapping*.

He doesn't know about last night.

He doesn't know about...anything.

Maybe I should feel relieved, but all I feel is like throwing up.

"Can we talk about this later?" I mumble.

His gaze sweeps over my face a few times before he nods. "But we will talk about it."

Once we get the dogs fed, surrounded by their cages and the happy noises of them devouring their meals, I sink into the chair propped against the far wall, my eyes trained on Squirt's cage.

"More differential equations?" Sam asks, leaning against the counter in the center of the room.

"I'm just worried about Squirt."

"But Jada said she didn't find anything concerning about the guy adopting her, right?"

I shake my head, frowning, and hug my arms to my stomach. "I just have a really bad feeling about it."

Just as the words leave my lips, the bells above the

front door chime. My stomach drops to my feet. The faint sound of Jada's voice leaks back into the room, and after a few minutes, she and Ryan appear through the door.

Just like before, everything about Ryan's presence is dark.

I can't decide if it's just my own paranoia. If I'm the only one who notices the air leave the room when he enters; if I'm the only one who gets shivers down my spine at the sight of his eyes. Maybe there's nothing wrong with him; maybe there's just something wrong with me. But I know I'll never forgive myself if I let that man walk out the door with Squirt and something happens to her.

Sam stands at my side now, his hand on my back. I can feel his gaze on my face, but I can't look at him. I'm far too occupied tracing the decreasing distance between Ryan and Squirt. I feel like I'm going to be sick. Squirt has already finished her dinner, and now sits in the back of her cage, watching Ryan warily.

Jada moves toward the cage to take her out, a leash in her hand—one of the red ones we only use when people adopt an animal. I feel like I just swallowed something sour, and it's now eating away at my insides like acid. I want so badly to step in, to tell Jada to stop, wait, *please*—

"Wait."

Jada freezes in front of Squirt's cage. Ryan's sharp gaze cuts to where Sam and I stand.

Sam is now a step ahead of me, his hand raised. "Wait," he repeats.

"Sam?" I breathe.

"Is everything all right, Sam?" Jada asks.

He shakes his head, slowly, presses his lips together, and lowers his hand. "I—I'll pay you double whatever he offered for Squirt."

My heart stops in my chest.

I look pleadingly at Jada. Her gaze flickers from Sam to Ryan to me. "He has already filled out all of the necessary paperwork. Squirt belongs—"

"I'll pay you triple," Sam says and turns to Ryan. "And I'll pay you whatever you would have paid for her."

Ryan stands stock still, his face that disturbing expressionless mask again. There's a forced calmness in his demeanor, in the way he regards Sam before turning back to Jada. He flashes what I assume is meant to be a charming smile. "I'm not interested in getting paid. I only want the dog."

Jada sighs, her hand resting on the cage. Squirt, oblivious to the rising tension in the room, licks her fingers through the bars. "I'm sorry, Sam, Mare." She unlocks the cage, brings Squirt to her chest, attaches the red leash to her collar, and walks her over to Ryan.

"But—" Sam starts.

I rest a hand on his arm. "It's okay." It feels very far from okay, but I swallow my paranoia and doubts and anxiety and nod at Ryan. "Just please take good care of her."

"Let's go finish up your paperwork and payment at the desk," says Jada.

Ryan gives me a swift nod and follows Jada into the hall. My eyes linger on Squirt, and she watches me over Ryan's shoulder until they round the corner and disappear from view.

"You didn't have to do that," I say quietly to Sam. "But thank you."

"Are you okay?"

"No," I admit, leaning into his chest, enjoying what may possibly be the last time he's willing to be this close to me. I could go on pretending that nothing happened. I could keep seeing Sam, always terrified and waiting for the other shoe to drop. But he deserves better than that. Hell, *I* deserve better than that. I sniff, swallowing back the tears, and wipe the few that managed to squeeze out from my cheeks. "Sam, we need to talk."

20

Once my shift is over, Sam and I head outside. It's still drizzling, but I don't mind. I kind of like it. The cold water stings as it hits my arms, but I need it right now. I need something to distract me from what I'm about to tell Sam.

He shields his eyes from the rain. "Do you want to get in the car—?"

"No," I respond a little too quickly. Sam looks slightly taken aback. "I just mean, I need the fresh air," I explain.

He nods, but the severe expression on his face doesn't let up. It isn't anger, exactly. But it sure as hell isn't happy. "Are you going to tell me what's going on now?"

I close my eyes and let out a slow breath. "You're going to hate me when I tell you."

"Mare, there is nothing you can say to me right now that will make me hate you. I'm just worried, okay? Is this about me? Am I not taking a hint or something?"

"No, no, it's nothing like that," I assure him. "It has nothing to do with you, I swear. I was dodging everyone's calls."

"But why? I haven't heard from you in *days*. You just disappeared off the face of the earth."

Staring at his face, I realize that as much as I don't want him to know about the pact, I don't want to lie to him more.

So I tell him. We stand there, dripping wet and shaking from the cold, and I tell him about the pact, and Ashley, and the volunteer list. About the photocopies around school, and the way my teachers couldn't look me in the eyes. I tell him about Harper and the girls in the locker room, and how angry she was with me when she found out about the pact. I tell him about Ashley kidnapping me and leaving me in the middle of nowhere.

But I don't tell him about James. I *can't*.

Because I'd only done it thinking Sam and I were already done. And if my entire life was going to crash and burn anyway, I figured I might as well take Ashley down with me. But now, looking at Sam's face, the logic feels like two puzzle pieces that just won't quite fit together.

He waits quietly until I'm finished. When I glance up, he's staring at me, his eyebrows drawn.

"Saying it out loud, I know how stupid it sounds—"

"It doesn't sound stupid," he says quietly. He shakes his head several times, but now he won't look at me. His gaze is trained on the mountains somewhere behind my head.

"Please say something."

"I'm a little thrown," he admits. "I'm just trying to

understand." He takes a step back, and then another, putting more and more distance between us. I want to reach out for him, beg him to stop moving away, but then he turns and starts walking in the opposite direction.

"Sam?" My voice breaks.

He stops walking and puts his hands on his hips, but he doesn't turn around. "This pact you have with Johanna," he calls, still facing away from me. "Is that what we are?"

"No!" I rub my hands against my arms, bringing warmth back to them. "I mean, that's what it started as. It's the reason I managed to pluck up the courage and talk to you that first day, but almost the second I started to get to know you again, it stopped being about that. Honestly, I hadn't even thought about the pact in weeks until I saw in on my locker. It hasn't been about that in a long time, I promise."

He still doesn't turn around. All I want is for him to turn around.

"Sam?"

"Just let me see if I have this straight. You and Johanna signed a pact. This Ashley girl got her hands on it and plastered it all over the school. Then she essentially kidnapped you and deserted you in the middle of nowhere. And instead of telling anyone or asking for help, you cut off everyone who cares about you and chose to deal with all of this on your own?"

"Sam—"

Finally, he turns. "I just need some time to think. I'll call you later, okay?"

"Okay," I whisper, the words barely audible over the rain.

He lifts his gaze to meet mine, just for a second, before turning and slipping into his car. I wrap my arms around myself as he pulls out and stand there, the rain dripping down my face, staring at the place his brake lights were long after he leaves the parking lot, before finally forcing myself to move and get inside my car.

I stare straight ahead for several beats, my eyes unfocused. At some point, I must have started crying, because I feel the tears dripping from my jaw. I fish my phone out of my pocket and rest my forehead against the steering wheel as I bring it to my ear.

Johanna answers on the first ring.

"She's *aliiiiive!*"

"Jo?" I sniffle and wipe a mixture of rain and tears from my face.

"Yo, what's happening? What's wrong? Are you *crying*? Mare, what happened?"

"Can I come over? I could really use a friend right now."

"Of course! What's going on?"

I press my forehead against the steering wheel and close my eyes. "I did something stupid, Jo," I whisper. "Something really stupid. And I think I just ruined everything."

∼

Jo's front door swings open before I even make it out of the car. She's barefoot and in workout attire, but she comes sprinting toward me across the crushed rock driveway just the same. I barely manage to open the door before she throws her arms around me and yanks me out of the car.

She squeezes me tight. "You're my best friend in the world and I love you forever, no matter what. You know that, right?"

"Yeah, Jo. I know."

"Okay." She squeezes me again before pulling away. "Let's go inside."

We end up in her bedroom, in the exact places where we signed that contract so many nights ago. She sits in her bubble chair and spins around and around like she always does.

"So, I'm guessing Sam found out," she says.

I flop back onto her bed and stare up at the ceiling. "He said he 'needs time to think.'"

"Fuck him," Johanna says lightheartedly and nudges my knee with her toe. "I'm sure it'll turn out fine, Mare."

I groan and throw my arms over my face. "He doesn't even know the worst of it, Jo."

I feel the bed shift and she jumps in beside me. "The worst of it? Is this the *terrible, terrible* thing you were telling me about on the phone?" Her tone is teasing, but when I don't smile, she stops wiggling around. "What happened?" she asks.

I peek one eye out to look at her. "I sort of...did something last night."

"Did *something* or *someone*?" she jokes.

I wince.

"Oh my God! Did you *do* someone?"

"*No.* I mean, almost. But we stopped, okay? Nothing happened."

"Okay, up. Up, up, *up.*" She pulls on my arms until I sit up. "Spill. I want every detail. Does *Sam* know? Is that why he's mad?"

"He isn't *mad.*" I keep saying that, but honestly I'm not sure. Maybe he was angrier than he let on. "And no, he doesn't know."

She scrunches her nose in confusion. "Okay, so, what happened then?"

I flop over and hit the bed face first.

"*Tell me,*" she whines.

I fish my phone out of my pocket, find the first of the pictures, and hand it to her.

There's a sharp intake of breath, and then silence. "Mare," she says in an overly calm voice. "Why. *The hell.* Do you have pictures of you in bed with *Ashley Miller's* boyfriend? Shit, has she seen these?"

"He left a note in my locker a few days ago with his number. I didn't know who he was, not really. And after the whole kidnapping thing with Ashley, I was just so *mad* and frustrated that people were treating me like shit for something I didn't even do, so I guess I just figured I might as well do it. So I went over there, but I couldn't go through with it."

Johanna is quiet for several moments. "Mare...are you

sure she doesn't already know? That she wasn't the one to..."

"The thought crossed my mind, but I don't think so. I think he's been cheating on her."

"So what exactly were you planning to do with these pictures?"

"I don't even know anymore." Sighing, I sit up again and take the phone from her. "Revenge, I guess." I laugh bitterly. "Which is clearly not my style, because I don't even know how to do it right. This isn't me." I stare at the pictures on my phone for a second. "I don't want to stoop to her level. And what can I even do with these? She'd probably somehow manage to spin it and make *me* look even worse."

"True. And you know how badly I want that bitch to go down for something, but I don't think this is the way to do it."

I laugh and put my face in my hands. "When did everything get to be such a mess, Jo?"

She rubs a hand on my back. "I've been wondering the same thing."

"Why did we even sign that damn thing in the first place? Nothing good has come out of it."

"It made sense at the time," she mumbles. "I guess growing up, and watching all of these movies and TV shows, I had expectations for high school. You know, going to parties and football games and dances and pep rallies. I never snuck out of the house, or ditched class with my friends, or got detention—not that I really want to do any of those, I just assumed they would be a part of this piece of my life. High school just didn't turn out to be anything like I expected."

"You can say that again," I mumble.

"But you know what? Who cares? We're almost done anyway, so just screw it. Screw everything."

"I thought trying to screw everything was what got us into this mess in the first place."

Jo gasps, but she's grinning. "*Damn*, Meredith killing it with the sex jokes. I've taught you well."

"You know what's stupid? We didn't even need boys for any of those things. *We* could have gone to the pep rallies, or the games, or the dances. Having sex with some random boy wasn't going to change the fact that we never did anything."

Jo squints at me. It's the look she gets in history class when everything's going over her head. "Mare. We are *so. Stupid.*"

"That's what I'm saying—"

"No, no, no. I mean, *yes*, you're absolutely right. But I mean, we're stupid because we made the wrong pact. We had the right idea—kind of. We just made the wrong pact. So all that means is we need to make another one."

I actually laugh out loud. It comes out harsh and full of sharp edges. "Are you *insane*? One pact has caused enough problems. Why the hell would we make another one?"

"Screw boys and virginities." She scoots over so we sit facing each other on the bed. "Let's make the pact that we should have made in the first place. One where we'll do all of the things we never did in high school. You and me."

I shake my head, but a small smile has begun to form on my lips. "What would we do?"

She shrugs. "We'll go to a party—just think about the looks on the Pretty Committee's faces if we showed up! We can be each other's dates to prom. We'll go to some sports game that we don't really care about and eat hotdogs or whatever disgusting food they sell there. We don't need *boys*."

Now she's grinning, and despite my best efforts, a small, stupid grin has found its way onto my face, and we probably both look stupid, but I couldn't care less, because I've been waiting all this time for a boy to come around and tell me all the words that I need to hear. Words full enough to fill whatever void still remained in my chest. And I'd never even considered that I could fill it with something else.

"Okay," I agree.

"Okay?"

"Okay." I roll my eyes, still smiling. "It's a deal."

She holds out a hand to shake. "By graduation," she says.

"By graduation."

21

It's just past ten o'clock on Saturday night and Sam still hasn't called. And since Johanna refuses to let me sit around in my bedroom wallowing for the rest of the weekend, she talks me into doing something absolutely insane.

I can't believe I'm doing this.

"Believe it," Jo says from the driver's seat.

I hadn't realized I'd spoken aloud. The streets outside our windows are dark and flooded with traffic. My leg jostles against the dashboard, pumping out a nervous rhythm in tune to the country song on the radio. It's going to be fine. Really.

Jo laughs. "It *will* be fine. I'm taking you to a party, Mare, not your execution. Chill out."

I really need to stop saying things out loud without realizing it.

"Sorry." I force my leg to stop bouncing. "I just can't believe we're actually doing this."

"Of course we are. We made a pact. And lord knows we always follow through on our pacts." Jo winks at me and turns on her blinker. "Hey, put that thing away." She snatches my phone from my hands and shoves it in her purse. "No checking for texts or calls from Sam all night. We're going to have fun. Just you and me. No boys, remember?"

"Got it."

As Jo pulls into the neighborhood, suddenly my skinny jeans and semi-provocative tank top ensemble doesn't seem like such a good idea. These houses are *huge*. Mansions would probably be a more appropriate word. They have balconies and wraparound porches and three stories. Their *garages* look like they could fit my house inside.

I feel like I should be wearing couture, or at the very least, heels. Why did I ever think flip-flops were a good idea?

"Jo. Where the hell are we?"

"I think the real question is where the hell am I supposed to find a parking spot?" she mutters.

The entire street is jam-packed with cars. They dot the surrounding lawns, double and triple-parking one another. Jo drives past the house—easily distinguishable from the music pouring out onto the lawn and the red Solo cups scattered along the ground. Bright lights blaze from every window, and a group of clearly intoxicated teenagers lounges on the front porch as more stream in and out the front door.

Jo turns to the adjacent street and lets out a small noise of frustration to find this one just as crowded.

"Looks like we're walking, babe."

"Why are there so many people? Where are they all coming from?"

"This is a Madison Prep party, right? So that means it's gonna be a ton of kids from there *and* Northfield."

Great. Two times the amount of drunk teenagers.

Another five minutes or so pass before we find a spot—it's in front of a fire hydrant—but by then Jo's response is a simple, "Oh, fuck it."

We follow the sound of music up the block, and I can't help but wonder how they haven't gotten a noise complaint already. "Whose house even is this?" I ask, wrapping my arms around myself.

"James Dean."

I quirk an eyebrow.

Jo shrugs. "Apparently that's what everyone at Madison Prep calls him. Honestly, I don't know his real name. Just that his parents are loaded and he's the kid to go to if you want some coke."

My eyebrows inch further up my forehead. "You ever take him up on that?"

Jo snorts a little. "Not yet."

"How did you even know about this party?"

"Cecilia from photography club," she says simply.

As the house comes into view, my muscles tense, almost stopping me short on the sidewalk. Jo urges me forward with a small tug on my hand. I don't know why I'm so nervous all of a sudden—why my heart is trying to leap out of my chest and make an escape.

"A hundred bucks says no one here even knows about the pact," Jo says under her breath. "And even if they do, they probably won't recognize you."

"Is that because they won't know me, or because they'll be too drunk to know any better?"

"I'm guessing a combination of the two."

It's difficult to discern if people really are staring at me or if it's my own paranoia as we step into the house. There are people everywhere—clustered in the various rooms loosely connected in the wide, open floorplan, clogging the stairway and the hall leading to what I assume is either the laundry room or the garage, lounging against the banister, grinding against each other in the corners. It's so much sensory overload that Jo and I pause in the doorway for several seconds, taking it all in.

A guy in nothing but a tight-fitting pair of boxer shorts and a loosely knotted tie comes barreling down the stairs. A drunken grin occupies his entire face as he stumbles into the foyer and grabs the first girl he can get his hands on, who just so happens to be me. I'm torn away from Jo and tucked against this strange man's side before I realize what's happening. Suddenly I'm eye-to-nipple with his chest.

"Hot tub!" he announces and presses his hand to the small of my back as if to lead me out back. His skin is hot to the touch. I'm not sure if he thinks I'm someone else or if any female company will do. Jo wraps an arm around me and slips me away as the guy turns and shimmies through the crowd toward the back door. If he noticed that he lost his companion, he doesn't show it.

I meet Jo's eye and we both burst out laughing. Her mouth moves in what appears to be a question. I point to my ear and shake my head, the pulsing music drowning out her words.

"Drinks!" she yells and jabs a thumb over her shoulder.

Nodding, I fist my hand in the back of her T-shirt so I won't lose her as we snake our way through the mass of sweaty, dancing bodies.

A huge bowl of red punch sits on the counter surrounded by Solo cups lying on their sides. Beyond that winks several cases of beer, some soda, and a keg. The noise is duller here, but still prominent enough that Jo and I have to yell to communicate. A group of three skinny, nervous-looking guys hovers on the opposite side of the kitchen by the chip bowls. Freshmen, probably. Other than them, Jo and I are alone.

Jo doesn't even hesitate before picking up two red cups. "I'd steer clear of the punch," she says. "Probably more than just a little spiked." Instead, she mixes some Coke and another dark liquid, hands it to me, then does the same for herself.

"So, what do we do now?"

She shrugs. "Dance? Socialize?" She tips back her cup and swallows. "Drink?"

"Huh." I try the drink, which surprisingly isn't disgusting. It burns a little on the way down, but I find the corners of my mouth twisting into a small grin.

The song shifts into some upbeat pop tune, and

Johanna starts jumping up and down. "I love this song!" She grabs my wrist and pulls me toward the living room. "Let's dance!"

Holding our cups close to our chests so people don't knock into them, we plunge back into the crowd. More people are dancing now. Spinning and bobbing, hands waving in the air, jumping—though some people are just straight up dry-humping one another.

We weave our way in, and instantly the room feels warmer. The people around us are really getting into the music, their expressions serious as they bob their heads. Some scream out the lyrics—though it all just blurs into one stream of unintelligible words in my head.

Johanna wastes no time. She jumps around, the hand not holding her drink pumping up and down in the air. I bounce along beside her, laughing as she spins and shakes her hips.

"I love this song!" she shouts again.

The music pounds so loudly, it feels like it's vibrating my bones, reverberating in my chest. Sweat collects on my lower back, between my breasts.

The song changes once, twice. Jo and I don't stop dancing.

"I'll go get us some more drinks!" Jo offers when she notices that both of our cups are empty.

"I'll come with you."

"Nah!" She waves a hand and starts cutting through the crowd. "I'll be right back!"

She's gone before I can respond. Taking a deep breath, I nod. I don't need her by my side every second of the night. I'm perfectly capable of being on my own, of being around other people my age. I can absolutely do this.

And, surprisingly, this has been kind of fun. Way more fun than I was expecting. The music is decent, the drinks are free, and no one has called me a whore yet.

But after about a minute of standing there alone, nodding along to a song I've never heard and surrounded by people I don't know, I come to the conclusion that I cannot, in fact, do this. People keep looking my way. They're just glances, but every time I make eye contact with someone, heat flashes through my chest. And then nausea is building in the pit of my stomach and threatening to boil over. Suddenly the room feels hot. So, so hot. How can anyone *breathe* in here?

The couple dancing next to me disappears, heading for the kitchen, offering me an opening to escape. I look up and my entire body goes still. Across the room, red Solo cup in hand and foot propped against the wall behind him, is Sam. He's wearing black jeans and a gray band T-shirt. He leans over, saying something to the tall blonde guy on his right.

I can't move. I can't *breathe.*

He looks so calm, so content. Like everything is fine. Like what happened between us hasn't affected him at all.

I have to get out of here.

The crowd of people has constricted again, filling in the gap of the departed couple. Before I can escape, Sam looks up, and for one horrible second, we make eye contact.

I have to go I have to go I have to go.

I break free from the crowd and look around wildly for

the bathroom or some empty room or *something* away from all of this. I turn for the front door. At least then I'll get some fresh air.

I'm nearly there when an arm grabs my shoulder and turns me around. My heart leaps into my throat. Did he come after me?

"Sam—?"

I choke on the words. The guy looking down at me definitely isn't Sam. I have no idea who he is, but he's looking at me like he knows me. He's tall, with tousled black hair, a hazy look in his eyes.

"Do I know you?"

"Nope," he says cheerfully. "But I know you. Meredith, right?"

"How...?"

Laughing, he shakes his head. "Sorry, that came out creepy. I'm Derek. I'm a friend of your friend's. She was looking for you."

"Jo? Where is she?" I glance around Derek's shoulder, but can't see anything through the clumps of people. I try to peek around to where Sam had been moments before, but he's gone.

"You want me to take you to her?" he offers.

I hesitate.

"I'm a tall guy," he laughs. "Probably a lot easier for me to spot her in this mess than it is for you." He makes a gesture with his hand to illustrate how short I am. "No offense."

"None taken. Sure, I guess. That's actually really nice of you, thank you."

"My pleasure." He salutes me and extends an arm. When I don't move, he adds, "So I don't lose you in the crowd."

Conceding, I take his arm and follow as he weaves through the room. Seeing Sam has left me shaken. I just want to find Johanna and get the hell out of here. Instead of heading straight for the kitchen though, he veers right down a hallway. We pass the couples making out against the walls and keep going until we reach the end. As he opens the last door on the left, an odd feeling tickles the back of my neck.

"Jo's back here...?"

He holds the door open. "Yeah, go on in."

The moment my foot crosses the threshold, I know something isn't right. Not only is the bedroom empty, but every nerve in my body is tingling like screaming alarm bells, urging me to run.

I whip around, but he's followed me into the room and closed the door behind him. He leans against it, swaying slightly on his feet, and watches me.

"My friend will be looking for me," I say, my voice stretched thin, and point to the door. "I should probably go back out..."

"I think you'd have more fun in here with me," he says, taking a step toward me. I immediately step back, my heart leaping to my throat.

This just makes him laugh. "Oh, I see. You want me to chase you. I'm down. Let's have some fun."

He advances, drunkenly stumbling forward, and I try to skirt around him. He catches me by my upper arms, fingers digging in hard, like he's using me to keep himself upright.

"Let me go." I try to pull out of his grasp, but his fingers just dig in deeper. The panic growing in my chest is on fire.

"You are a little tease, aren't you?"

His mouth reeks of whiskey as he shoves his lips on mine, slobbery and rough. I try to pull away, but he swings me around and backs me toward the bed. My lips are sealed shut, but he keeps trying to break in with his tongue. When that doesn't work, he bites my lower lip, hard, and the shock of pain makes me open my mouth.

He seems to take this as encouragement, groaning.

"Stop—" I try to shout, but we fall onto the mattress, and his weight knocks the air from my lungs. He pins me down, and I can taste the alcohol radiating off of him, feel his sweat soaking through his clothes and pressing against my body. "Don't touch me." I try to sound authoritative, calm, but it comes out shaky.

I try to kick, roll, squirm, *anything* to get out from under him, but nothing works. My futile attempts at escape only grant me a drunken, slurred laugh.

"Get off!" I squeeze the words out through gritted teeth.

This only seems to encourage him, like this is all some role-playing game, and shoves his mouth back against mine. His hands roam over my body, and every time he finds a new piece of skin to touch, I flinch.

I have never felt terror like this—pure, untainted horror clawing at my chest. I squeeze my eyes shut and feel the tears stream down the sides of my face. My entire body is trembling, and I try to take a deep breath to calm myself.

Then everything goes quiet. The noise around me feels distant, echoey. My body goes still. I can barely feel his weight anymore. Everything slows down; everything goes numb. And in the very back corner of my mind, in the barest whisper, I hear, *not like this.*

"Shit," he mutters, and suddenly his weight lifts from my body. I don't care how or why, but it does, and I don't hesitate. I roll to the side, off the bed, and hit the floor on my side. Pain flashes through my body, as if from a distance. With shaking hands I hurriedly pull my clothes back into place. Looking up, I see Derek swaying on his feet, looking rather confused. He must have drunkenly tripped or something.

After he finally manages to regain his balance, his gaze falls back on me. He starts a slow smile—I guess that's the only good thing about him being this drunk. Everything about him is slow. He takes a step forward and I leap onto the bed. He laughs, but I don't stop. Launching myself from the bed, I jump toward the door, shrinking away from his grabbing hands, and make a run for it into the hall. I trip over my own feet, my legs buckling beneath me through my sobs, and I grab the doorframe to steady myself.

My back slams into the wall, and it knocks the wind out of me. I look up and Derek's face is suddenly much, much more serious. His hands grip just below my shoulders, hard enough to bruise.

"What are you playing at?" he spits.

I try to wrestle away, but he tightens his hold, forcing out a yelp of pain.

"No one likes a tease who's all talk," he murmurs, leaning in close, his breath hot against my ear. "You shouldn't promise unless you can deliver."

I have no idea what he's talking about, but I know I need to get away from him *right now*. I open my mouth to scream, but he clamps a hand over my mouth.

"What the hell is going on here?"

Derek leans back just enough for me to see Sam at the end of the hall, coming toward us.

"Nothing, bro. All good here!" Derek calls. His voice is back to the friendly tone he'd used on me before.

I manage to pull out of his grip in his distraction and slip under his arm, the tears now flowing freely down my cheeks, whether from terror or relief, I'm not sure.

Sam's entire face shifts when he notices it's me, but I have no room left in my chest to feel anything when I see him. So I run. Past him and down the hall. The only thoughts in my head are *get out get out get out get out*.

But even after I reach the living room full of people, I still feel like I can't breathe. People are still dancing, laughing, kissing, drinking. Their faces blur and the edges of my vision are black, the darkness pushing in.

I shove toward the door, desperately trying to catch my breath.

"*There* you are." An arm shoots of the crowd and grasps me around the elbow. I let out a little shriek and wrench away, breathing hard.

Blinking, I look up and realize it's Johanna standing in

front of me. I spin in a quick circle, surveying my surroundings. No sign of Derek. Of Sam.

Jo raises her eyebrows at my outburst and scrutinizes my face. "You okay?"

A head shake is my only response as I turn for the door and plunge out into the night. Johanna's footsteps and calls follow me, but I don't pay attention. The fresh air hits me in the face, and I'm desperate for more of it. A girl in a bikini top lounging on the front lawn gives me an odd glance as I pass.

"Mare, wait *up*," Jo calls as I jog down the block and turn the corner, desperately searching for the car. I'm less than half a block away when she catches up and pulls me to a stop. "What is going on?" she demands.

She barely has a chance to get the words out before I crumble into a puddle of tears in her arms. "Please take me home," I sob. "Please just take me home."

22

Jo drives me home in silence. She opens her mouth several times, but seems to think better of it, and closes it again. I'm still shaking, can still feel his hands on my skin, his breath on my neck, the way my fear turned so hot and tight in my chest that I couldn't even find my voice to scream. Mercifully, Jo pretends not to notice. When we finally pull up outside my house, she cuts the engine, but doesn't unlock the doors.

"Are you sure you don't want me to come in with you?" she offers. "I don't want you to have to be alone. We could have a sleepover. Like old times."

"Thanks, but I'd really rather just be alone." My voice doesn't even sound like it belongs to me anymore.

I know she's staring at me, but I can't look at her.

"Call me in the morning?" she asks as I manually unlock the door and throw it open.

I give her some kind of noncommittal reply and hop out.

"Mare—"

I close the door and head for the house.

It's quiet and dark when I head inside, everyone else already asleep. I immediately jump in the shower, still fully clothed, and turn the water as hot as it can go. For several minutes, I just stand there, the water burning as it hits my skin. *Good.* I want to burn away this feeling and the memories and this whole goddamn night.

Eventually, I strip my clothes off and throw them in a wet heap on the floor.

But even after I get out and wrap myself in my robe, I still don't feel clean. My skin is raw and red from the hot water and scrubbing, but it still feels as if insects are crawling beneath the surface. I can still feel his hands on me, and it makes me want to peel the flesh from my bones, if only so I wouldn't have to feel it anymore. But I can't get away from it because *it* is *me*.

So I shuffle back to my bedroom, still dressed in my bathrobe, and bury myself under the covers. Something hard digs into my hip, and I wrestle under the covers until I find the culprit. My cell phone.

I have four missed calls from Sam.

I squeeze my eyes shut and images from the party drench my vision red. And then I see James' face, and Ashley's, and the looks of all the Pretty Committee girls when they left me standing alone in the middle of nowhere.

Sam standing against the wall, staring at me with a blank expression.

I burrow under the covers and hope that somehow sleep with erase the memory of this night. Or at least bury it into the back corners of my mind in a place I don't have to see it.

So, I sleep.

I sleep for what seems like days, and when the morning rolls around, I make no move to get out of bed. Even when I hear Harper getting ready next door and Maman starting breakfast in the kitchen, I just roll over and press the pillow over my head.

When Harper pokes her head in to tell me breakfast is ready, I pretend to be sick so I don't have to go to church. I have nothing left in me. There's no way I could handle being surrounded by that many people. Or smiling and mingling and pretending like everything's *just great*.

I'm not sure how much time passes after that. I don't move, but I also don't fall back asleep. Judging by the French Opera I hear drifting up the stairs, Harper and my parents are back.

Sam's picture pops up on my phone as he calls, yet again. I don't even hesitate before hitting decline this time. With a deep breath, I roll myself out of bed, wrap myself in a blanket, and head down to the kitchen, my stomach growling. I can't even remember the last time I ate something.

Maman and Papa are sitting at the counter, reading the paper together and chatting. Harper sits at the table, nibbling on some leftover French toast.

When I enter, the room goes silent. Harper stops chewing, Papa sets down his coffee. Maman removes the reading glasses perched on her nose.

"Are you feeling better?" Papa asks.

"A little." At first I attribute their odd behavior to me ditching church this morning, but it becomes quickly apparent that it's something more. "Is everything okay?" I ask as I take a seat across from Harper and pull a piece of French toast onto a paper plate.

"Everyone is saying some girl from our school got raped the other night, apparently," Harper says.

I go still in my chair as Maman and Papa pace over to the table and fill the remaining seats. There's no way they could be talking about what happened. There's no way they could know about that—there's no way *anyone* could know about that.

Except for Sam. Depending on the assumptions he made about what he saw.

Maman nods grimly, pursing her lips. "What a terrible thing."

"How do you know that?" I try to make my question casual, but my voice still comes out accusatory.

"This girl from our school apparently saw some of what happened. She tried to go to the police or whatever, but they said they couldn't do anything if the victim didn't come forward to press charges. But this chick wasn't having that, so she started posting all of this stuff on social media, saying we need to raise awareness for sexual assault and things like that. And so of course, half the people in the school shared her post because they'd look like dicks if they didn't—"

"*Harper*," Maman and Papa chastise.

She holds up her palms in apology. "*Anyway*, pretty much everyone knows by now. I'm surprised you didn't."

"I haven't checked any social media lately," I mumble and set my fork back on the table, my appetite suddenly gone.

"Well." Papa clears his throat. "Your mother and I just want you to know that we're here for the two of you, if you'd like to talk about it. We realize this can be difficult, especially if it's someone you know, and maybe it's even a little confusing. But I know God will give us the strength to get through this and bring us closer as a family, just as I'm sure He'll place His hands on the family of that poor girl."

"Who was it?" I ask Harper. "The girl who posted all that stuff online?"

Harper shrugs. "Nora something? Patterson, maybe?"

"Blonde hair? Just had a nose job? Always has perfect eyeliner?"

Harper somehow manages to raise her eyebrows and narrow her eyes at the same time. "Yeah, actually."

Nora's Ashley's right-hand woman/sidekick/robot-slave who does anything Ashley wants. She also couldn't be less interested in activism.

"She claims she has pictures, though," Harper goes on. "And that if the school district and police department and whoever else she thinks needs to get involved don't do anything, she's going to start posting them to—and I quote —*deeply impact the community to spark change on a larger scale.* That's some serious bullshit if I've ever heard some—sorry," she adds when Maman and Papa open their mouths to object.

The room spins and I grip the edge of the table to steady myself. Nora has *pictures?*

Ashley has to be behind this. She has to.

"Meredith, honey, are you okay?" Maman reaches over and touches me on the elbow, and I nearly jump out of my skin. The touch is light, but it's enough to send me to my feet.

"Yeah, yeah. My stomach is just a little upset again. I don't think I would be able to keep it down if I tried to eat, so I'm just going to go back to bed."

"We hope you feel better," Maman offers. "I'll bring you up something later!"

I excuse myself and disappear upstairs. Barely seconds after I close the door behind me, it reopens, and I turn to see Harper in the door.

I raise my eyebrows. "What? So now you're talking to me again?" The words have less of a bite to them than intended, and it comes out rather monotone.

She shrugs. "You were at that party, weren't you?"

I'd told Maman and Papa that Sam was taking me out to dinner, knowing they'd never be okay with a party full of underage drinking and drugs. Blinded by their adoration of Sam, they'd believed the lie immediately. Harper, however, obviously hadn't been convinced.

"Does it matter?" I try to keep my expression blank.

Apparently I suck at it, because upon seeing my face, Harper's expression softens.

"Oh, no."

"What?" I demand and cross the room to my unmade bed.

"Would you just drop the bullshit?" she hisses in a whisper and follows me. "Just tell me. Tell me if it was you."

I tense at the head of my bed, covers clutched in one hand. How the hell did she come to that conclusion so quickly? There were hundreds of people at that party. It could have been anyone. I say as much out loud.

"You've been acting weird. More than usual. More than just the stuff with the pact. Like something happened." She steps around into my line of sight, frowning, and lowers her voice. "*Did* something happen?"

I look away, ignoring the burning sensation rising in my eyes. I don't want to talk about this. Not with her. Not with anyone. Especially not after the way she reacted to the pact. If I have to hear her say I was asking for this, too, I swear I'm going to lose it. "Look—" I start, and flinch at how rough my voice comes out.

She steps forward and pulls me into a tight hug, wordlessly. I'm too broken to object, so I just slacken into her embrace.

"You know you have to go to the police," Harper says. When I don't immediately respond, she grabs my arms and shakes me. I wince; clearly the places Derek grabbed *had* bruised. "You have to report this."

So I can have one more person not believe me? So I can

be interrogated about what I was wearing, if I was drinking? So I can have some grown-ass man, who has no idea what it feels like to be completely powerless, look me in the eye and tell me it was my fault?

"Who was it?" Harper demands.

I shrug, swiping away the tear that somehow made it onto my cheek. "I don't know," I say. "I'd never seen him before. Some Madison Prep guy. Derek something."

Harper's entire body goes rigid. "Tall? Dark hair? Built like a linebacker?"

I squint at her. "I mean, yeah, I guess."

Harper takes a step back and sits on the edge of my bed. "Meredith," she says quietly. "You have to report him."

"Do you know him?" I demand.

"No." She shakes her head. "But my friend Melanie, from dance class—you know her. She's my year, works in the library at school. She went on a date with some senior named Derek from Madison Prep a few Fridays ago. She wouldn't shut up about him beforehand, but then after—"

She meets my eyes.

Melanie. That's who I'd seen crying in the library last week.

Which means it wasn't just me. This is something he *does*. Something he's done to who knows how many girls?

"They might not take my word for it," I say hoarsely.

"Maybe if she didn't have to do it alone, we could get Melanie to talk, too," Harper offers.

My stomach churns. Melanie's a freshman. She's *fourteen years old*. And by the sounds of it, no one found her just in time, like Sam did for me. And for it to have been someone she'd *liked*, someone she'd probably been so excited to go out with, to have a senior interested in her, only to find out...

I feel sick. I feel sick to the very core of my being.

"Okay," I croak, pushing to my feet. I look around the room, anywhere but Harper's face. "Call Melanie. See if she'll agree to go with us tomorrow after school."

"Okay." Harper gets up to leave, but pauses by the door. "Mare?"

Finally, I look at her. "Yeah?"

She shifts her weight and pauses before saying, "For what it's worth, I'm really sorry about what I said about the pact. I was just upset. I didn't mean any of that."

I give her half a smile. "I know, Harp."

23

Monday is the first day since the pact got out that I'm not the center of attention at school. People still stare, and guys offer to have sex with me, but it's not nearly as bad as the past few days were. Most people are occupied with the latest scandal—the mysterious rape (or almost-rape) victim. The gossip is airborne, and everyone knows. Now everyone wants to know who the girl is. Everyone wants to know who the *guy* is. And by now, everyone's just egging Nora on to post the pictures, like this is all some kind of game.

Every time I close my eyes, flashes of that night assault me.

His fingers digging into my arms.

Slamming me back against the wall.

His teeth in my lower lip.

His hands pulling at my clothes while his weight held me down.

How I couldn't move. I couldn't scream. I couldn't *breathe.*

I'm just glad no one's made any guesses as to who the girl is; otherwise I'd be the center of attention all over again. If people knew it was me...I can't even imagine how much worse things would get.

When I make it to fourth period, most of the seats are already filled, and to my surprise, Johanna is sitting in one of them. She hasn't been to class since the incident with Mr. Graham. I hurry over to her, ignoring the whispers and looks that follow me as I cross the room.

"You're here," I say under my breath.

Jo is staring intently at her desk, probably to avoid making eye contact with Mr. Graham. He has his back to us, seemingly reading over the notes he has scrawled across the board, but again, I think it has more to do with not wanting to look at Jo.

"So are you," Jo acknowledges. She sneaks a peek at me sideways, her fiery hair obstructing the majority of her face. "How are you holding up? Is it as bad today?"

"I'm okay," I say, pulling a notebook from my bag. As far as Johanna knows, I'm still just upset about the pact. And strictly speaking about that, I *am* okay. She'd texted me as soon as she'd heard the rape rumors, to make sure that wasn't why I'd been so upset at the party. And...I lied, letting her believe it was just a drunken overreaction from running into Sam.

I don't know why I didn't tell her. Why I don't want her to know. Why I don't want *anyone* to know. I feel stupid and embarrassed enough without an audience.

I look away from her. "It seems like everyone's moved on to the next scandal."

"It was only a matter of time," Jo mutters. "These people are like piranhas. They can't resist fresh blood."

"What about you?" I lower my voice and nod my head sideways at Mr. Graham. "Are you all right?"

Her cheeks redden to match her hair. "He hasn't even looked at me since I walked in. But if he just wants to pretend nothing happened and go on like usual, then that's exactly what I'm going to do."

As she says it, Mr. Graham steps up to the front of the class to begin his lecture, his eyes avoiding our side of the room. He manages to keep it up the entire time he talks, as if some kind of magnetic force repels his gaze every time he gets close to Johanna. When he starts passing out papers halfway through the period, Johanna's head snaps up, panic filling her eyes as she watches him get closer to our desks.

"I'm going to the bathroom," she mumbles, and quickly scurries out of the room. Mr. Graham shows no sign of noticing her abrupt departure.

I have half a mind to go after her when Ashley turns around in her chair to face me. Her expression is innocent enough—it almost looks *friendly*—but there's something off in her eyes. "I know it was you," she says under her breath, still smiling.

I don't react. I don't break eye contact. I don't even breathe.

The corners of Ashley's mouth twist, and her next words come out as a quiet snarl. "If you think pressing charges is going to make your life anything but a living hell, think again. I'll see to it myself." She pauses and sizes me up with a flick of her eyes.

The shock is so heavy that I can't even muster up the energy to feel angry. I thought she'd *want* everyone to know it was me; that would just give her a whole new spectacle to entertain herself with. Isn't that why she's had Nora making so much noise about this? Unless Nora went rogue and did this on her own.

But then why hasn't Ashley spread this news around like did the pact? It clearly isn't because she suddenly has amiable feelings toward me, and it isn't an act of mercy. So the only logical explanation is she has something else up her sleeve, something worse than being tormented in the halls as I walk from class to class. After all, she already gets to witness that. Maybe she's grown bored of watching her monkeys rattle my cage.

I open my mouth to respond, but nothing comes out.

"If you think you can get away with dragging my brother's reputation through the dirt, think again. I won't let that happen. So go ahead and tell the police about Derek. Our family knows every attorney in this state. We'll bury you."

Derek.

Derek is...her brother?

I wrack my brain. I didn't even know Ashley *had* a brother.

I have to remind myself to breathe.

I must take too long to respond, because she shakes her head with a disgusted expression. "What did you expect was gonna happen?" she nearly spits. "Of *course* someone went after you." And with that, she turns away.

Of course someone went after you, as if this is my fault. As if her own brother hasn't been going around raping girls for sport. My mind flashes back to that day in the library, the way she'd looked at Melanie crying. She *knew*. She knew what happened to her. Did she threaten her to stay quiet too? Seething hot anger shoots through my system. My hands are shaking so badly that I can no longer grip my pen to take notes.

I'm done standing by and letting Ashley get away with murder. If no one else is brave enough to stand up to her, then it might as well be the one person in this school who has literally nothing left to lose.

24

I'M SUPPOSED TO WORK AT THE SHELTER TODAY BUT CALL and cancel at the last minute. What was once my solace, my place to get away from all things high school and my parents breathing down my neck, has transformed into a painful reminder. I don't think I could handle walking through those doors to find Squirt's cage empty, not after everything else that's already gone wrong.

Not even the UC Davis acceptance letter I received today—something that would've brought me to happy tears a few weeks ago—is enough to lift my spirits. It doesn't matter much anyway. Not with news of the scholarships I applied to still a week out. There's no use getting excited about a school if I'm not sure I can go yet.

I texted Harper earlier to be ready. That I'd pick her and Melanie up after school and the three of us would go straight to the police station.

But when I pull up to the house, I hesitate before

getting out of the car, my phone in hand. I scroll through the pictures from that night at James' house, my insides twisting at the sight of them. This whole plan was a terrible idea, and I should probably just delete them before anyone else gets hurt.

But then I hear the words Ashley snarled during class echoing in my head, and all I can think about is how badly I wish she knew what this feels like.

I glance up and spot Sam through the windshield, waiting on the front porch. I quickly lock the phone and shove it back inside my backpack, the guilt flushing hot against my skin.

"Is this becoming a regular thing with us?" Sam asks as I head up the driveway. "I don't know what to think, Mare. You apologize the first time for ignoring my calls for days, but then you do it again." He pauses. Glances at the ground. Back to me. "Are you okay?"

I nod, but don't respond at first. Because it isn't him. It isn't his fault. I haven't wanted to talk to anyone lately. It just so happens that everything in my life went to shit all at the same time, and Sam got caught in the crossfire.

"I'm sorry I haven't returned your calls," I finally say.

"Mare, don't you get it?" He sighs and runs a hand through his hair. "I couldn't care less about the calls. I'm just *worried*. Especially after—"

"There's just been a lot going on lately, Sam," I cut him off.

"Is this still about the pact and the kids at school..." He trails off, wincing. "Or what happened at the party?"

My mind spins and pictures flash behind my eyes—the

posts Nora has plastered all over the internet, Ashley's threats, Derek pining me down, James kissing my neck, the Pretty Committee laughing out the windows as they drove away...

I press my knuckles to my temples as if I can force the memories out of my head. "I can't do this right now, Sam. I just—this is all me, okay? This has nothing to do with you."

"The 'it's me, not you' speech? Really?"

"No! I just—" I sigh and press my knuckles harder against my skin. I just want to scream, *I can't do this right now,* but if I push him away one more time, I'm worried he won't come back. I take a few deep breaths before saying, "Do you want to come inside and talk?"

We're two steps into the house when I notice them. My parents are standing at the end of the foyer, blocking both the stairs and the hall to the kitchen. Their arms are crossed, expressions severe. I'm not sure what's more unsettling, their seemingly choreographed stance, or the fact that they're both home at three in the afternoon. It isn't unusual for Papa, but Maman usually doesn't get home from the boutique until around six.

Sam and I freeze, and for a moment we all just stand there staring at each other.

"Um, hi," I offer, slipping my backpack from my shoulders and setting it on the ground. "Is everything all right?" I glance behind them, wondering where Harper and Melanie are.

Maman heaves a mighty sigh and glances at Papa. "We'd like to speak with you."

Sam shoots me a worried glance, the tension from the

last few minutes replaced by an entirely new kind. "Um. I can come back—"

"That won't be necessary," Papa cuts in, his voice surprisingly sharp. "It would probably be best if you're here for this discussion as well, Samuel."

Samuel?

Exchanging another glance with Sam, we follow my parents through the hall and join them at the kitchen table. My gaze bounces from Maman to Papa and back again, trying to gauge the severity of the situation. Based off their rigid body language and Papa's out of character formalities, it's bad.

Maman pulls out a sheet of paper from her purse, smooths out the wrinkles, and lays it on the table between us. I lean forward to inspect it, and my heart careens into the pit of my stomach. It takes me half a second to recognize the document.

I just want to go back and punch drunk me in the face for signing that goddamn thing in the first place.

"It was in our mailbox," says Maman. "Your father called me after he read it and I came home straight away."

I want to crawl under the table, curl into a ball, and die.

This is the moment I've been dreading—more so than the kids at school finding out, than Harper finding out, than trying to find a way to explain things to Sam. And the sheer disappointment, heartbreak, and betrayal in my parents' eyes solidifies exactly what I'd feared.

I say nothing. Even if I wanted to, even if I could mentally formulate words to try and patch up this situation, my throat feels so tight, I don't think I'd be able to squeeze anything out.

"I just don't understand," Papa says, shaking his head. To my horror, he looks as if he's about to cry. "What is this, Meredith?"

"It's nothing," I gasp out, my voice shrill. I snatch the paper from the table and smash it into a ball. This damn piece of paper has caused more damage than I ever could have imagined. I can't let it destroy my family, too. "It's *nothing*, I swear."

"There's no need to be defensive. We just want to talk about it. We just want you to be honest with us," Maman says calmly, laying her hands on the table. "We're just trying to understand, *ma bichette*. Please explain it to us."

My doe. She hasn't called me that since I was kid.

"It's nothing," I repeat, squeezing the paper in my fist in anger. Anger at Ashley for being so damn vindictive, but also at myself for getting into this situation in the first place. "It was just this stupid joke Johanna and I made a while ago. It isn't *real*. It's nothing to take seriously or worry about, I promise you."

Their eyes shoot to Sam, and the accusation there is clear.

"I thought we raised you better than this," Papa mutters, shakes his head, and looks away as if he can't stand the sight of me.

"Is *that*," Maman points to the paper in my hand, "what *this*," her finger wags between me and Sam, "is about?"

"Absolutely not," Sam jumps in, and I'm suddenly grateful he's here. Maman and Papa are probably still trying to remain civil in front of him, which makes me wonder how much worse this would be if I were alone. "With all due respect, Mr. and Mrs. Beaumont, Mare and I are dealing with this, and I can assure you that piece of paper means nothing anymore." Sam waves his hand as he says it as if to illustrate its insignificance.

I look to him in surprise. If he's defending me, that must be a good sign, right?

Papa's eyes snap back to us, anger stiffening the lines of his mouth. "The two of you have *dealt with this?*" He puts air quotes around the words. "Have the two of you already done it?"

Sam's eyes go wide. "Sir, that's not what I meant—"

Papa is on his feet. Red creeps up his neck. I don't think I've ever seen him so livid. "How could you do this?" he demands. "How can you go against all you believe in like this? I thought you were stronger than this, Meredith. That you knew better. Corinthians 6:18—"

I put my face in my hands. "Papa, *please*, no Bible verses right now."

"Flee from sexual immorality," he continues as if I hadn't spoken. "Every other sin a person commits is outside the body, but the sexually immoral person sins against his own body. Or do you not know that your body is a temple of the Holy Spirit within you, whom you have from God? You are not your own—"

"*Stop*," I beg, clenching my hands into fists so tight that my nails bite my palms, but he just talks louder, his voice raising with each word.

"Galatians 6:19—but when you follow your own wrong

inclinations, your lives will produce these *evil* results: impure thoughts, eagerness for lustful pleasure...anyone living that sort of life will not inherit the kingdom of God. Those who *belong* to Christ have nailed their natural evil desires to his cross and crucified them there—"

"Stop it! Just stop it! I don't want to hear anymore!" I explode, jump to my feet, and slam my hands on the table. Anger wells in my chest, all-consuming. I'm momentarily blinded by it, and the words are flying out of my mouth before I can stop them. "Can't you see that I don't *care* what the Bible has to say about it? What it has to say about anything? I don't believe in any of it, and you shoving your beliefs down my throat won't change that!"

The moment the words are out, it's clear there's no taking them back. Papa's eyes have gone so wide they look as if they might fall out of his head. Maman has one hand pressed to her chest, as if I just broke her heart and she's trying to hold the pieces together.

But they're silent.

For the first time in eighteen years, I have the floor. This is it. My chance to finally put the bomb that's been threatening to explode inside of me out in the open.

I take a deep breath to calm myself and continue in a more level voice. "I respect your beliefs and your views. All I'm asking is that you respect *mine*, and accept that they're different than yours. I understand that this is important to you, and if it makes you feel any better, Sam and I haven't had sex. But if and when I *do* decide to take that next step, whether it be with Sam or someone else in my future, it's *my* decision. It's *my* body. *My* life."

Papa closes his eyes, as if each word that leaves my mouth hits him like a bullet to the chest.

"I love you both, and I never wanted to hurt you. You have to believe that."

"*Believe?*" Papa nearly spits the word. "You've just made it abundantly clear that you don't *believe* in anything, so why should we believe in you?"

I try not to let him see just how much those words hurt me. "Just because I don't believe the same as you do, it doesn't mean I don't believe in something," I say softly. "Religion isn't the only way to believe in something, Papa."

"I don't understand," he whispers. "Why would you turn your back on the church? On your *family?* Why would you put your soul at stake over this? Your eternity? God loves you, Meredith, even if it's hard to see right now. He sent his son to *die* for you. The Bible tells us—"

"Why can't you just *hear me?*" I demand, tired of being spoken over. Tired of no one listening when I talk. Tired of using my silence as an excuse to let people walk all over me. "I. Don't. Believe. And I don't *want* to. There's nothing you can say that'll change that. I'm not just having doubts. It's not a phase, or me being rebellious. I don't care what *the Bible tells us* because that *book*—and that's really all it is, a book—has made me feel *terrible* about myself all my life. I can see that believing in it helps you and comforts you and is true for you, but it's not true for me. I have the right to choose what I believe, and if you loved me half as much as you claim to, then you'd respect that."

He shakes his head in sharp, fast movements. "Get out of my house."

The room goes completely silent. At first, I'm certain I've misheard him. I knew he'd get mad, quote some scripture, maybe lock me in my room for the rest of my life, but *this?* Surely he can't be serious.

But his gaze is hard, unwavering.

"Maman?" I whisper.

She won't even look at me.

"Papa." My gaze pingpongs between the two of them, but it quickly becomes apparent that nothing I say will get either of them on my side. The anger fizzling in my stomach surges up, filling my entire body with its heat. "So that's it, then? You can't control me and beat me into submission, so you just throw me out so you don't have to deal with it? How very Christian of you," I spit.

"I said *get out of my house!*" Papa booms.

I jerk back. He never raises his voice. Never.

"What's going on?" Harper appears in the doorway, her wide eyes flickering around the room.

"Come on, Mare, let's just go," Sam whispers.

"Get out!" Papa yells again, snatching the crumpled pact from the table and throwing it into the hall.

"Papa!" Harper gasps.

I follow Sam into the hall before Papa can scream again. He marches after us, his footsteps booming against the floor. As soon as Sam and I reach the porch, I turn, an ache spreading out from my chest. "Papa—"

He slams the door in my face.

25

When I climb into Sam's car, I feel like my body is on autopilot. Papa's glare through the window follows us down the lawn, and when it becomes clear he isn't going to stop until we leave, Sam starts the car and heads out of the neighborhood.

"Mare—" He stops himself.

"I'm sorry," I whisper. "About not returning your phone calls. I know it sounds cliché and stupid, but it had nothing to do with you. I was just dealing with a lot, and I didn't talk to anyone—not just you. I just needed some time."

"You could have just told me that."

He's right, of course. I'm not sure why it didn't even occur to me. Apparently, no matter what I do or how hard I try, someone is unhappy and it's never enough.

"I've had a lot on my mind, okay?" is what comes out instead. I don't mean for my voice to sound so defensive, but I'm tired of being treated like I'm the only one who's done anything wrong. "I've been dealing with some really shitty stuff, and calling you, or anyone else, wasn't exactly on my priority list." I bite the words out as hot, angry tears trail down my cheeks. I know I'm not angry at him and I'm not being fair, but it's like my voice doesn't even belong to me anymore. "I don't have to keep in contact with you every second of every day."

"I never said you did—" His grip tightens around the steering wheel and he lets out a slow breath through his nose. "I was only worried for your safety. When Johanna's calling me because she hasn't seen you all day and your parents call because you didn't come home, and then at that damn party—I don't think it was so unusual for me to be concerned. You could have been kidnapped, for all I knew—and you actually kind of were. So if you want to get mad at me for caring about you, go right ahead. But don't talk to me like I'm some overly-clingy boyfriend who can't take a hint." He shakes his head several times. "Why don't you call Johanna and ask if she's home? I'll take you there."

My cheeks burn at his raised voice. Whether it's from anger or shame, I'm not entirely sure. I pull out my phone, but my hands are shaking so badly I can't even unlock it. Johanna's going to want to know why I need to stay at her place, and she won't be satisfied until she gets every detail, and I'm really not in the state of mind to be interrogated right now.

"I'll do it." Sam pulls up to a red light, reaches over, and takes my phone. And I let him.

The moment I hear the faint *click* of the phone unlocking, I realize what a huge mistake that was. Because the last thing I did on my phone was look at those pictures of me and James.

I reach out to snatch the phone back. "Sam—"

His entire body has gone still. His hand is tightly fisted around the phone, his eyes locked on the screen. "What is this?" he asks very, very quietly.

In the back of my mind, I've always known that all these things I've been doing are wrong. That I've been on a self-destructive downward spiral. But now there's so much momentum that I don't know how to stop. I guess I always assumed that in the end, I would simply hit the bottom. I'd be a shattered, broken mess, yes, but I could accept that. If I was the only one who got hurt, I could live with that. But now, looking at Sam, I realize that I'm not the only one who got hurt. Not even close.

"Sam, it's not what it looks like, I swear—" I reach for the phone, but he jerks away.

"Is this why?" he demands and holds up the phone for me to see, as if I don't already know what he's looking at. "Is this why you've been avoiding me and ignoring me? Why didn't you just tell me that you met someone else? Yeah, I wouldn't have been happy, but at least I could have accepted it and stopped making a fool of myself, chasing after you—"

"Sam, no, you don't understand—"

"Then help me understand. Help me understand, Meredith. Because excuse me if I'm a little confused by the sight of you in bed with some random half-naked guy."

"I—" I freeze, mouth open, eyes wide. I had a reason. I

had an explanation. There are a million things I could say, a million ways to try to explain this, but none of them seem good enough anymore. None of them make as much sense as they had at the time.

I've spent all this time feeling sorry for myself, thinking I'm the victim. And maybe I am or maybe I'm not, but either way, that's no excuse. That doesn't give me permission to crash land my life and take everyone around me down, too. That doesn't make any of this okay.

Tears fall down my cheeks.

He tosses the phone back to me and looks away. "I'll take you to Johanna's."

"Sam," I plead. I don't know what I'm pleading for, what I want him to say. "Sam, I can explain," I say helplessly.

"No, I really don't think you can."

We sit in silence for the rest of the ride.

SAM DOESN'T STAY. HE DROPS ME OFF OUTSIDE JOHANNA's house, and the second I close the door, he pulls way without looking at me. The moment he leaves, there's an empty space in my chest where his presence used to be. The farther away he gets, the more the ache spreads.

I sink onto the porch step, staring at the end of the driveway where Sam's car disappeared behind the tree line. My chest aches so badly that I clutch at it with my hand as if I can physically push away the pain. But it doesn't stop.

And this overwhelming fear that it never will washes through me.

When the door swings open and Johanna steps onto the porch, I turn my head, just a little, and ask: "Do you have anything to drink?"

She hesitates in surprise, her lips pursed, but eventually nods her head to the side, motioning for me to follow her to the kitchen. "Water? Soda?"

I heave myself up and shuffle after her. "No, I mean like a *drink* drink."

A single eyebrow lifts. "Damn. It's that bad?"

I collapse into a barstool and lay my head on the counter. "Get me drunk and I'll tell you all about it."

"I can do that."

She sets a cup down in front of me. I don't even ask what it is before swallowing it in a single gulp.

"My dad kicked me out of the house," I say, motioning for her to pour me some more. "And Sam just found the pictures."

"*What?*" she demands. "We'll deal with the Sam thing in a minute, but what the hell do you mean, *your dad kicked you out?*"

I stare at the glass. "What do you think I mean? He said *get the hell out of my house* and slammed the door in my face."

Johanna shakes her head, her expression still stunned. "What on earth did you do to make *Pastor Beaumont* angry enough to throw his own daughter out? He's, like, the least angry-prone human being on the planet."

"You think I don't know that?" I mutter, waving my empty glass around, still desperately waiting for a refill.

"You know I'm all for the poor decisions," she says, taking the glass from me and filling it with a brown liquid, "but maybe drinking away your problems isn't the answer."

Ignoring her, I eagerly down the second drink. It burns when it reaches my chest, and for a moment, it's almost enough to block out the other pain lingering there. "I think it's a wonderful solution."

"What happened?" she pushes. "With your dad?"

His angry face flashes behind my eyes again, the red tint to his neck, the vein popping out of his forehead.

The way he slammed the door in my face, no emotion in his eyes.

"Someone left a copy of the pact in my mailbox for my parents to find," I say hollowly, staring at the red numbers of the clock on the oven until my eyes unfocus. "They flipped out, of course. Quoted some scripture. Told me I was going to hell. Accused Sam of *deflowering* me, then told me to get the hell out of their house."

"'Someone?'"

I shrug. "Ashley, I'm assuming."

Jo's face scrunches together. "I know she's a bitch and all, but didn't she have her fun spreading it around the school? What pissed her off enough for *more* retaliation?"

It was a warning. I can feel the alcohol burning through me, and already I feel lighter, as if maybe I won't suffocate under the weight of all the shit going on today after all. But the very next second, it all comes crashing back, and suddenly the weight is even heavier than it was before.

"Are you okay?" Jo asks when I don't respond. She reaches over and gently plucks the glass from my hand.

I stare pointedly at my confiscated glass. "Another one of those would make me more okay."

"Yeah, I don't think so," she says. "I'm cutting you off."

"I've only had two drinks!"

"Drinking for fun, I endorse. Drowning your sorrows is a completely different story. This," she jostles the glass and gets up to put it in the sink, "isn't going to make your problems go away or make you feel better."

"You don't know my problems, so how do you know what's going to make me feel better?" I mutter, too numb to flinch at the bitterness in my words.

"Talk to me," Jo offers.

I shake my head and press my face to the counter.

"Your parents will come around. You know that. They'll cool down, apologize for overreacting, and you'll work it out."

I'm glad she's so sure, because I'm not. She also doesn't mention Sam because there's nothing comforting to say about that one.

She takes a deep breath and blows the air out of her cheeks. "Okay, so you don't want to talk. That's fine. How about we just hang out tonight then? We'll get our minds off everything. It'll be a girls' night, just like old times."

"Jo—"

"I'm not taking no for an answer." She hops up and heads toward the stairs. "I'll get the DVD, you grab the ice cream in the freezer, and meet me in the TV room."

She disappears before I can protest.

The setup is the same as always: Johanna starts *The Princess Bride* and angles the TV toward the plush couch in the corner, where the two of us snuggle into the blankets until we combine to make one giant burrito. We demolish the pint of cookie dough ice cream within the first ten minutes, then break out the potato chips, though I can't taste any of it. I rest my head against Jo's shoulder and blankly stare at the TV, desperately trying to muster up some laughter at the funny parts, but all I feel is numb.

I don't talk, and she doesn't ask me to. When I sniffle, she just tightens her arm around me and shoves more food in my face. I can't help but think of my first date with Sam, snuggled under the blankets, his arm around me, the movie in the background. He was the first person I'd actually let *see* me since Johanna. And he'd taken everything I said in stride, so I have no idea why I thought I couldn't trust him with any of this. It's like I knew I finally had something good, but I was so comfortable with the way things had always been that I subconsciously self-sabotaged myself to keep things as they were. And now, nothing is like it was. I don't have Sam or Squirt or the respect of my teachers or parents.

"Can you slap me?" I mumble.

Jo pulls her head back to look at me. "Huh?"

"I'm wallowing in self-pity and I need something to snap me out of it," I explain, voice flat.

She purses her lips as she considers this. "Okay."

I close my eyes, bracing myself, but instead of slapping me, she gives me a little shove, and I roll straight off the couch, taking the blankets with me. I hit the ground butt first, my arms so tangled in the blankets that they're stuck to my chest.

Johanna lets out a snort of laughter. "You look ridiculous!"

I try to wrestle my way out of the blankets, fail, tumble onto my side, and my laughter joins hers.

Just then, the doorbell rings.

"Just leave it," Jo says, waving her hand. "Nothing is interrupting girls' night."

But then it rings again. And again.

I finally untie myself from the blankets and stand.

"Oh, for fuck's sake," Johanna mutters and jumps up from the couch. "This better be a girl scout with free cookies."

I search through the blankets for the remote to pause the movie as Johanna shuffles down the hallway. After locating the fallen bag of potato chips, I resituate myself on the couch.

I wait several minutes, but Jo doesn't come back. I strain my ear to hear what's going on down there, but can't make anything out. And now I'm starting to get restless, so I pad over to the front of the house to investigate. As soon as the front door swims into view, I freeze. Sam is standing on the welcome mat with a strained expression.

"You came back," I say. I almost smile as I glance to Jo for an explanation, but her face matches his. The color is gone from her complexion, and the creases around her mouth and forehead are deep.

There is nothing kind about the way Sam looks at me. "I didn't come back for you," he says. "It's Squirt."

"Squirt?" I ask, surprised. Of all the things I was bracing myself for him to say, that one hadn't even crossed my mind. But the loss is still fresh enough that hearing her name sends a twinge through my gut.

"I think..." Sam trails off, his forehead creasing. "I think she may be in trouble."

26

Sam's been on the phone for more than twenty minutes. He's standing by the front door with his back to us, speaking fast, gesturing around wildly with his hands as if the person on the other line can see him.

"Who does he know that can help us find a *dog fight?*" Johanna whispers.

"No idea," I mumble, my eyes tracing his form as he paces back and forth. Every few moments, my gaze flickers to the large iron clock above the television, as if by monitoring it I can force the seconds to pass more slowly. Every second we stand here waiting for whoever Sam's speaking with, the anxiety crawling under my skin gains velocity. I have never fully appreciated how precious time is until now. Anything can happen in a second, a minute, an hour. Life-changing things. Life-*ending* things. And with each passing moment, the possibility of there not being anything left to find of Squirt expands cruelly in my mind.

I didn't come back for you.

Despite everything, I can't keep replaying those words in my head, and the cold look in his eyes when he said them.

"Hey." Jo nudges me with her shoulder. "Stop torturing yourself. There's nothing else we can do right now but wait."

"You heard what Sam said." I rub my temples with my fingers. "Ryan was arrested for dog fights. They found *dozens* of dogs in his possession, but Squirt wasn't one of them. He could have sold her off anywhere. Jo, she could be *anywhere*." I trail off as my hands begin to shake. "Why is it that everything that could possibly go wrong seems to happen all at once?"

"On the bright side, at least you know you're getting it all over with at once. Once all this clears up, what's really left to happen?"

If her words were meant to make me feel better, they failed.

"Maybe we should call the police again," I offer.

Jo rubs my back and sighs. "They're already doing everything they can, Mare. Everyone is going to do everything they can."

"I have a lead," Sam says as he hangs up the phone, though his face hasn't seemed to catch on to the good news.

"Then why do you look like someone just clubbed you?" Johanna asks.

"There's just no guarantee, okay? I don't want to get your hopes up—"

"You have an address?" I interject.

"Well, yeah, but—"

"Then what are we waiting for? Let's *go*." When he doesn't move, I take the car keys out of his pocket. "We can talk about this in the car, but please can we just *go*? If I have to stand here for another second I think I might explode."

"Okay, okay." He takes the keys from me.

The sky is already the color of a bruise when we step outside, the sun well into its descent behind the heavy cloudbank. Johanna hops in the backseat while Sam slides behind the wheel and I join him in the passenger seat, punching the address in my phone for directions.

He hesitates for a second, looking sidelong at me. I wonder if he's also thinking about the last time we were sitting here.

But then my phone starts barking out directions, and Sam peels out of the driveway, spitting up dirt and rocks as he goes. We fly through the neighborhood and head straight to the highway. Luckily, the roads are relatively empty.

Normally, the way Sam is driving right now—swerving and pushing the speedometer well past the speed limit—would make me nervous. Tonight, I'm grateful.

Sam and I lock eyes, just for a moment, but that look seems to communicate everything we haven't been able to say. He's still angry with me, hurt. And I still don't know how to fix everything. How to fix *me*. But tonight is about Squirt. I don't have enough emotional capacity to worry about anything else. For now, we'll put it aside.

"So who exactly did you call?" I ask, breaking the eye contact. My phone informs me our destination is over an hour away, and I try not to let that freak me out.

Sam makes a face, his eyes snapping back to the road. "He's an old...*acquaintance* from school. I haven't spoken to him in at least two years."

Not that it really matters right now—the only thing that matters is finding Squirt—but I can't help my curiosity. "How does he know about this? And where exactly are we going?"

"He said it's some sort of warehouse. And. Well." Sam lets out a long, slow exhale, as if bracing himself for his next words. "He's not a good guy, okay? He's always been messed up with some pretty sketchy stuff."

"You mean he *participates*—?"

"No," Sam says firmly, then sighs and rubs his eyes. "Kind of. In his own way. He would never actually hurt the dogs, but he's the kind of person with dollar signs in his eyes, you know? He's always working whatever system he can squirm into to make a buck. Bets, mostly. That's always been his thing. He said he's only ever been to a few of these, but apparently this warehouse is the closest one to us where these kind of people frequent, so it's our best bet if Ryan lives around here. His best guess is it'll start around ten or eleven."

"And you're sure there's even one going on tonight?" Johanna pipes up from the back seat.

"He seemed pretty sure."

"Did you ever *go* to one of these things with him?" Jo demands.

"No, of course not." Sam shakes his head, his face twisted in disgust. "I never even knew about this part of his life until tonight. I just hoped with his track record he'd know something, or at the very least know someone else who could help us."

"How do you even know this guy?" Johanna asks, propping her elbows against the center console and leaning forward. "Sounds like a total skeeve."

Sam shifts in his seat, his grip tightening on the wheel. "I made some bad decisions my first two years of high school. I wasn't...myself."

As much as my curiosity is screaming and clawing in the back of my mind for more details, it's clear from Sam's face and body language that the last thing he wants to do is talk about this.

I'm also the last person who has any right to demand anything of him right now.

"We don't have to talk about it if you don't want to," I cut in before Johanna can ask any more questions. She's probably not even aware of it, but Johanna has always lacked a filter when it comes to grilling people. Left to her own devices, she'd push and push until you were flattened against the wall, all of your secrets scattered across the floor.

With a *humph*, Jo pushes herself back into her seat and glances out the window, clearly not satisfied.

Sam visibly relaxes once she's no longer breathing down his neck, but there's something different about his demeanor, as if that slight admission drained something from him.

"What does it say?" He nods at the phone in my hands.

I latch onto the change of subject. "Stay on this road for another eight miles or so, then we're gonna take a right."

"What exactly is the plan once we get there?" Jo asks. "Pop in, ask the civilized gentlemen in there if they happen to have a dog named Squirt, and then go on our merry way?"

"Your sarcasm really isn't helpful right now," I snap.

"Sorry." She holds up her palms in surrender. "It's how I deal with stress. But seriously, what's the plan?"

I look to Sam. I hadn't thought that far ahead. *Getting there* had been my main priority, blinding me to everything else.

"I'm not sure," he admits. "I have no idea how these things are run. Best case scenario, they keep the dogs in some kind of kennel thing, we sneak in, and grab Squirt if we see her."

"And the worst case scenario?"

He shrugs. "If she's with whoever bought her—maybe try to bribe him to get her back? I don't know, Mare. I'm sorry, I just don't know. I think we're gonna have to play it by ear."

Those were possibly the least comforting words I could hear right now. But it looks like they're the only ones I'm going to get.

∼

The exit pulls off to a ghost town. Empty streets, flickering streetlights, broken windows. We drive for what feels like a long time, and I keep looking out the window for signs of life, but none appear. Eventually, the GPS directs us to a warehouse at the end of a gravel road, its windows boarded up with stained planks of wood and its walls covered in multicolored graffiti. Trash blows across the ground in the wind.

"Well," Jo says from the backseat, her voice lowered despite being completely alone in the middle of nowhere. "This is about as sketchy as sketchy gets."

Sam drives around to the back of the warehouse, maneuvering through the weeds and avoiding patches of broken glass on the ground. There are a few cars parked back here, but not enough to transport the amount of people I assumed would be here tonight.

"Does this look right to you?" I ask.

Sam shrugs and parks under the only working streetlamp, glancing around. "Maybe they're afraid a bunch of cars parked around a seemingly abandoned warehouse will draw too much attention?"

Seems reasonable enough, but then does that mean we're walking into a warehouse full of sadistic people, or just a few? With only a few, if Squirt really is here, it'll be a lot easier to find her. But on the other hand, with a lot of people, it'll be easier to slip in and out unnoticed. I glance at my phone. It's just past ten, so the fights may or may not have started already. Navigating the entire way here really drained my phone, though, and I'm down to seven-percent battery.

The gravel crunches underfoot as we make our way to the backdoor. Sam pulls out his phone to use as a flashlight and leads the way while Johanna pulls her sweatshirt tightly around her body. She and I walk with our hands clasped together and follow closely behind Sam. He tugs on the door, but it doesn't budge. A part of me wants to bang on it until someone opens, but we can't draw attention to ourselves. Not before we get what we came here for. Cupping his hands around his eyes, Sam leans against one of the windows with wooden planks crisscrossing its surface and peers inside.

"I don't like this," Jo whispers, looking around at the dark lot.

"Shh." Sam's back stiffens. "Do you hear that?"

We freeze, and the wind howls around us. Crickets chirp somewhere in the distance. And then I hear it—a faint hint of clapping, cheering, shouts.

"Can you see anything?" I ask.

Sam shakes his head. "It's dark as hell in there. They must be in the basement."

"Should we try a different door?" Jo suggests.

Sam yanks on the handle once more before heading around to the side of the building, motioning for us to follow.

The next door is also locked. We take turns pulling on it, but it doesn't move

"How does anyone get in here?" Jo mumbles.

Sam turns his face toward the sky and narrows his eyes. A few feet up and to the right of the door there's a window.

The glass is shattered, but it hasn't been boarded up like the others.

"Think you guys could give me a boost, and then I'll pull you up?" Sam suggests.

The window is about seven feet off the ground—not ridiculously high, but high enough that I worry how much it'll hurt if I fall through to the other side.

Wedging his foot in our linked hands, Sam grips the bottom of the window, kicks off the frame of the door, and hoists himself up with a grunt, the flex of his back and arm muscles visible through his shirt. Balancing himself in the window, he pauses and glances inside. Whatever he sees must be satisfactory, because he wedges his right foot on something on the other side, his left foot in the corner of the window, leans down, and extends his hands to us.

"Go ahead." I nudge Jo forward.

She stands on her toes, reaching her hands toward him, but their fingertips only just brush.

"Here." I link my hands and give her a boost, and pushing off the wall as she saw Sam do, Jo grips Sam's forearms and scrambles up. They fumble awkwardly around one another once she reaches the top, trying to fit both of their bodies in the narrow window frame.

"Can you get down from here?" Sam asks her.

Jo eyes whatever she sees on the other side, nods, and then disappears from view.

"*No, Paul. I'm not going to say it again. Tonight.*"

My eyes go wide at the approaching voice. Footsteps crunch around the corner, coming closer.

"Hurry," Sam whispers, reaching his hands toward me. Even on my toes, I can't quite reach him.

"*Yes, Paul. In full. Every cent. Tonight.*"

The footsteps are getting closer, quickly. Much too quickly.

"Jump!" Sam urges, straining to reach lower.

I jump, and our hands brush, but I slide out of his grasp. His head whips in the direction of the voice, his eyes wide with panic. "Come on, Mare," he whispers. "You can do it."

Swinging my arms to help propel myself up, I jump as high as I can. Our right hands connect, but my left slips through his grasp again. My entire body jolts as I swing to the side, flashes of pain sparking up my shoulder.

"*Shit*," Sam hisses through his teeth, his face creased in strain. He waves his left hand frantically. "Take my hand. *Hurry*."

Finding purchase with my feet against the doorframe, I manage to position myself well enough that Sam grabs my hand and pulls me up. Just as he yanks me into his arms, both of us squatting in the window, a man talking on a cell phone rounds the corner. Sam and I are both panting, but he presses a finger to my lips as the man pauses directly beneath us.

"*You have until midnight,*" the man says into the phone. "*Not a minute more.*" Ending the call, the man shoves the phone into his pocket and slips out a cigarette in its place.

I glance inside the warehouse where Johanna is standing seven feet below us. A slash of moonlight through the window illuminates half of her face. There's a shelf a few feet below the window that looks like it's holding on by a single nail. It must be the way she climbed down. Sam and I exchange a look. If we make any noise at all, we'll get caught before we even make it downstairs.

We're so close, I can feel his breath on my cheek. One hand is still tightly gripping my forearm, the other braced against my hip. We stare at each other for a second, then Sam nods his head to the side, which I interpret as *you first*.

Still holding onto his hands for support, I slide down the wall, reaching for the shelf blindly with my feet. Suddenly, I feel Jo's hand on my ankle, guiding me. My foot connects with the wood, and it lets out a soft groan.

We freeze. The wall is now obscuring my view, but Sam glances back at the man outside before nodding at us to continue.

Holding my breath, I plant my feet on the shelf, and slowly release Sam's hands, letting the plank of wood take my full weight. When it doesn't break, I grab Jo's hands, and she helps me hop the rest of the way down.

With another glance outside, Sam slowly begins to lower himself from the window. Hands clasped around the frame, he dangles from the edge, and I guide his feet to the right place as Jo did for me. Gingerly, he tests his weight on the board before releasing the window. When the shelf holds, we all exhale. My heart beats dangerously fast in my chest.

I reach my hands out to help Sam down. As he turns to face me, the shelf makes that horrible groaning sound, louder this time. The nail yanks free from the wall, and the board breaks out from underneath him. It clatters to the ground, and Sam lands on top, his feet connecting with the wood in a loud *clap*.

We freeze and exchange a wide-eyed glance.

"Who's there?" the man outside calls.

Sam points at the far corner of the warehouse where a small sliver of light is poking out. Jo and I link arms again as we maneuver through the metal beams and crumbling foundation, trying to avoid the planks of wood and loose nails scattered across the ground. Sam's phone cuts a sliver of light through the darkness, illuminating just enough to see a few feet in front of us.

The door behind us rattles.

27

"Go!" Sam urges as we reach the other side. The light is coming from the bottom of the stairs. *The basement.* Bracing myself for whatever we'll find down there, Jo and I clutch each other tighter and hurry down, Sam close behind. The stairs feed into a narrow hall with a dirty, crumbling brick wall on one side and a rusty chain-link fence on the other. The noise is noticeably louder down here. Clapping, cheers, and dog snarls seep toward us.

Sam edges around us, killing the light on his phone. The hall branches off into a few separate rooms. I try to ignore the sight of dried blood smeared on the floor, the heavy scent of sweat, sewage, and something metallic. Sam pauses at the first room. Judging by the volume of the noise, this is where everyone is. Jo and I peek around his shoulders, and sure enough, the room is wide and surrounded by studio lighting kits that cast odd shadows around the crowd.

And it really is a crowd. There are at least fifty people, if not more. They're all clumped together in the back, surrounding what I assume to be a fight. But none of the spectators have any dogs with them.

"You think they're holding the dogs somewhere else?" I whisper.

"Looks like it." Sam continues down the hall, light on his feet. Cringing at the strangled barks sounding from the room, I hurry after him, Jo's hand a vice around my wrist.

"We have to call the police again," I whisper. "Report this. We can't just save Squirt. All of these other dogs—"

"I agree." Sam nods. "We should call them just before we leave here. That way they won't show up and cause a bunch of panic before we can find Squirt, and also so we don't get caught up in the mess trying to get out."

Jo and I nod our agreement as we pause at the opening to the next room.

"This is it." Sam hurries inside.

This room is smaller, with a narrow path down the middle, framed on either side by dozens and dozens of rusty cages stacked atop one another. Nearly all of the cages are full. The dogs don't bark or growl as we enter the room. Most don't even look up. As I get closer, it becomes clear why.

"Oh, God." Jo lets out a soft sound and turns away, covering her eyes.

Many of the dogs are mangled, fresh blood still dripping from their wounds. Some are missing chunks of skin, of flesh. But the worst is their eyes—some are just plain *missing*—but they all contain this absolute sadness. Helplessness. I choke on my next breath, horror seizing my chest at the idea of Squirt being hurt like that.

"Wait there." Sam points at the door. "I'll find her."

The dog closest to me lets out a low whine, and it's the most heartbreaking sound that it's all I can do not to unlock every single one of these cages and take my chances trying to escape with all of them.

"This doesn't even make sense," I whisper. "Some of these guys are so small. Why would you want a small dog in these fights? They don't stand a chance."

Sam gives me a pained look across the room. "Bait dogs."

"*Bait* dogs?"

Sam continues down the line, peering into each cage.

My phone starts ringing, and we all jump at the sound.

"Shh!" Johanna hisses, glancing at the door behind us.

Harper's name flashes across the screen. I quickly hit *ignore*, my heart racing. I can't tell if it was really that loud, or just felt that way in the silence. "Sorry. Thought I turned the sound off." As soon as I store it in my pocket, the phone starts vibrating again. I glance at the screen. Harper again.

"I found her!" Sam calls from the end of the line.

I take off at a sprint. By the time I reach Sam, he's unlocked the cage, but Squirt won't let him pick her up. Instead of her usual jumpy, friendly self, she's cowering in the back corner.

But it's definitely her. I'd bet my life on it.

She's not in nearly as bad of shape as some of the other dogs, but the skin around her neck is raw and red, and there are scratches on her face. The sight sends so much rage through my system that it almost knocks me over. Instead, I kneel down so I'm at eye level and hold my arms out to her. "Hey, baby, it's all right. It's me. Come here, Squirt. You're okay. You're okay now."

She rises to her feet uncertainly, her eyes flickering from my hands to my face. She has to recognize me. She must.

"Squirt," I say, trying to sound cheerful. "Come here, girl."

Her tail gives a tentative wag.

I close the rest of the distance between us and scoop her into my arms. It's clear she's lost some weight, and she was already quite light to begin with. I let out a low sob the second she's in my hands.

"Let's get the hell out of here and call the police," Jo whispers.

Clutching Squirt tightly to my chest, I follow Sam and Jo as we make our way through the cages. It absolutely breaks my heart to leave the others here, but there's no way I can get them all out right now.

You're going to call the police, I remind myself.

But that still doesn't feel good enough.

As we're passing the first room holding the spectators and fights, my phone slips out of my back pocket. I feel it the moment it leaves my body, and hear it as it hits the floor. Luckily, it stays in once piece. Unluckily, someone is calling me again. The phone vibrates against the concrete floor, and the noise echoes in the large space.

I snatch it from the ground. When I straighten, I see

several people in the room have turned around, looking straight at me. Their gazes shoot from the dog in my arms to my face. One of the men actually bares his teeth.

Shit.

"Run!" Sam grabs my arm from behind and yanks me after him. Jo sprints up the stairs first, and Sam pushes me in front of him to follow her. I'm out of breath by the time I reach the top, clutching Squirt so tightly to my chest that I worry I might be hurting her. I hear footsteps behind me. Far too many to belong to Sam alone. The three of us dart across the dark room, no light from Sam's phone to guide us this time.

Our progress is too slow. They're gaining on us. The loose planks of wood slam against the ground beneath our feet.

"Stop them!" someone calls.

Panic pounds in my chest, in sync with my racing heartbeat. When we finally reach the opposite side of the room, we feel desperately along the wall for a door handle.

"Found it!" Jo whispers and yanks on it, accomplishing nothing but creating more noise.

The footsteps are so close behind us now. Beams of light reach us, momentarily blinding me. "Where do you think you're going?" a faceless voice sneers.

Sam nudges Johanna aside, grabbing the wooden plank blocking the door, and pries it loose. He hisses in pain as he does so, but then the door is open and fresh air hits me in the face.

"Go!" Sam shouts.

Jo takes off across the parking lot, looking around

wildly for the car. I remember parking beneath the one functioning streetlamp, but now it's pitch black. The bulb must have blown while we were inside.

Sam curses, encourages us to keep running, and fishes in his pockets. Light explodes from his hand as he pulls out his phone, illuminating our path.

"There!" I point.

Jo reaches the car first, yanking at the door handle, but it's locked. Just as I'm about to yell at Sam to unlock it, I hear a loud *thump* behind me.

I whip around to see a woman with a shaved head and a snake tattoo curling around her neck tackle Sam to the ground. He struggles his way out from under her and throws the keys in my direction.

"Got one!" The girl calls back to her companions. To my horror, even more followed us than I realized. At least ten.

Scurrying after the keys, I scoop them off the ground and throw them to Jo. I set Squirt down and she takes off running toward the car.

"What are you going to do?" Johanna demands when I start heading the opposite direction.

The girl kicks Sam in the ribs before he can get to his feet, and he lands on his side with a painful exhale. "What're you punks doing here, huh?" she demands, then looks at Squirt. "Think you can *steal* from us and we'll just let you get away with that?"

"Get away from him!" I yell, surging forward. I know I can't do much damage, but I distract her long enough for Sam to push himself to his feet and get out of her reach.

"Start the car!" he yells to Jo.

As I reach the woman, fist raised to do I-don't-know-what, she beats me to it. I have never been punched in the face before, and God, I don't ever want to experience it again. Pain laces through my head, momentarily staining my vision black.

"Mare!" Sam catches me before I can hit the ground.

Tires squeal, and I turn to see Sam's car heading straight for us. He yanks me out of the way and the headlights flash across the woman's face as the vehicle barrels toward her. Her friends have caught up. Some are holding knives. The woman jumps back just as Jo yanks the car to the side, blocking her off from us.

"Get in!" she screams.

Sam and I both jump into the backseat and she takes off before we shut the door. I climb over Sam to get to the next seat over, and he yanks the door shut as Jo peels out of the parking lot and speeds down the main road.

Sam and I collapse against our seats, breathing hard. My face throbs in sync with my pounding heart. I pull Squirt onto my lap, trying to calm her trembling little body. She lets out a low whine.

"Well, that was the most terrifying experience of my life," Jo says calmly from the driver's seat. "Why couldn't we have just finished *The* fucking *Princess Bride?*"

28

THE SHOCK WEIGHS HEAVILY IN THE CAR, LEAVING US ALL speechless as Jo barrels down the empty road. When I pull out my phone to call the police like we planned, a notification informs me the call that nearly killed us tonight was another from Harper. There's also a text from Maman: *I'm so sorry. Please come home tonight. We'll sit down and talk about this. Just please come home. Love you xx*

The moment I unlock my phone, the battery dies.

"I'll do it," Sam offers, pulling his own out.

I climb into the front seat to help Johanna with directions. Once we manage to find our way back to the highway, Jo seems confident enough to get us home.

"My place?" she asks.

I glance at the dead phone in my lap. "Mine, actually."

A quirked eyebrow is her only response.

"My mom texted me," I explain. "It sounds like they

want to apologize. Like they want to have a real conversation."

"And you trust that after what happened last time?" Jo asks, not unkindly. "Hell, what's been happening the last eighteen years?"

I lean my head against the window as Sam starts talking on the phone. I can't help but think how differently everything could have turned out if I'd just given him a chance. I won't make that mistake again.

"I have to at least give them a chance," I say. "I owe them that much."

IT'S WELL PAST MIDNIGHT BY THE TIME WE GET BACK TO our side of town. Squirt is asleep in my lap, and we sit in silence. I turn around in my seat to see Sam leaning against the door with his eyes closed.

"Sam?" I whisper. He straightens and opens his eyes. "Can I borrow your phone? I should call Harper, tell her I'm on my way back."

He hands it to me, and I lean my head against the seat as I listen to it ring.

"Hello?" her groggy voice answers. I must have woken her up. I can easily picture her—rat's nest hair, bleary eyed.

"Hey, Harp. It's me. I'm sorry, my phone died—"

"Mare!" she screeches so loudly into the phone that I have to pull it away from my ear. "Oh my God, Mare! I've been trying to get ahold of you all night!"

"I know," I sigh as Jo pulls into my neighborhood. "I'm sorry, but I'm almost home now, so we can talk about it—"

"*What?*" she almost yells, and I hear shuffling in the background. "No! You can't come home, Mare. Do you hear me? *Don't come home.*"

I sit up straight. "What are you talking about? Is everything okay?"

"Wherever you are, just turn around and get as far away from here as you can. They're waiting for you to show up. That's what they want. That's what I've been trying to tell you! You can't come back here!"

"Harper, take a deep breath. You're not making any sense. Who is waiting? What are you talking about?"

Jo pulls onto my street, and I spot three black SUVs parked outside of my house.

"Stop the car," I say hollowly.

Jo's eyes are fixed on the cars, too, and she slams on the breaks in the middle of the road.

"Mare, what's going on?" Sam demands.

The headlights of the SUVs alight at once.

"I overheard Maman and Papa on the phone," Harper says so quickly that the words stumble over one another. "They were talking to some kind of camp. Like a Jesus camp or something. You know, the bootcamp ones that help reconnect you with God or whatever? Do you remember Silvia from church—?"

I don't hear anything she says next, my eyes fixed on the cars waiting in our driveway. A black hole erupts in the pit of my stomach. This can't be happening. They wouldn't do this to me. They wouldn't.

"Is that who's in those cars outside the house?" I whisper. "Are they here to *take* me?"

"You're here?" Her voice is shrill again. The front door of our house flies open, and Harper steps onto the porch in her little plaid PJ shorts, her phone to her ear. Lights flicker on upstairs. "Get out of here!" She waves her arms at us from the porch. "Go!"

The SUVs pull away from our house. One pulls out, blocking the street in front of us so we can't advance, one comes right toward us, and one disappears down the other side of the street, probably to circle around and block us in.

"Get us out of here!" I gesture wildly at Jo, tears in my voice. She throws the car into reverse and backs us straight into the next street.

Terror snakes its way through my chest. I can't let them can't take me. I've seen the documentaries and read the articles about those camps. They basically torture and abuse the kids there until they're so emotionally, physically, and mentally drained that they'll agree with any bullshit the "counselors" tell them to believe. The betrayal guts me, and my breaths start coming in short gasps. Maman said they wanted to talk. But really, it was just a trick to get me back here. If they can't force me to believe like they do, they'll send me to someone who can.

As Jo shifts the car back into drive and makes to exit the neighborhood, the other SUV rounds the corner, blocking our way.

Jo curses, tries to make a U-turn, but the SUV that was following us blocks her path. We're boxed in. The men in the car closest to us jump out and start toward us. Jo hits the locks, and they all sink into the doors with a *click*. A tall man in a black cap leans over and raps his knuckles against the window. Another stands just outside my door, peering in at me.

"We're here for Meredith Beaumont," says the one on Jo's side. His words are muffled by the closed windows, but between the aggressive intensity of his voice and reading his lips, the message is clear. "Her parents signed a waver and a contract. She's coming with us. There's no need to make this difficult."

Jo cracks the window, not even an inch. "She's eighteen, shithead," Jo yells, and the man finches back at the volume. "You can't take her if she doesn't want to go. Sam, call the police."

"Already on it," Sam says, the phone to his ear, glaring through the window at the man outside my door.

"Her parents have the right to make this choice for her," the one with the hat continues calmly. "Now unlock these doors."

"Unless you want me to start honking the horn and screaming that you're trying to kidnap or rape us and wake up the entire neighborhood," Jo says through her teeth, "I suggest you get the hell away from my car."

I hear Sam explaining the situation into the phone behind me, but my eyes never leave the man just outside my door. His eyes are locked on me, too. My heart pounds against my chest. The only thing between us is this measly window. What if he just breaks it and drags me out?

Jo places her hand on the horn. "Get the *fuck* away

from my car! You're not getting anywhere near my friend. Not on my account."

Both men take a step away. "We can wait," says the one closest to me. "But we're not going anywhere."

"What you said is true, right?" I whisper. "They can't take me? Not if I'm eighteen?"

"They can't and they won't," Sam assures me, leaning into the front seat. "I just got off the phone with the police. They're on their way. No one is taking you anywhere you don't want to go."

"I just can't believe my parents would do this," I whisper. And really, I can't. We disagree about a lot of things, but this seems too extreme for them. Too desperate. Too impulsive. How long have they been planning this? Or did they make the call after Papa threw me out?

He reaches forward and grabs my hand. "It's going to be okay."

I start at the unexpected contact, then meet his eyes. For a second, he looks at me the way he used to.

Someone knocks on the window beside Sam's head. We all jump and my body tenses, prepared to see that man again, but instead, it's my father.

He peers in at us, his bathrobe tied around his waist, his hair rumpled. "Meredith!" he calls. "Come out of there, now!"

I shake my head, my throat tight. "No."

"Can't you see that we're doing this to *help* you? We just want to help you, sweetheart."

Behind him, I glance Maman and Harper on the sidewalk. It appears as if Harper is trying to get to us, but

Maman is holding her back. Harper's face is tearstained and creased with anger and determination, and I press my fingers against the window's surface.

I try to communicate through my look how grateful I am that she tried to warn me. If I hadn't known—sure, I would have thought it strange that those cars were in front of my house—but what if I'd gotten out of the car? Would they have grabbed me right there on the sidewalk, shoved me in their car, and peeled off down the street before anyone could do anything about it? She may have just saved my life.

As terrified and angry as I am right now, all I can think about is how I can't leave Harper in that house. If Maman and Papa find out she likes girls, could this be her next? And if that happens, she wouldn't have the protection of being eighteen and having the right to make her own choices. Could they just snatch her out of bed and ship her off?

Seemingly noticing Sam for the first time, my father turns his attention on him. "Samuel," he says, his voice almost exasperated. "Surely *you* must see why we're doing this? The importance of Meredith finding her way back to the church? What she's doing, how she's living, it's *wrong*. As parents, the only thing we want in the world is the best for our child. We're just trying to save her. If you love her, you should want that for her, too."

"And if *you* loved her," Sam snaps. "Then you'd respect her decisions and let her live the life that she chooses for herself. You wouldn't try to force her to into something she doesn't believe in."

"With all due respect, Mr. Beaumont," Johanna adds, turning around in her seat. "This," she gestures to the men surrounding us, "is batshit crazy, and you should know that. *This* is wrong. Not your daughter."

He shakes his head and looks heavenward, as if we're all lost causes, too clueless and ignorant to see the wisdom of his ways, and turns away, rejoining the rest of my family on the sidewalk.

I reach my arm toward Jo. She takes my hand and squeezes.

"Thanks," I whisper.

"We're here for you," Jo says, surprisingly sincere for once. No sarcasm. No wicked grins. "Always. If they want to take you, they're going to have to go through me."

"And me." Sam agrees. "But as you showed us in the parking lot earlier, obviously you can take care of yourself."

I laugh, wincing at the memory of getting punched.

"How's your face?"

"How are your ribs?" I retort.

We make eye contact again and his expression softens. I'm not forgiven—even I know I don't deserve that—but he still stuck around when I needed him most, which is more than I could have asked for.

"Look." Sam points out the back of the car. We turn and watch as the cop cars pull up the street.

29

It feels like we stay locked in the car for hours, though it's probably no more than twenty minutes. Even after the SUVs pull away, I can't bring myself to get out of the car. What if they come back? What if they just wait until the police leave before turning around, plucking me out of my bed at three in the morning and disappearing with me halfway across the globe? No one would be the wiser.

My gaze finds my family through the window. Harper is in the same place, now sitting on the curb. My parents stand a little further off to the side, talking with one of the police officers. Papa is nodding slowly, arms folded over his chest. Maman is crying and pacing back and forth.

"I need to talk to my sister. Will you guys wait here for me?"

"Of course," says Jo.

As I approach, Harper leaps up from the curb, sprints

forward, and meets me halfway. Throwing her arms around my neck, she nearly tackles me to the ground, but I cling to her just as tightly. We stand in that embrace, silently, for a long time. I feel her face press into my shoulder, her fingers dig into my back.

"Thank you," I finally whisper. "You saved me tonight."

"You would've done the same for me."

I pull away to look at her. "I would," I agree. "In a heartbeat." Which is why I need to figure something out for her. With me about to move out of the house, I can't just leave her here with them, not after this.

She must read something on my face, because her expression falls. "You're not coming home, are you?"

"No, Harp. I'm spending the night at Johanna's. But so are you."

"Yeah?" There's a note of uncertainty on her face. I never let her hang out with me and my friends. Ever since I reached my teen years, we went from doing everything together to me excluding her whenever my friends were around. Whatever reasons I had before seem so stupid now.

I squeeze her shoulders. "Yeah. Come on."

She notices Sam in the backseat of the car and pauses. "Wait. Can I run back to the house and get something first?"

Brow furrowed, I release her. "Sure."

With a quick nod, she turns and runs up the street to the house. As soon as she's gone, my parents and the police officer approach me. I refuse to look at my parents, and instead focus on the cop. His face is cracked with age, his hair tired and gray, but he has kind eyes. Understanding eyes. And it might just be because I'm so tired, but I could have sworn there was a little anger, maybe even disgust, at what my parents tried to do.

"I don't think it's necessary to make a formal report about this," he says. "I've talked it over with your parents, and they agree."

"Of course they agree!" I snap. "That just means they get away with it, and can do it again."

"Meredith," Papa admonishes, but he has lost all right to parent me right now.

The officer seems unfazed by my outburst. "You're eighteen years old. I've made it very clear that if they try anything like this again, we'd know, and they could get into some very serious legal trouble."

"And my little sister?" I demand. "Who's going to protect her? Who's going to stop them from shipping her off when they don't know how to deal with her anymore?"

"Meredith," Maman breathes. It isn't admonishing this time, but heartbroken at the accusation. Dark tracks of mascara trail down her cheeks, and I can't help but notice the amount of distance she's put between herself and Papa, her body angled away from his.

The cop exhales and glances at Harper as she comes running back down the street, a folder tucked under one arm. "How about you come into the station in the morning and we can talk about this some more? After we've all gotten some rest?"

After we're all in agreement, I nod for Harper to join Sam in the backseat, and she eagerly obliges. As I turn to loop around to the passenger side, Maman makes as if to grab my arm and stop me, but I yank away.

"Meredith!" she pleads, her voice raw. "I understand that you're angry, but we're still your parents."

"What you tried to do to me is unforgiveable," I say in a low voice. "So don't expect me to act like nothing's changed between us. Yes, you're my parents. You will always be my parents. But that doesn't excuse what you just did. I'm not sure if anything will ever excuse what you just did."

I slam the door.

30

It's well past two in the morning by the time we make it to Johanna's house. She, Harper, and Squirt immediately dart inside, leaving Sam and me on the porch. I perch myself on the first step, looking up at the stars, and Sam does the same, except he sits as far away from me as the porch permits. For a while, we don't say anything. Johanna's house is removed enough from the city that the view is nearly as good as it had been at the drive-in. This tiny reminder just sends a pang through my chest.

"You came back," I squeeze out, my throat tight.

Sam shifts, his arms crossed over his chest, gaze trailed forward. "As soon as I saw that news report, I knew I had to do something. For Squirt."

For Squirt. As in: *not for you.*

I can't blame him for being angry. I haven't given him a single reason *not* to be angry. But still, the short way he snips the words *for Squirt* feels like getting punched in the face all over again.

I lock my jaw to hold the tears back. "I know that nothing I say now is going to fix this, but I just want you to know how sorry I am, Sam. You got caught in the middle of the mess that is my life right now, and that wasn't fair to you. *I* wasn't fair to you. And I don't have an excuse. I just screwed up." My voice shakes around the last four words. Unable to look at him, I keep my gaze trained on the tree line in front of us.

"Thank you for apologizing."

I wait for him to continue, but we just lapse back into silence.

Despite everything, I can't help my curiosity. I clear my throat. "About what you said in the car..."

The left corner of his mouth twists up. "I was wondering when you'd ask about that."

"You don't have to tell me. I was just—"

"It's okay." He lets out a long breath. "It's like I said, I wasn't myself. My dad's drinking started to get bad freshman year. Really bad. Worse than it is now. And I was angry. I was just so *angry*. So, like a punk, I started acting out. Drugs. Skipping class. Fighting. I almost got kicked out of school. Junior year, I realized I was basically turning into the man I was so mad at, so I started turning things back around. Well, I'm trying to."

I'd always assumed Mr. Johnson had a drinking problem, if dinner at our house was any indication. But hearing it aloud, and the raw edge to Sam's voice when he says it, makes guilt tighten my stomach. It twists further when I think about all the times we talked about my problems, and how he was always there. How I don't think I could say the same thing for me.

"Sam, I had no idea any of that was going on. I should have—"

"It's okay," he says quietly. "We'd stopped hanging out by then."

"I'm not just talking about then. I mean *now*, too. I'm just sorry you've had to go through it at all."

He shrugs. "Life, I guess."

"Life, I guess," I agree quietly. I look at his profile, and I can tell he's grinding his teeth. "About the pictures," I blurt, running my sweaty hands up and down my jeans over and over again. "The ones on my phone. It wasn't—there wasn't actually anything going on there. I don't even know him. He's Ashley's boyfriend—I went over there after the whole kidnapping thing to get back at her. I was just so mad. It was stupid—it was a stupid plan I made in the heat of the moment. Not that it's an excuse. Anyway." I realize I'm rambling and force myself to take a breath. "I just thought you deserved an explanation, is all."

He doesn't say anything at first. He stares straight ahead, his jaw working.

He doesn't look at me. More than anything, I just want him to look at me, to feel that familiar sense of calm that washes through me when we lock gazes. When he finally does turn, I suddenly wish he hadn't. There's no anger in the lines of his face, but his eyebrows are pulled together, his eyes slightly wide. As if he doesn't even recognize me anymore.

I'm not sure if I recognize me anymore.

I can't think of a single thing to say that's good enough, so I settle for, "Sam, I'm so sorry." It comes out as less than a whisper. I know what I need to do. What I have to say next. But the words are in direct conflict with what my heart is screaming for, and the warring longing and logic have my chest so tight, I can barely breathe. "I think I have a lot that I need to figure out on my own right now." My body feels hollow as I say it, like someone just punched a hole through my gut and let everything drain out. But Sam has already been through so much—his mom leaving, his father's drinking problem, the problems at school. I can't let myself become another problem. And right now, I don't think I'm capable of being more than another item on that list. It wouldn't be fair to him, but it also wouldn't be fair to *me*. "And I don't think I can do that if I'm with you. It wouldn't be fair to either of us."

He stares straight ahead and bobs his head once. "I was thinking the same thing."

The words sting more than I thought they would. Of course after all I put him through he agrees. But a small part of me hoped he wouldn't.

"This is probably for the best," he sighs and runs a hand through his hair. "We both have finals coming up, and graduation, and getting ready for college. Maybe we both need to just focus on ourselves." The white light of the moon illuminates half of his face, sending the rest into shadow.

I don't know what else to say but desperately want to fill the silence and keep Sam talking. Because as soon as this conversation is over, he's going to leave. And I'm not sure if I'm ready for that.

"I'm really sorry I put you in the middle of all of this."

The corner of his lip curls. "You certainly know how to keep things interesting, Beaumont."

A cautious smile prods my face. "I don't know if I'll ever be able to thank you for what you did for Squirt."

He bends his knees and loosely knots his arms around his legs. "You were right. It's impossible not to fall in love with that little one. I'm just glad she's alright."

Finally, he looks at me. And everything unsaid between us rests behind his eyes. I want to reach out and touch him, just to feel his skin one more time. I want to rewind and go back to our first date. Everything that felt so complicated then seems so simple now.

He stands, brushes his hands off on the back of his pants. I stand, too, wrapping my arms around myself.

"I guess this is it, then?" I ask quietly.

Wordlessly, he steps forward and wraps his arms around my shoulders, pulling me against him. My throat tightens so much, I nearly choke on my breath, and I rest my head against his chest, arms still wrapped around myself. I feel his heart beating against my ear, steady and strong, feel the warmth of his body soaking into my own. His familiar scent washes over me, and I breathe it in as deeply as I can, trying to store as much inside of myself as I can before he leaves.

I wonder if this is the last time. If this is the last time I'll ever feel this. The last time I'll ever be this close to him.

All I can think is, *I could have loved him*. And it's this loss, the loss of possibility, that hurts the most.

"I hope everything works out for you, Mare," he says into my hair. "I really do."

I don't respond. I can't.

And with that, we break apart. I watch as he climbs into his car and hesitates before pulling out onto the road, waving at me once through the windshield. He pulls out of the driveway before I have the chance to wave back.

I stay out on the porch long after he's gone. It isn't until I start shivering from the cold that I finally coax myself into going back inside. Harper and Jo are in the living room, *The Princess Bride* aglow on the screen in front of them.

None of the nearby vets or animal hospitals are open at this hour, so I leave a message at the one closest to Jo's place so we can take Squirt in the morning. Until then, Squirt seems content enough, curled up with a blanket on the plush chair in the corner.

Harper's folder sits on the coffee table in front of us, its contents strewn across the surface. She finished the illustrations for Sam's book, and they're *amazing*. She used watercolors, so the images seem to bleed onto the page gracefully, the colors beautifully blended and rich.

Sam never got to see them.

We all technically have school tomorrow—well, today, I guess. In fact, my alarm back home should be going off in a few hours, but I don't think any of us are planning on going. With graduation being so close, it doesn't matter all that much for Jo and me. I do feel a little guilty about being a bad influence on Harper, but after everything we've all been through, I think we deserve a mental health day.

One more thing to check off your list, I think wryly. *Ditching school with your friends.*

Jo and Harper look up when they hear me walk in, both taking in the sight of me, alone. Jo just holds out an arm and makes some room for me on the couch. I crawl in, tucking myself into the leftover corner of the blanket, and the three of us stay like that until eventually we all fall asleep.

"W<small>HERE IS SHE</small>?" J<small>ADA EDGES INTO</small> J<small>OHANNA'S HOUSE</small> before I have the chance to fully open the door. A bright red scarf is knotted around her hair, a perfect match to her silk pajamas. My eyes are still half glued shut with sleep and I stumble aside as she hurries through the door. I blink a few times and realize she's barefoot.

"Who is it?" Johanna garbles from the couch.

Jada starts toward Jo as I glance at the clock on the wall. Not even 5:00 a.m.

"You got my message?" I ask, shuffling after her, my words coming out slow like my mouth isn't awake enough to form the words yet.

"Of course," Jada chirps, her energy identical to her usual demeanor at the shelter, as if the fact that the sun hasn't risen yet doesn't bother her in the least.

Jada heads straight for Squirt, who is still cuddled up with a fuzzy white throw blanket on the leather chair in the corner. Harper and Johanna wrestle out of the blankets and roll to their feet.

Squirt stirs from the noise, and her tail gives a few hopeful wags at the sight of Jada.

"Hi there, baby girl," Jada coos, crouching in front her to inspect her injuries.

"She seems okay," I say, pausing beside Harper and Johanna by the couch. "But we were going to take her to the animal hospital when it opens at eight."

Jada makes a humming noise as she gingerly touches Squirt, inspecting the blood dried in her fur and the scratches on her face. She lets out a low whine when Jada picks her up, but doesn't try to stop her.

"They look like minor injuries," Jada says, turning back to us. "But you should definitely still take her to the hospital just in case." She swallows, meeting my eyes. "When I saw the news about Ryan, Mare. I swear, my heart dropped into my stomach. I had no idea—but you did. I should have listened to you. I'm so sorry—"

"It's okay," I cut her off, my eyes suddenly burning. Everything that's happened in the past twenty-four hours threatens to burst out of my chest in the form of ugly sobs and heaving breaths, but I'm not about to do that in front of an audience. I wrap my arms around myself like I can physically hold it all inside. "She's okay, and that's all I care about."

"Where's Sam?" she asks, looking around. Sam had been the one to leave her the voicemail in the car since I'd been too shell-shocked to be of much use.

The room gets very quiet, and for one horrible second,

everyone looks at me. Johanna and Harper look away when I meet their eyes, and sensing the energy shift in the room, Jada nods slowly.

"I'm going to go make some coffee!" Johanna announces.

"I'll help," Harper adds, almost immediately, and the two disappear into the kitchen.

I stare after them a little too long, just so I don't have to meet Jada's gaze again. There's something about the way she looks at people, like she can see everything and just chooses not to comment on it. And I know if she looks at my eyes, she'll see everything I don't want to talk about right now. About my parents, and Sam, and the dog fights. We didn't give her any specifics on the phone, just that Squirt was hurt and we weren't sure what to do, but pairing that with the news report on Ryan, she'd clearly put two and two together.

In fact, I have the sneaking suspicion that she's put two and two together about a lot of things.

"Sit down," she says, her voice soft and kind, though it's definitely not a suggestion.

I sink into the couch, pulling the blankets around myself for an extra layer of protection as she perches in the chair across from me. Squirt settles into her lap, her head propped on Jada's forearm so she's facing me. She closes her eyes and lets out a small sigh.

I wait for the words to come. Wait for her to ask me. But she just looks at me, a slightly sad smile on her face, as she strokes Squirt's fur. "You look so sad, my love," she finally says.

And that's all it takes. The tears come, fast and hard and violent. They stream so quickly down my face, it feels like a downpour, and I wipe a sleeve across my face, trying to absorb some of the moisture.

"Oh, no, baby girl, there can't be anything in this world worth that many tears." She gently sets Squirt on the chair and gets up to come sit beside me. She tucks me into her side, like she can shield out the rest of the world. I lean against her shoulder, the tears on my cheeks soaking into her silk pajamas and leaving gross, eye-shaped imprints.

But still, she doesn't ask about it.

Honestly, I'm not sure what I would say if she did. There's too much. There are just too many things wrong to point a finger at any one thing anymore. It's all accumulated and grown and amassed to encompass everything.

"Will you come to the police station with me?" I whisper, sniffling and wiping my face again. "After we drop Squirt off?"

Her body stiffens. "What on earth did you get yourself into, child?"

I laugh a little, though it comes out sounding more like a sob. Because that's all I've been asking myself for weeks.

31

The hardest part is leaving Squirt at the vet's office. They said she'd be all right but wanted to keep her overnight for observation, just in case, and gave us a couple of different medicines to use until her wounds heal.

After leaving the vet, we head straight for the police station, Jada, Jo, Harper, and I tucked neatly inside Jada's sedan, the only noise the faint rumble of the AC. I stare out the window as we drive, my mouth dry and my mind in overdrive. I'm not sure what I'm dreading more, dealing with my parents or Ashley's brother. It occurs to me that I'm constantly referring to him as *Ashley's brother*, even in my own head. I guess I don't want to remember his name. I don't even want to think it. For whatever reason, it feels marginally easier to deal with a nameless man than an actual human being as my attacker.

Attacker.

I feel guilty calling him my rapist, since it wasn't as bad

for me as it was for Melanie, and who knows how many other girls. Then I realize how stupid that is—that *I* am the one feeling guilty about this right now.

My parents and the officer from last night are all standing by the front desk waiting for us when we enter the station.

Jada gives my hand a firm squeeze as I leave her and Jo outside to wait. The officer leads me and my family into one of the private rooms and shuts the door. The seat is cold beneath my legs and I grip the bottom of it with each hand, zeroing my focus on the bite of the metal against my palms. Harper reaches over, pries one of my hands from the chair, and intertwines it with her own under the table.

Honestly, I'm not even sure what I want the outcome to be in all of this. As much as I don't want Harper in that house, possibly in danger because of something about herself that she can't help—but Maman and Papa would surely try to change if they knew—I also don't want her taken away from her family. Where would she finish high school then? With a foster family? I don't want that for her. And it's not like she can come with me to college.

"I think the last thing anyone wants is to bring child services into this," the officer says, spreading his hands on the table. "But if your daughter wishes to press charges, and she *does* have the right to if she so choses, then—"

"I don't want to press charges," I say quietly, the intense anger I'd felt last night ebbing away. I still feel hurt and betrayed—I don't think those feelings are going away for a long time—but I don't want revenge. It hasn't done me any favors before. "I won't press charges," I repeat, louder this time. "But *if*, and only if, the two of you swear to me you'll never pull something like this again. Not on me. Not on Harper. No one."

"Yes," Maman agrees immediately, her eyes darting to Harper, visibly shaken by the mention of child services. Maybe it hadn't occurred to them earlier that their actions might cost them their kids. In their eyes, they really did think they were doing the right thing, no matter how twisted it was. Papa reaches for Maman's hand on the table, but she pulls away, tucking it into her lap.

"Papa?" I demand.

He won't meet my eyes, and at first I think he isn't going to reply. But then, quietly, he says, "Of course."

"I need your word. A written statement," I wave my hand at the officer, "swear on the Bible. *Something*. I need to actually believe you aren't just lying again."

Hurt flashes across his face, but he nods. "I'll do whatever you ask me to do, as long as it means we won't lose either of you."

I glance at the officer, who looks back, eyebrows raised. The decision is up to me. "I don't need a written report of what happened last night. But I *do* want a written statement from him. And if I ever find out that you lied and pull something like this on Harper when I'm gone, I *will* press charges."

They both look so shocked that this is even happening that all they can do is nod. Once the officer finishes up the necessary paperwork, my parents stand to leave the room, but Harper and I remain seated. Harper reaches over and takes my hand again.

Maman pauses at the door, looking back at us quizzically.

"There's something else we want to talk to him about," Harper explains.

The officer just raises his eyebrows in surprise.

"We'll be out in a bit," I add.

Once the door closes and we're alone with the officer, I feel the weight of that night crash back into me. The memory of his hands on my skin, his weight pressing me into the mattress, the helpless hysteria I felt when I realized I wasn't strong enough to fight him off if I had to.

The sight of Melanie bent over in the library, trying to silence her crying.

Ashley's threats to stay quiet.

"What did you want to talk about?" the officer asks, spreading his hands out. He looks friendly enough. Understanding, even. But that does nothing to lessen the absolute terror of not being believed. If I have to hear one more time about how any of this was my fault, or how I was asking for it, I think I very well may just disappear.

"Before that," I say. "We called about a dog fight last night. You wouldn't happen to know what happened with that, would you?"

He cocks an eyebrow and flips the page in his notebook. "I can find out."

"Thank you."

Harper squeezes my hand in reassurance, and I have to clear my throat before speaking. "What would we need to do to press charges against a rapist? We have a couple of girls willing to come forward."

If the officer is surprised, he doesn't show it. He just leans back in his seat and nods. "I can get you the paperwork. And I'll need to get a statement from each of the girls."

It makes me wonder how many other girls Derek has hurt and scared into not coming forward. If they'd be willing to join in if they heard that Melanie and I spoke up first. I'm not sure if just two names will be enough, but for now, it'll have to be.

32

I SPEND THE NEXT WEEK LIVING OUT OF A SUITCASE AT Johanna's house with Harper running interference between me and my parents. We haven't spoken since the police station. And no matter how many texts they send, voice messages they leave, or letters they make Harper give me at school, the betrayal in my chest is just as hot and tight as it was the first day. Johanna keeps telling me to give it time, but it seems like no matter how much time passes, I'm no closer to forgiving them. I'm no closer to trusting them again.

They arrested half a dozen people at the dog fight warehouse that night and rescued twice as many dogs. It should feel like a win, but the knot of guilt in my stomach about leaving the dogs behind doesn't lessen, because there was way more than half a dozen people there, and way more than a dozen dogs. Which means the fighting is not going to stop. And some of those dogs didn't make it out.

Johanna's parents are out of town on another trip, and I'd never really noticed how quiet their house was during the day. No siblings blasting music like Harper does during her workouts, no parents laughing in the kitchen. No neighbors near enough to hear mowing their lawns. Squirt's been pretty exhausted since the whole ordeal and has filled her days with napping on the couch, so not even the tiny clicks of her paws against the wood floor break the silence.

Jo is upstairs changing out of her school clothes. I stand in front of the fridge, eyeing the calendar tacked to the surface with a small reflective magnet. Jo's parents' travel schedules are mapped out with yellow highlighter and black sharpie, the destination of each trip scribbled in crunched cursive letters. There's nothing to differentiate work trips from vacations, but I guess in the lives of a pilot and flight attendant, it might not really matter. What is obvious, however, is the ratio of days they've been gone—twenty-five—to the days they've been here this month—five.

The doorbell rings and reverberates through the house, breaking me out of my thoughts.

"I've got it!" I call, taking a step back from the fridge. Squirt's tags jingle as she lifts her head to watch me head toward the front door.

The very last person I expect to be waiting on the other side is Ashley Miller.

She looks almost back to her usual self today, her blonde hair straightened, wrists covered in tiny gold bracelets. She's wearing jeans with tan wedges and a maroon shimmery tank top to match the glitter on her eyelids. Her lipstick is so dark it looks like blood. She's twirling her hair between two fingers when I open the door with so much fervor, it looks like that single motion is grounding her to the spot.

I keep my hand braced around the door. "What are you doing here?" I ask.

Her face contorts like it wants to look condescending, but she freezes halfway into making the expression, maybe thinking of better of it.

She hugs her arms around herself, her confident energy suddenly dissipating. "Can we talk?"

The anger stiffening my shoulders relaxes at her tone, quiet and resigned. "What do you want, Ashley?"

Her trademark expression breaks through the mask, just a crack, lifting a single eyebrow. "Are you planning on slamming that in my face?" She eyes my hand on the door.

I drop the arm and step out onto the porch, closing the door behind me. "Okay, I'm listening."

She huffs like I've inconvenienced her and paces over to the bannister.

"I heard about what happened with your parents." She doesn't look at me when she says it, her attention focused on the mountains in the distance. "I didn't think...I didn't realize..." she huffs again, but it doesn't seem to be from annoyance this time. "The point is, I didn't think it through. I didn't know it would be that big of a deal, and I wish I hadn't done it. I'm sorry, okay?"

At first, I'm too stunned to move. The word *sorry* in her voice is so foreign to my ears, my brain almost can't understand it. As soon as my chest thaws from the shock, however, a hot surge of anger takes its place.

I was just ruining your life for fun. Didn't realize it sucked so bad, lol sorry—isn't exactly going to cut it. I open my mouth to say something, but she keeps talking.

"Anyway, that's not why I'm here. It's...I heard about your case against Derek. Obviously. And—"

"If you're here to try to threaten me out of pressing charges again, you can just—"

"That's not why I'm here." She finally turns around to face me, and for the first time, I notice how dark the circles beneath her eyes are. She crosses her arms over her chest, a look of determination hardening the lines of her face. "If you need someone else to testify or whatever, I'll do it."

If I thought I was shocked before, it was nothing compared to the utter bafflement that silences me now.

"I'm tired, Meredith," she says, as if this explains everything. She leans back against the rail and smooths her hands over her hair. "Look, I don't expect you to understand. My mom...well, it's always been family over everything. No matter what or how badly someone screws up. Anyway. I've seen it happen. The first time, I was fourteen and didn't really understand it. All I knew was Mom wanted us to keep it quiet, and she said she'd deal with it. And I thought maybe he'd learn. Maybe he'd, I don't know, grow up? But he hasn't stopped. He got kicked out of Northfield sophomore year, but they kept the whole thing quiet. He's never had to own up to anything. My point is, I can't do this anymore. I can't keep watching it happen. So if you need help with your case, I'll help."

I stare at her. I stare at her for what feels like a very long time, and judging by the way she starts to fidget, it *is* a very long time. As her words sink in, a confusing cocktail of emotions wars in my chest. I don't want to understand what it's like to go along with what your family wants even when you don't agree with it. I don't want to understand feeling stuck and not knowing what to do. I don't want to understand regretting choosing wrong. I don't want to feel anything but hatred for this girl who did everything in her power the last few weeks to burn my life to the ground. But at this point, I'm angrier with myself than I am with her.

I'm angrier with my parents.

"Who's at the—?" Jo steps out on the porch in oversized gray sweats, a grungy blank tank top, and her second-day hair piled in a bun. "What the hell are you doing here?" she demands.

"It's okay—" I lay a hand on Jo's arm.

Ashley's eyes flicker from Jo to me before taking a step back towards her car. There's something in her eyes as she looks at the two of us that actually makes me feel a little sorry for her. I've never really thought about how good of friends the girls in the Pretty Committee likely were—or rather, how *not* good. She might have dozens of minions, but she doesn't have a Johanna.

"I was just leaving anyway." She locks eyes with me again before getting in her car. "My offer stands."

TWO WEEKS LATER

It's only eight o'clock in the morning and it's already past ninety degrees. My dress sticks to my back and legs beneath my graduation gown, and my makeup is probably melting off my face. I readjust the heels on my feet for the thirtieth time that morning. I just want so badly not to trip on my way to the stage. Although, all things considered, what's one more humiliating moment in front of my peers?

Squinting against the sun, I locate my family sitting in the stands of the football stadium.

Maman and Papa sit with Harper between them, and when they catch my eye, they flash hesitant smiles and wave. Things are still strained between us, but a week ago, I moved back in. I haven't heard a Bible verse since, but I catch them watching me often. And there's a lot of awkward silences. There's still a part of me that mistrusts them, and I'm not sure if that feeling is ever going to go away.

Johanna's parents sit beside my father, sporting their impressive new tans from whatever vacation they've just returned from. When I mentioned their attendance to Johanna—who is now sitting to my right—she'd merely rolled her eyes, saying something about how she almost didn't recognize them since it'd been so long, but she'd been trying to fight a smile. It sounds like they're planning on spending the entire summer here—their normal favorite vacation time—so they can spend Johanna's last summer before college together. Well, except for the surprise trip to Paris they're taking her on next week, but she doesn't know about that yet.

She reaches over and grips my hand tightly. Both of our palms are sweaty from the heat.

"I can't believe it! We're actually *graduating*," she squeals.

I grin back and squeeze her hand. This day had been a deadline in my head for so long, and now that it's come, and neither of us have completed the task we'd set out to do, I feel oddly liberated. Because I don't *care*.

By the time they actually start calling names, it must be a hundred degrees. Once people return to their seats with their diplomas, they immediately double them as fans. Luckily, with the last name Beaumont, I'm called toward the beginning—and sans catastrophe, I manage to get my diploma, and the slight breeze it offers makes the rest of the ceremony a little more bearable.

Then Johanna's name is called, and she hurries up, grinning, her red hair flowing down her back in perfect curls. I swear she's the only one here who looks good in the graduation hat. On her way back to her seat, she flips off Mr. Graham behind her diploma—luckily he doesn't see—and winks at me.

When Ashley's name is called, she makes her way to the front, taking her time, looking as confident as ever. She has to pass our seats on her way back, and for a second, we lock eyes and exchange a nod. I would never describe our relationship as friendly, but at least now there's noticeably less malice.

"What was that about?" Jo murmurs.

I clap along as the remainder of the names are called and shrug. "We've just come to an understanding, is all."

"What's that saying again?" she teases. "When hell freezes over?"

I smirk. "Stranger things have happened."

After the hugs and pictures and tears, Jo heads off with her parents, and I climb in the car with Harper, Maman, and Papa. Jo's graduation party starts in an hour, leaving us just enough time to go home and change. Papa waits until we're parked outside of the house before pulling the envelope out of his pocket.

"What's this?" I ask as he hands it to me.

A shrug. "Open it."

I do, slide the contents out, and freeze.

Maman and Papa exchange a soft smile.

I hold the airline tickets up with a shaking hand. "Why am I holding four tickets to California?"

"Well," Maman says. "We know how much you wanted to go to UC Davis, and even with the scholarship, that school has quite the hefty price tag. So we talked about it, and we're willing to pay for *half*, so you'll have to get a job. But we thought it would be nice to have the whole family there to help you move in."

Harper leans over, eyes wide, and grabs one of the tickets. "We're going to California?" she squeals. Clearly she was not in on the surprise.

I meet Papa's eyes in the rearview mirror. "Thank you," I mouth.

There are tears in his eyes, but he just nods.

"Now let's go inside!" Maman calls, throwing open her door. "We have a party to get ready for! Mare, Harper, I brought home some dresses for you to choose from…"

Harper and I share a groan as we head for the door. The house quickly turns into a flurry of activity as everyone gets ready and Maman tries to relocate where she'd put both my and Johanna's graduation gifts.

A notification on my phone flashes. Detective Brown, the officer on my case, left me a voicemail, but I'll listen to it later. The case has moved quickly, and things are going well, especially once the word got out and three more girls came forward in addition to Ashley. But it's not something that I want to think about today.

I'm not letting anything get in the way of having a good day.

Even though I did think about Sam earlier. Just for a little bit. I imagined him sitting in the crowd at graduation with my parents, or walking into Johanna's party with me, his hand in mine. I imagined having to say a tearful goodbye as we packed up our things and headed our separate ways to colleges on the opposite sides of the country.

We haven't spoken since that very, very long night.

I've thought about texting him more times than I care to admit, but every time, I've thought better of it.

Because now I've started to patch things up with my family, I have a generous scholarship to help get me through my dream school, an adorable emotional support Maltese who is just as excited for college as I am, and I have a plan. Not one to lose my virginity or fulfill all of these milestones stupid romantic comedies made me think I needed. Not to find a boyfriend or get revenge on the high school mean girls.

I have a plan for *me*. And that is so much better.

Thank you for reading! Reviews are one of the best ways to support authors. If you enjoyed this book, please consider leaving a review on the site where you got it!

Continue with Johanna's story in *The Anti-Relationship Year*...

Johanna Palmer is very much over relationships. After a scarring experience her freshman year of college, she's decided she would much rather have something fun than something serious.

Her best friend Miller has seen it all—the tears, the parties, the drunken phone calls at four in the morning when she needed a ride. In fact, there might be several things Miller saw that Jo herself can't remember.

Things Miller can't forget.

With the whirlwind of senior year underway, Jo just wants to move on, get her degree, and land her dream job. But her past might not be as easy to outrun as she'd hoped.

The Anti-Relationship Year is a friends-to-lovers new adult romance novel that acts as a companion to The Anti-Virginity Pact.

SIGN UP FOR MY AUTHOR NEWSLETTER

Sign up for Katie Wismer's newsletter to receive exclusive content and be the first to learn about new releases, book sales, events, and other news!

www.katiewismer.com

ABOUT THE AUTHOR

Katie Wismer is a die-hard pig lover, semi-obsessive gym rat, and longtime sucker for a well-written book. She studied creative writing and sociology at Roanoke College and now works as a freelance editor in Colorado with her cats Max and Dean.

When she's not writing, reading, or wrangling the cats, you can find her on her YouTube channel Katesbookdate.

You can sign up for her newsletter at katiewismer.com, or check out her instructional videos on writing and publishing on Patreon.

patreon.com/katiewismer
instagram.com/katesbookdate
goodreads.com/katesbookdate
bookbub.com/authors/katie-wismer
facebook.com/authorkatiewismer
amazon.com/author/katiewismer
twitter.com/katesbookdate

Made in the USA
Monee, IL
24 June 2021